To the memory of my grandparents
Engebret Engebretsen Lobeck and Martha Persdatter Nordby Lobeck

and for my grandchildren
Seth, Marit, Greta, Aidan, Connor, Samantha

I will strive to live so
That I may kindle a light
So they who may come after me in the world
May walk in a better light than I.

Written by E.E. Lobeck as preface for his book of poetry *Forglemmigei*
(Norwegian for "forget-me-not"), 1894.[1]

Contents

Hon. Engebret Engebretsen (E.E.) Lobeck (1864-1922)
Minnesota House of Representatives, 35th and 36th sessions, 1907-1910
Minnesota Senate, 39th and 40th sessions, 1915-1918
Candidate for Governor of Minnesota, 1912
Candidate for U.S. House of Representatives, 1898, 1916, 1918

Acknowledgments

This book would never have come to fruition without the editor, Patrick Henry (www.IronicChristian.org), trained historian, former professor of religion at Swarthmore College and executive director of the Collegeville Institute for Ecumenical and Cultural Research, and, since 2007, a monthly columnist for the *St. Cloud Times*. He encouraged me to think beyond just a family chronicle, and gently – but relentlessly – nudged me with his knowledge, expertise, advice, and friendship.

Growing up, I had the advantage of frequent time spent in the childhood home of my mother, Constance Petra Lobeck Kahl, which was the home of the E.E. Lobeck family in Alexandria, Minnesota. Many of the old-timers were still living and reminisced about the period I have written about. I listened to conversations – except when they were speaking Norwegian – and I was curious about the career and personality of E.E., my grandfather, who died several years before I was born. He sounded too good to be true. I followed along to the cemetery, visiting graves, and listened to the pain in their voices when speaking of him. He was much loved and died too young. So why did it seem so tragic to his children, even when they were well into their 80s and 90s?

That question stayed with me into adulthood. When my mother died, in 2000 at age 96, one of her siblings, Martha, was still living. She began to tell me many things and sent me some family documents. I was intrigued and decided to explore E.E.'s life. This book is the result of my quarter-century journey through letters, diaries, documents, travels, history, pictures, newspapers, and relatives unknown to me previously.

All my life I had heard of Trysil, Norway, as the birthplace of my grandparents, E.E. and Martha. In 1999 my husband and I sold our business and retired. We took a trip to Norway the following spring to visit Trysil, and also the birthplace of my husband's father in Risør. We wandered into Trysil with a one-page ancestral chart and the plan to find the farms where E.E. and Martha were born.

The first person we met while strolling down the village street was Marit Øvergaard, who looked at my paper and said, "Come with me. You are related to nearly everyone here." Marit called her mother, Jorun Øvergaard. who gathered her *Trysil-Boka*, history narratives of the farms in the area, and furnished me with much history. The Øvergaards are descended from my great-grandfather Embret P Lobeck's brother, Halvor. The evening culminated with coffee in the Norwegian twilight at midnight in the home of my great-great-grandparents, Halvor and Marie Strandvold, who emigrated to America in 1868.

Per Oscar Strandvold asked many questions about the Holmes City area of Minnesota. I didn't know the answers. I promised to search them out for him when I returned home.

Back in Minnesota, I contacted Roger Ostby. He, too, knew of E.E., and put me in touch with Arne Sørli in Oslo, descendant of Johanna Viken, my great-grandfather's sister. Arne also introduced me to Magne Teppen, who translated most of the articles from *The Reform* newspaper that are in this book.

Magne's sister, Ragnhild Teppen, and her husband, Asbjørn Hildemyr, generously presented us with the latest *Trysil-Boka*. When I mentioned that E.E. had written a lot of poetry that needed translating, Asbjørn, who holds degrees in linguistics, volunteered.

Roger Ostby put me in touch with Ivy Ostby Hjornevik of Austin, Texas – her grandmother married my great-uncle. We exchanged information constantly, helping each other with genealogy searches. She came to Minnesota yearly to attend the Solorlag Stevne and stayed an extra week visiting cemeteries and mining courthouses and history centers.

Ivy introduced me to Gunnar Kolstad in Trysil, who answered and researched lots of my questions. He made a trip to Minnesota to research Tryslingers here.

Hilding Sponberg, director of Trysil Historielag, and Frank Bjørseth of Østby, soon to retire as head of the Østby Historielag, are mentioned on the beginning page of this book. They have worked hand in hand and provided wonderful experiences and research for me.

Often I contacted Kari Odden of the Trysil Bibliotek, who looked up answers for me and found family connections in Trysil for 60 of us who attended the Trysil Stevne in Norway in 2008.

The names mentioned have genealogical ties to me. Our ancestors knew each other a couple of hundred years ago.

I also thank NAHA (Norwegian American Historical Association), based at St. Olaf College in Northfield, Minnesota, for allowing me to spend hours with original copies of *The Reform* newspaper. I photographed each of E.E.'s "Under Blyanten" articles, published in Norwegian in Gothic script, and forwarded to Magne Teppen to translate.

Minnesota History Center has been a treasure of newspapers on microfilm from all over Minnesota, hence the *Park Region Echo*, *Alexandria Post*, and *Alexandria Citizen* in endnotes.

Membership to Solorlag gave me access to a myriad of documents and bygdeboks. (Each district of Norway publishes a bygdebok that narrates the history and people in that district, e.g., *Trysil bygdebok*.)

The Holmes City/Farwell area still has many properties that were settled 150 years ago by Tryslingers. Attics were full of information and pictures ferreted out by a small group named Trysil Historielag USA/Canada; they maintain a website, https://www.trysilhistorielag.com.

Sadly, Per Oscar Strandvold, Arne Sørli, Roger Ostby, Magne Teppen, Ivy Hjornevik, and Gunnar Kolstad – valuable contributors all – passed away before this book was finished.

Last, but not least, thanks to my wonderful husband, who accompanied me on my pursuits and allowed me generous amounts of time and space and a listening ear to accomplish finishing *Across Minnesota in All Directions*. I regret that he did not live long enough to hold the book in his hands, but I am grateful that he knew it was on the verge of publication.

Preliminary Notes

- Many moments in this story are grounded in Lobeck family papers in the possession of the author. If an anecdote or quotation lacks an endnote reference, chances are very good that the source is in that collection.

- Every effort has been made to identify persons E.E. Lobeck mentions in his quoted writings. Many such searches were successful. A few of the actors in the story remain elusive.

- Money appears often. To give a sense of what the sums were in terms of today's purchasing power, each amount is followed by a bracketed equivalent in early 2020s dollars, determined by the Bureau of Labor Statistics CPI calculator, https://data.bls.gov/cgi-bin/cpicalc.pl, and for years prior to 1913, https://www.in2013dollars.com/.

- When an endnote contains more information than simple source reference, the number is in italics.

- Given the central importance of Temperance, Prohibition, County Option, and Women's Suffrage in this story, the terms are capitalized throughout, even when a quoted source has them in lowercase.

- Nearly all the translations from Norwegian are by Magne Teppen, of blessed memory, and Asbjørn Hildemyr.

- This book was in its final stages when I and my editor were alerted to the stunning book – seismic revisionist history – *Smashing the Liquor Machine: A Global History of Prohibition*, by Mark Lawrence Schrad (Oxford University Press, 2021).

  This is a history of Prohibition the way you've never heard it. And you've likely never heard it because most writers on Prohibition have been looking for the wrong things in the wrong places at the wrong times, using the wrong assumptions to ask the wrong questions and draw the wrong conclusions.

What Schrad does is to "decolonize" and "de-exceptionalize" a whole dimension of American history "by situating it in its proper global context."

My contention is that the global war on the liquor traffic was a transnational normative shift about the inappropriateness of benefitting from addiction and misery of the masses, precipitated in many countries undergoing the upheavals of industrialization and colonial domination. It was an attempt to put the welfare of society ahead of the needs of the state. Whether the beneficiary was the state monopoly, foreign colonists, or the so-called liquor trust of corrupt and conniving capitalist brewers and distillers, Temperance advocates fought to put the individual ahead of profit. … The transnational social movement which embodied and promoted this normative shift, championed Prohibition and other alcohol control policies to harness the power of the state in order to constrain the worst excesses of the predatory liquor trade on behalf of the good of the people.

In short:

Everywhere, the Temperance-cum-Prohibition movement harnessed the moral and material resources of organized religions into a broad-based, progressive movement to capture the instruments of legislation and statecraft against powerful, established political actors.

The Temperance and Prohibition movements have more in common with opposition to the British opium trade (and the wars they spawned), or contemporary efforts to reduce the social harms from cigarette smoke, or holding politically connected "Big Pharma" companies responsible for the opioid epidemic, in which predatory pharmaceutical companies reap obscene profits from the misery of their addicted customers. This is a far cry from traditional characterizations of Bible thumpers "legislating morality."[2]

What Schrad provides is nothing less than an explanation for what we – shaped by the wrong things, wrong places, wrong times, wrong assumptions, wrong questions, and wrong conclusions employed and promoted by most writers on Prohibition – found surprising: that E.E. Lobeck could plausibly make this claim at the 1912 Minnesota Prohibition Party convention:

For forty years and more the Prohibition Party has been struggling against fearful odds, fighting the battles of the people against the legalized drink traffic and corporate greed. We sent our words into the wilderness and it took years before the echo came back, but now we are heard. Our planks are eagerly snatched up one by one and incorporated into the platforms of other political organizations, except the plank calling for the destruction of the liquor traffic, this the greatest curse of all the curses of humanity. They do not dare to touch that – they evidently believe that we have the first mortgage on that plank. But aside from this we should be glad that our principles are taken up and advocated today by the greatest men in the nation – and we ought to be proud of the fact that the Prohibitionists have been doing the political thinking in the country for the last twenty years. Every advanced idea that has been brought forward by the Republicans and Democrats of late has for years been shining like a beacon light to progressive statecraft in the Prohibition platform.

We also now understand that E.E.'s calling on Abraham Lincoln as an ally in the Temperance cause was not a stretch.

And Schrad makes clear that it was not merely by chance that E.E. and his wife, Martha, very active in the Woman's Christian Temperance Union, were so united in both their Prohibition and their Women's Suffrage work. E.E. and Martha, individually and together, were emblematic of the Progressive Era.

As a coda to these Preliminary Notes, and by way of reinforcing Schrad's thesis, here is an item from the July 18, 1874 *Scientific American* (Vol. 31/3, 40) – a journal not known as a hotbed of Bible thumpers – in a section called "Medical Notes," under the heading "Alcohol," reprinted from the *Boston Journal of Chemistry*. At the time E.E. Lobeck was not yet quite ten years of age, and it would be 46 years before the 18th Amendment was ratified.

As the result of the chemical change which sugar undergoes in passing downwards towards a dead, inorganic condition, a substance is produced which has been the cause of more sorrow, crime, and suffering than all other evil agencies that have afflicted the world. It has caused tens of thousands of murders, and uncounted instances of robbery, theft, arson, incest, and suicide; it has brought misery and want into millions of households; it has filled almshouses and asylums with wretched victims; it sends a never ending procession of crime-stained men and women to prison and the gallows. What an awful indictment this is to bring against a substance which stands so closely allied in chemical relationship to innocent sugar! Alcohol is not a natural product; it can only result from a spontaneous change which is excited in saccharine liquids under the influence of a ferment. If in the order of things this chemical change had been impossible, the human race would have been saved from shedding tears, the aggregated volume of which reaches to that of a river. But alas! Atoms of carbon, hydrogen, and oxygen are permitted to group themselves in a way to form the maddening liquid; and the great enemy of human happiness confronts us in all our domestic, industrial, and commercial relations. If through disarrangement of Nature's laws, the vinous fermentative process should suddenly cease, and not another drop of any kind of spiritous liquors be produced, no sensible harm would come to any industrial or art process, and no absolute want in medicine would be encountered. Carefully viewing the matter from the standpoints of the chemist, physician, and artisan, we unhesitatingly declare that the world in its present advanced stage has no need of alcohol; it is simply convenient, but not necessary. Why not then make a determined effort to rid the country and the world of the monster? Although alcohol results, as we have said, from spontaneous changes, yet the aid of man is necessary to form the various liquids containing it into attractive and permanent beverages. The fermentation of the juices of grapes and other fruits produces alcohol; but if let alone, Nature will not allow the spirit to remain except for a brief space of time. Nature abhors not only a vacuum, but manifestly one of her products, for alcohol is so unstable in its attenuated combinations that, if left to itself, it speedily runs down into the harmless form of acetic acid.

If man ceases to interfere in the series of natural changes which saccharine liquids spontaneously undergo, alcohol will not survive long enough to do mischief. Why not then compel the great army of men, engaged in isolating and compounding the agent, to let it alone? Alcohol is a poison; it acts inharmoniously with vital processes in the animal organism. In its purest and best form, it slowly undermines the constitution, and hinders or arrests metamorphosis of tissues; in its vile associations, as presented in these modern times, it kills with the certainty and almost with the rapidity of strychnine and arsenic. We ask again, why not attempt to arrest its production, and thus strike a blow at the root of the evil? There is virtue and moral force enough in most of, if not all, the States to compel legislatures to enact laws prohibiting its manufacture. This is the point to which we must, sooner or later, come. All the laws ever made, or that ever will be made, conjoined with all the prayers of all the well intentioned women of the country, will never stop the gnawings of human appetite, or prevent its gratification, so long as rum, whiskey, wine, malt liquors, etc., are imported and manufactured under the sanction of law. Alcoholic beverages must cease to exist, before the world will be released from the terrible thraldom which they exercise over human appetite. In making a remedy for the enormous evils caused by alcohol, nothing absurd or impracticable is associated with the suggestion, and the time is not far distant when the poison will be placed under a ban, as regards its importation and manufacture, which will give a forced emancipation to the tens of thousands of slaves now in subjugation to the monster.

Prologue

Opening the Door to the Past

"Are you ready to go by 9:00 a.m.? Dress warm."

It's May 31, 2005, in Trysil Hotel. Hilding Sponberg has arranged quite a day for my husband and me.

We drive east, climbing slowly up to Østby. We stop at the home of Frank and Grethe Bjørseth. By now a cold light rain makes us glad we have dressed warm. Frank is coming with us, but he has to make us ready: knee-high rubber boots and thick hand-knit stockings.

Off we go on the dirt road leading from Østby to Løvbekksetra. The dirt road turns onto a narrower old logging road. Eventually, Hilding pulls the car to the side and parks. Nothing but trees in sight.

Frank takes his satchel, we take our cameras. The four of us form a single line with Frank in the lead. We walk over uneven ground and reach a stream, Dulpbekken, narrow but deep and cold and punctuated by raindrops. Two narrow logs span the stream. Frank goes first. Now, my turn. "Just hold both arms stretched out on your sides and it will balance you." I do as I'm instructed and make it across.

Once we're all on the other side of the stream, I see the reason for the knee-high rubber boots. We slosh through bogs and then, up on a little rise, between all the trees, I see the størrøse built by my great-grandfather in 1848.

We walk around the little størrøse, touching and listening while Frank and Hilding describe the construction and history of the building and the current plans for restoring it.

"You must open the door," Frank says. "This is your house, built by Embret P Lobeck." I remove the barrier and step inside: the big stone for fire building, the beam over the door with "EPS 1848," the plank benches, the table.

Frank opens his satchel and brings out a guestbook, candle and holder, flask of hot coffee, and a tin of "trysilsnipp." And here we sit, surrounded by my history, drinking coffee and enjoying pastry and writing in the guestbook.

The floodgates of memory are opened, but the memory requires research. I've heard some of the stories, but to know the full tale of what started in this remote part of Norway and became part of the saga that is Minnesota, I must ferret out letters, diaries, newspapers, photographs – all the flotsam and jetsam that lies upon the shore of the past.

This book is the record of what I have found in tracing the lines – genealogical, historical, social, religious, political – that radiate out from what started in that moment I signed the guestbook.

Chapter 1

From Norway to America

In my hand I hold a silver pitcher, given to Engebret Persen Lobeck (also known as Embret) in 1813, on the occasion of his baptism at two weeks of age. This family heirloom points to the role religion will play in his long life of 83 years.

Embret's father, Per Jonsen Tekta, became Klokker (sexton) of the Trysil church soon after Engebret was born. Per Jonsen's position was of influence almost equal to that of the "prest." He maintained church property, led the singing (he was known for his beautiful voice), kept church records, rang the bells.

Per Jonsen was also the ground of stability in the church. In a retrospective journal entry, written when he was eighty years, three months, and fourteen days old, Embret – who could be obsessively precise – noted a series of short-term pastors: one who was very old; a young one who died; one who taught the children arithmetic and writing but soon moved away; another who stayed "for two or three years." Finally, in 1825, when Engebret was twelve, "P. Irgens Dybdal came. He was the only one, I believe, who worked for the welfare of both body and soul all that he was able, and he stayed for twelve years. He encouraged them to clear up both the fields and meadows and to avoid drinking and dancing and the bad behavior that would result."[3]

When Embret was about seven, Per Jonsen built a new house called Sundstøen across the river from the Trysil Kirke. For many years Embret was known as Engebret Persen Sundstøen.

In 1837, when he was twenty-four, Embret earned his shoemaker's license. There were many shoemakers in Trysil. Almost all farmers fixed their own footwear, but some were better than others. A license required a severe test. Embret's passing it showed that he was a very good shoemaker. This skill was useful all his life. When he moved in his last years, his shoemaker tools were still among his possessions.

On October 20, 1845 Embret married Ingri Halvorsdatter Opseth Løvbekksetra. His father-in-law, Halvor Jonsen, gave the newlyweds the mountain farm of Løvbekksetra, situated in the forested mountains east of Trysil toward the border with Sweden. The mountains of eastern Norway, more rounded and gentle than the craggy, peaked mountains and fjords to the west, are nonetheless at a high elevation. Even in summer the temperature is much cooler and the wind much stronger than down in the valley where Trysil Inbygda lies.

Løvbekksetra lies on a flat spot beside a narrow cold stream and a narrow road connecting Østby and Ljørdalen. There is an old dwelling built in the old way with a one-room living, sleeping, cooking area, and a corner fireplace used for warmth and food preparation. This was connected to the animals' living space by a covered walk about three feet wide.

This small cabin probably dates from before Embret Persen's time. Although the exact date is unknown, a large white home had been added by the time Embret and Ingri moved there.

Embret and Ingri's time together was short – two and a half years. Their son, Ingerinus E Lobeck, was born March 28, 1848. Ingri died a week later, on April 4.

That summer, in memory of Ingri, Embret built a small cabin, called Størrose, about ten miles from Løvbekksetra. This cabin provided shelter for his two- to three-week stay while gathering hay and grasses to store for his animals during the winter months. There were many of these storage cabins or størrøs throughout the forests and pastures in Norway. Embret built his little cabin around a large stone which served as a fireplace for heat and warming food. Such structures were called ljørkoie – koie meaning small cabin and ljør, the hole in the roof for smoke from the fireplace.

The simple cabin had benches or planks along three sides. The board across the back served as seating for a table that could also be used as a sleeping space. There were no windows, but Embret spent all his waking hours outside. Inside was for sleeping. When his little størrøs was complete, he carved his initials and date on the beam above the door: "EPS 1848" (Engebret Persen Sundstøen – thus perpetuating his childhood surname for me to see in the 21st century).

Embret P Lobeck

Inger Lobeck

In the summer of 1848 Embret gathered his tools and traveled to his land in the woods. To get there he had to slosh through boggy ground – the same I traversed in 2005 – midway to his knees. Once there, the hard work of gathering hay began.

It was two years later, on April 15, 1850, that Embret Persen Løvbekksetra – note the place name as surname again – age thirty-seven, and Inger Olsdatter Støa of Nordgarn Støa (also known as Nylørdalen, about 15 miles east of Løvbekksetra), then a week shy of her eighteenth birthday, were married in the Trysil church.

Eking out a living must have been quite difficult – winter snows, cold, small parcels of tillable land. It certainly took hard work, strength, stamina, perseverance, and faith. Embret seemed to possess all these survival necessities. He and Inger welcomed their first child Per in 1853, Ola in 1855, Kari in 1859, John in 1862, and Embret, also known as Engebret E. (eventually, E.E.), in 1864. These five joined Ingerinus to make up the family of eight.

Faith becomes fraught

In 1845 Norway passed a Dissenter Law which officially allowed religious tolerance. Essentially, the State Church was allowing other Christians to worship and proselytize as they pleased.

This was a radical departure from tradition. The State Church of Norway was a department of the government. The salary of the "prest" was paid by the government. Churches were built and maintained at government expense. Church officials were often of the aristocracy, making for a "high church" feel.[4] The "low church" was a protest against the perceived abuses of the State Church. Somewhere in between was the "broad church," which encompassed most dissenters.

Some dissented because they disagreed with the law that only the educated clergy should be allowed to interpret the Bible. Many of them could read and didn't always agree with the "prest" in the way he interpreted God's word.

Others felt that the life of the "prest," often in the style of wining and dining, was inappropriate for God's representative.

And there were different views on baptism – infants or adults?

Embret was influenced through his father with Haugeanism, a religious movement started by Hans Nilsen Hauge shortly before 1800.

Hauge was an uneducated poor farmer's son. He traversed the country, claiming he was called by God to witness for Christ. A "spiritual awakening" or revival resulted. This was a threat to the State Church clergy, who laid claim to all things ecclesiastical.

Haugeans gathered in homes, quite informally though very seriously. Their meetings consisted of hymns, reading the Scriptures, and prayer. There were no clergy. The members were adamant about the autonomy of each congregation. But they were still connected with the State Church for anything requiring organization, administration, and recordkeeping, since the State Church was the official keeper of records as an arm of the government. And Hauge was careful never to have meetings that conflicted with state-sanctioned church services.[5]

This is the background for May 28, 1858, when seventeen people withdrew their membership from the State Church and fourteen of them organized the Trysil Frimenighed (Trysil Free Church) the same day. They did not accept Confirmation, which they viewed as perjury, nor did they believe that the reverend/pastor should wear clothes or robes that set him apart from the members of his congregation.[6]

Trysil was a long trip down the mountain from Løvbekksetra. To attend church would have required an overnight stay, which meant giving up working time when it was hard enough to survive. Those who lived at Løvbekksetra would probably attend church only three or four times a year. My grandmother, Martha Persdatter Nordby, who lived near the Trysil church, remembered many trunks stored at Nordby. They belonged to those who came from the mountains and were filled with the owner's "church clothes" for weddings, festivals, and church services themselves.

Around 1859 Embret formed a "Frimenigheds" congregation, Lutheran Free Church, at Løvbekksetra. In the main churchbooks at Trysil, daughter Kari's baptism on August 14, 1859, is recorded with a note that her father is a dissenter, and the old Norwegian churchbooks of dissenting congregations show Embret as the leader of the congregation.

Into this dissenting flock John and Engebret E (Embret), the two youngest sons of Embret and Inger, were baptized. These baptisms are recorded in the churchbooks of their father's Frimenighed congregation, not in the main Trysil churchbooks. However, in the "prest's" log of Trysil Church is written that he received a letter from Engebret and Inger Lobeck stating they dissented from the State Church – and that John and young Embret were baptized.

Church was central, but life was more than church. It was friendships.

Many years later Embret E recounted stories he had heard from his father (Embret P) and his father's good friend, Per Aas, about their exploits back in Norway.

They were boat mates, floating timber. Per Aas rowed, while Embret controlled the pole that served as both push and rudder. "When we used all our strength, we could lift the boat out of the water," said Per.

Hearing screams for help from another team whose boat had overturned, they speeded down the river. "We could only see the men's heads as they bobbed in the water, waving." Embret grabbed the men by the neck and pulled them into the boat.

One night Per and Embret were traveling together on the way home from Elverum. Embret tied his horse behind Per's sledge so they could sit beside each other and talk. Each had a new pair of woolen mittens, spun and knit out of goat's wool. "It is surprising how well these mittens, knit by True [Per's wife], grasp the shaft of the axe," Per said. "Aaaah, these mittens knit by Inger [Embret's wife] grasp much better," replied Embret. They stood on either side of the sledge. Per handed the axe shaft to Embret. Each tried to pull the axe out of the other's hand and be the winner. The sledge shook and creaked. The axe shaft, eventually, remained in Inger's mittens.[7]

Leaving home

It is unknown exactly why Embret Persen Lobeck and wife Inger decided to emigrate to America. Perhaps the burden of leading a congregation was becoming heavy. It seems more likely, though, that the lure of free tracts of land in America was the reason. Embret was probably thinking that with five sturdy sons, there would not be enough land for them to have a future in Norway. The odel system gave the eldest son inheritance rights to the farm, and America was making promises.

For whatever reasons, Embret gave Ole Nyhuus power of authority over his property, then packed trunks and left home at Løvbekksetra on April 11, 1867. Arriving in Trysil, the family stopped to say goodbye to Inger's mother and to Embret's sister, Johanna Viken, who wrote to young Engebret E in America in 1880 and mentioned that the only time she had ever seen him was when he came down from the mountains as a boy of three years to begin his big trip to America. Ten others from Trysil – including five children – were also making the journey to America.

Forty-five years later Engebret E Lobeck (E.E.) reminisced about that momentous day.

> One afternoon we set out over Kristiania fjord; the city disappeared little by little and finally was hidden in Mother Norway's bosom. There wasn't much conversation at first; mournfully the travelers saw the land disappear. The coastline around Kristiania began to fade in the distance and soon the night wrapped its cloak with benign folds over old Norway. Thus many of the travelers saw their fatherland for the last time.

> From Kristiania we took the steamer Odderen to Hull in England, from there by railway to Liverpool. From there on a big steamship called City of Paris and landed in Nyork [New York] on May 5.

> May 7, we went by train overland to Easton, Allentown, Reading, Harrisburg, Cleveland and over Lake Erie to Detroit, then to Grandhaven over Lake Michigan to Milwaukee.

> From there by train to Prairieduchin [Prairie du Chien] and then on the Missipin [Mississippi] up to St. Paul where we rested for a couple of days.

In St. Paul, several of the emigrant group decided to go to Christiania settlement near Northfield, Minnesota. Engebret Lobeck and family, with Jens Norlie, decided to go to Holmes City. Lobeck had met a man from Tolgen on the journey who was going to the Holmes City area, where a family member had settled. Perhaps his talk about the possibilities in Holmes City persuaded Embret to go there also.

Then by train again to St. Cloud. The fare from Kristiania cost $57 [$1,000 – throughout this book, money sums will be followed by their approximate value in 2023 dollars] per adult. And there the railway ended so we had to procure oxen and wagon which we and a family from Tolgen went together on and bought oxen for $175 [$3,300] and the wagon for $100 [$1,900] and took a part of the belongings, all the women and children and drove west over to Holmes City in Douglas County, in Minnesota, where we arrived May 29 where there were several Norwegians and Swedes together with Yankees who had taken most of the finest land, but no one had any fields yet and many had no houses, but four or five had planted a little that spring and some got a little wheat in the fall, but blackbirds took the most.[8]

Chapter 2

In America

This Trysil group of new settlers did not come to America uninformed. Representatives from shipping and railroad companies freely circulated information in Norway about the prospects and opportunities in America – overstating much, and silent about less desirable facts. A "Guide to Minnesota," consolidating this information, published in 1868 and reissued a year later, touted the seeming paradise of the state, praising its lakes, rivers and streams, rich warm loamy soil which would mature crops rapidly, abundant timber that would create wealth for generations, and its wonderful climate.

> It is claimed to be "the healthiest in the world." The testimony of thousands of cured invalids ... confirms this. ... Almost anyone who has resided here for any length of time can refer to numbers now enjoying ordinary health, who on first coming here were considered hopelessly gone with consumption, or other chronic disease. Minnesota is entirely exempt from malaria. ... Diarrhea and dysentery are not so prevalent as in warmer latitudes.

The handbook states that Minnesota has a low mortality rate, though not quite as good as Oregon, but better than California, Wisconsin, and Utah. This falling short of the best is explained:

> Were it not for the large number of invalids who come here too far gone to recover, and die here, Minnesota would show less mortality than Oregon. ... "A very large proportion of the persons dying in the city [St. Paul] are strangers, who have come here sick and almost dying, to receive the benefits of our salubrious climate, but only to linger a few months and then cease the struggle."

The Guide noted that railroads were being built throughout the state for easy access. The current population was estimated to be 450,000, made up primarily of Yankees, Brits, Germans, Norwegians, Swedes, and Swiss. Native Americans are not mentioned.[9]

Homesteading

Probably the most enticing information in the handbook to the new settlers emigrating from Norway and its odel system was how to "get a homestead."

> No State in the Union offers such facilities for getting a comfortable and valuable homestead as Minnesota. It is almost the only State possessing much agricultural land that can be secured by "squatters." Under the U. S. Homestead law any head of a family, or single man twenty-one years of age, can obtain 160 acres of public land by paying twelve dollars [$264] for it at the local U. S. Land Office. Title is perfect at the end of five years.
>
> During the five years the settler must, in good faith, "inhabit" and "cultivate" the tract. No particular amount or value of improvement is required; but the settler is to cultivate the land to the extent that his circumstances will reasonably admit of. Nor is he obliged to live on it all, or even the greater part of the time, especially if he is a single man and needs to work out to procure the means that will best enable him to develop his farm.[10]

Alexandria, Douglas County, Minnesota is listed as one of the U.S. Land Offices.

During the first few days the Lobeck family stayed with recent Norwegian settlers in the Holmes City area. There were some Indians in the neighborhood, and a few other settlers. For shelter, some had made dugouts, a few built log cabins. There was no work to be found in the area, so those who had oxen and wagons drove goods to St. Cloud, the closest market, from which they could be taken west to the forts set up for protection against Indians. Others supported themselves by trapping muskrats.[11]

That first summer, Embret Persen was not sure about settling in Douglas County. He decided to look elsewhere. Leaving Inger and the children with their Holmes City hosts, he yoked up his team and took the government trail in the direction of Otter Tail County, but when he reached the old fort at Pomme de Terre and from a hilltop looked west across the country – no settlers between there and the Rockies, he got lonesome … and at once he was on his way back to Holmes City. In crossing Chippewa River he discovered that the water was packed with fat and beautiful hogs. He grabbed a handspike and went down to see what was up and found that the river was teeming with fish – buffalo fish, mind you – and as no game warden was around, father manipulated the spike in such a way that after a while he had the wagon-box full of fish and came in triumph back to Gunder Knutson's. "America is all right!"*12*

The Lobecks found shelter for the rest of the summer with Gunder and Johanna Knudsen and family, Emmy, Mary Ann, and Albin. Three-year-old Embret enjoyed the summer, free of all the worries his parents must have felt. He enjoyed play with the Knudsen children, and Johanna was very good to them.

> When some of us small ones in the tumult of a fight received a scratch, she strewed brown sugar over the sore and at the same time put a pinch of the same in our mouths. With me it had the result that I became monstrously reckless in my play. If things got too bad, there was sugar to be had both for the wound and the mouth.[13]

During the summer of 1867 Embret bought three cows for $50-$55 [$1,000] each, paid $19 [$360] for a barrel of flour, claimed 160 acres of land in Section 21 of Holmes City township in Douglas County, cleared two and a half acres, bought lumber for his house, and began to build a home for his family. In the late fall they moved into their new house built of logs in the old Norse way with a sod roof. There was only a dirt floor that first year.

One day they saw familiar persons outside. Per Aas and his wife True had arrived – the first friends from Trysil – who brought with them the stories from earlier years in Norway that were recounted. Within the next two or three years many other friends and acquaintances from Trysil showed up in the neighborhood.[14]

One of E.E.'s happiest memories is of the first Christmas in America.

> Mother made a sort of soup cooked with "primost" [made with whey] and water, and besides that we had some bread and fish with potatoes. We still

did not own a lamp, so we got along with candles. All of us had had a bath and had on clean, white muslin shirts. "Christmas has come with healing for the anxious heart" was heard from our mouths. We each had a verse to say. Father, who was the oldest, began, and down the line I, who was the youngest, ended with "Food, in Jesus's name." When the meal was over we sat around the oven and talked and there was scarcely any of father's and mother's friends in Trysil, Norway who was not mentioned. "One wonders how it is with this one or that one this night."[15]

It was a bitterly cold winter, but the family had plenty of food. The woods were full of deer and occasional bear, the lakes of geese and ducks. Fish were always abundant, winter or summer, in Lake Rachel and other nearby lakes.

Weather was a challenge year-round. Heavy rains, flooding, tornadoes, hail, prairie fires, were added to winter's severe cold, blizzards, and heavy snows. Potato bugs and grasshoppers exacted a heavy toll on crops – and on stamina also.

Embret's first crop was 45 bushels of wheat and 50 bushels of potatoes. In summer 1868 he cleared another eight acres of land.[16]

By 1870 there were enough Tryslingers in the area to start a church and a school.

School districts were organized, congregations formed, ministers called, and the people went afoot four to five miles to get to prayer meetings and other gatherings of that kind in the evenings – singing both going and coming. As the population increased, strife and quarrels came. It was a mighty hard thing to get the schoolhouses and churches in the right places. Well do I remember a day when hard words were flying, fists were used and axes flourished at the foot of the hill between where Ole Mauseth and Ole Johnson now reside. A schoolhouse had been erected at that place and the people farther to the south came and demanded that the institution of education and learning should be moved. At the foot of the hill the battle was fought. A gentleman of some reputation led the forces for the faction that wanted the schoolhouse moved – and a genuine Viking, chunky, strong and fearless, by the name of Lars Isakson, was the leader for the other side. ... In that schoolhouse fight he stood like a wall, even if an ax was flourished over his head. ... Some small scrappings occurred about fishing places in the spring. An heroic battle was fought on a hill between two sturdy pioneers, because both claimed the right to a creek where the fish went to spawn. A handspike was used by one of the men, breaking the arms and legs of the other fellow and for many years that hill went under the name of "Slagter bakken," the butcher hill.[17]

Despite the small "scrappings," helpfulness and camaraderie were strong among the settlers. Embret often mentions in his journal that they shared farming chores and oxen teams and helped each other plant and reap and build houses and barns.

Sometimes, relations between the settlers and Yankees got fractious.

John Aasen and Jens Baekken scared up a bear. Frightened, the bear ran up a tree. John had his gun but Jens did not, so Jens told Aasen to stand at the bottom of the tree and watch the bear while he ran to get his gun. Aasen decided he didn't want to be at the bottom of the tree, as the bear was getting ready to jump down. He took aim and shot the bear which fell down stone dead. Upon examining the bear, they noticed something odd around its neck. It was a brass collar. The bear had been a "tame" bear owned by some Yankee who was not too happy when he found out his bear's fate.[18]

E.E.'s account of prairie fires is vivid.

> Men folks had to leave home to meet this foe while the women and children sat by the windows staring at the glare in the sky, fearing that both house and barn would go up in smoke. There were many who saw their buildings and the year's crops become the flame's prey. When the fire reached the high grass one could hear the rumbling din like distant thunder and everything in its path went up in smoke. … If the wind was from the direction where the light was seen, the people gathered in flocks and set backfires in order to stop the oncoming sea of flames.[19]

Despite the struggles, the 1870 agricultural census for Holmes City township shows that in the short time since immigration, the Tryslingers had begun to do quite well. Embret Persen had managed to clear over thirty to forty acres; his farm with livestock had a cash value of $1000 [$21,000]. He owned two cows, two oxen, two cattle, eight sheep, and two pigs. His cousin Halvor O. Strandvold also owned two horses as did Halvor Engemoen.[20] Horses were very expensive, because during the Civil War, which had ended recently, in 1865, so many horses had been killed or eaten.

During these early years some of the Tryslingers, including Embret's oldest son, Ingerinus, were often away several months working on railroad building. During the heavy work times on the farm they returned to help with the sowing or the threshing.

Church

Norwegian immigrants' baggage included church tensions.

Some sought to transplant the structure and ecclesiasticism of the State Church of Norway. Embret's cousin, Halvor O. Strandvold, provided the

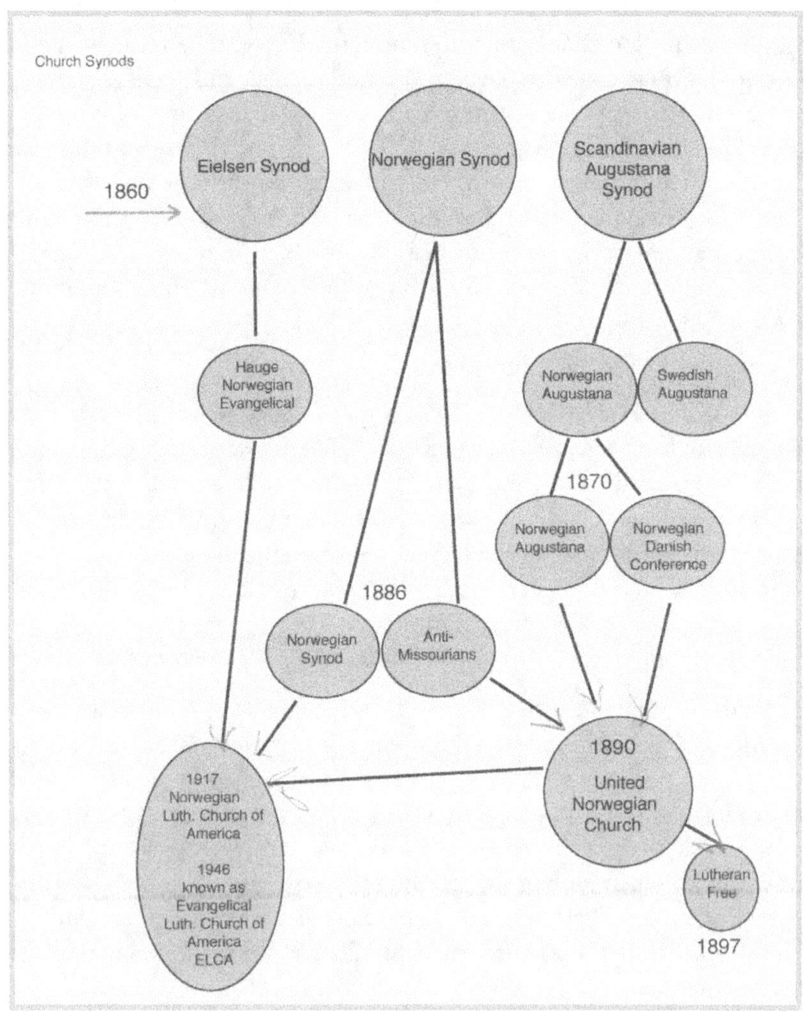

funds and his son-in-law, Andrew Knudson, provided the land to establish Trysil Church congregation across the road from Embret's farm. Oscar Lake congregation, a mile north of Embret's land, was comprised of mostly Swedish immigrants, more in tune with Embret's Haugean sympathies. Though the Lobecks had already been in Holmes City township for four years, Embret P notes in his journal on April 16, 1871, that "we joined the Swedish congregation in Oscar Lake."

The Oscar Lake congregation had been formed in 1866 in a home where the attendees sat on the joists of an incomplete floor and used an emigrant trunk for a writing table. In 1870 a log church building, 24 ft. x 30 ft. x 12 ft. high, was built on a hill. Rev. Jonas Magny, sent as a home missionary to Stearns, Todd, Douglas, Pope, and Ottertail counties, filed a report to the Conference that includes this about completing the Oscar Lake church building:

> At the ... congregational meeting it was decided that the debt on the church building should be paid this fall [1870], and to get the money needed for this each communicant was taxed fifty cents [$10]. For the finishing of the church interior and for the purchase of a stove a free will subscription was begun. Everything that is to be bought is rather expensive out here and cash is hard to get. ... [B]ut I found a way; I drove to Alexandria ... and secured a promise that wheat would be accepted for anything the church would need. Now the people were in the midst of threshing, and I grasped the opportunity to be along and shake the harvest tree. A subscription was begun and both enemies and friends were visited. Seventy bushels of wheat and thirty dollars [$600] in money were collected, the work was completed, all to everyone's satisfaction.[21]

There was competition between denominations.

> The shortage of pastors was a serious handicap in the attempt to organize congregations and gather the settlers around the Word of God. In 1873 it was reported that along the St. Paul and Pacific and the Sauk Valley railroad there were at least 5,000 Swedish settlers. Less than ten percent of these had been brought into the fold of the Minnesota Conference. It was stated that there was in many places a hunger for the Word of God, and since the Conference had been unable to meet the needs adequately the Baptists were doing what they could to gather the people.[22]

Aaron Wahlin, who had come from McGregor, Iowa with his parents and filed for 160 acres in Solem township, Douglas County, was not ordained. He continued his studies while serving as lay pastor for the fledgling Norunga and Oscar Lake congregations, and in June 1873 was ordained at the seminary in Paxton, Illinois. He was then called to be official pastor at Norunga, Oscar Lake, and Wennersborg.[23]

Inevitably, church problems surfaced. Embret Persen wrote that meetings were called day and night the first week of January 1872 to discuss "God's work and this Life's desire." He credits Pastor Wahlin. "a kind teacher," for leading, encouraging, comforting, and admonishing "with untiring zeal."[24]

In America there was no state church to perform administrative duties. The Haugeans had no organizational structure. They soon found they would need to establish a structure and provide a means to train people to be administrators.

The distinction readily visible only a few miles apart, between the Trysil and Oscar Lake churches, was writ large. There were now two Lutheran synods: the Norwegian Synod, modeled on the State Church of Norway, and the lay people's synod, called the Eielsen Synod after its founder, Elling Eielsen, a Haugean, and the first Norwegian Lutheran minister in the United States.

Lutheran congregations and synods managed to disagree and splinter. Those who disagreed with both the Norwegian and Eielsen Synods formed a Norwegian/Danish Lutheran Conference and a Norwegian Lutheran Augustana Synod. Eventually, after bitter struggles and even court cases in the 1890s, these synods and Anti-Missourians formed the Lutheran Free Church, with which Augsburg Seminary and St. Olaf College were associated.[25] (Embret's sons, John and E.E., later attended Augsburg.) E.E. would himself, with 700 others, attend a conference in Minneapolis on June 10, 1897, that permanently established the Norwegian Lutheran Free Church; E.E. was appointed to the Temperance committee, along with his old professors and friends from Augsburg, Reimestad and Nydahl, Casperson and Anderson.

Lutheran fluidity is evident in the Lobeck family's church hopping.

In April 1874 they went to services at Norunga congregation, and another Sunday to the Moe church and listened to "Pastor (Lauritz A.)

Carlson of the (Norwegian) Synod and Pastor Saugstad of the Conference discuss dogmas and feelings towards one another. Pastor A. Wahlin was there as a listener."[26]

Carlson was prest in Alexandria, Saugstad of the Trysil church of the Norwegian Synod. A predestination controversy was dividing the Norwegian Synod and the "Open Declaration" issued by Professor Sven Oftedal of Augsburg and the Conference Synod. Oftedal emphasized congregational liberty, stressed Lutheran confessions, favored frank discussions of dogma, and issued a scathing statement against tendencies toward Romanization.[27]

In January 1876 Pastor Wahlin became ill and was unable to come to church for over a month, but on March 5 "Pastor (Peter) Carlson[28] from Carver County was here and preached and Wahlin was well enough to be in church. This time there was a deacon's meeting to hear the many who had complaints against Wahlin, especially Nils Vatterud, but the complaints lacked foundation so were laid aside."[29]

However, over the next months other pastors often presided over the services. Wahlin's old parents stayed with the Lobecks during the summer of 1876, while Pastor Wahlin moved to Cannon Falls and took a congregation there. On October 5 "Pastor Wahlin came up here from Cannon Falls. He was here about two weeks, and on October 15 he married Jennie Solberg and left right away with his wife and old parents."[30]

Despite the wrangling, the familial relationship between the Norwegian and the Swedish Lutherans of this community was evidenced by their constant intermingling and attendance at each other's services.[31] Each group belonged to both churches' Ladies Aid, attended and hosted the Reading Society that was begun by Trysil's minister, Saugstad, and in 1886 both churches worked together to form a Temperance society (nearly 40 people signed up). Even ministers crossed lines. On Christmas Day 1877 Pastor Christian Saugstad preached at Oscar Lake and later in the morning at Trysil church.[32]

And Embret still exercised some of the authority he had had in the Frimenighed in Norway. Ole Støen's journal entry for April 28, 1890, states that "Engebret P Løbek baptized our child by the name Petra."[33]

Weather and death and grasshoppers

January 1872 was mild, but February brought severe cold and a snowstorm in which some neighbors froze to death. Stories were told for many years about how some tried to survive by tipping over their wagons and wrapping themselves in blankets and empty sacks while the blizzard raged for three days and nights around them.[34]

Winter returned again with fury in 1873. Ola Lobeck wrote about one of the big blizzards, January 7-10. (The term "blizzard" had first been used for such storms just three years before.)

> When I came out of the door the dense snowfall was so thick that I could see nothing. ... I continued until I thought I was midway between the house and the barn. I stood there a long while and anticipated that I would catch a glimmer of one or the other, but I saw nothing because the air was so thick with snow. ...
>
> Staring hard, looking down, I could see my own feet. Just as soon I could not see them and I felt very alone. I could not make out anything above my waist and down to my knees. I gave up, and struggled to return to the house. ...
>
> Many people froze in the storm. Many, who were out, froze both hands and feet. Several were crippled for life. Some went to the barn to see about their animals and got lost and disoriented and stayed outside, others went for wood and got lost and some were in the woods and didn't get home and many of them died.[35]

A newspaper account in the Jan. 18, 1873 *Alexandria Post* tells of a 15-year-old boy a few miles from Lobecks, who had been driving a yoke of oxen and was found near his home standing against a fence, dead, his oxen also dead. Tracks showed he had been within 200 feet of his own home and unable to find it. The storm resulted in the deaths of 70 Minnesotans, hundreds of cattle lost, and trains stuck for days in high drifts.[36]

There was good reason Embret Persen included the recipe for curing cold feet in the margins of his journal.

> A cure for cold feet or other cold parts of any limb. If it is the feet, soak them in a basin of warm water, as hot as you can tolerate. Mix in a tablespoon of mustard and throw a blanket over the legs so they don't cool off too fast. After 5-10 minutes take the feet out and dry them and put the

patient in bed under a couple of blankets and when he has lain down have him drink a large glass of lemonade as warm as possible – or a glass of warm water with a spoonful of pure wine and a little sugar. Eat sparingly of ordinary food. Baked apple and other fruit, bread and butter, baked potato, and raw oysters are good.[37]

A couple of weeks after the storm, Embret Persen Lobeck and Ole Støen made a trip into Alexandria to the land office. With money borrowed from Halvor O. Strandvold at 12 percent interest they bought more land, about four miles from the Lobeck farm. In April the Lobecks tapped over 100 maple trees and made syrup, began planting crops, and set out thirteen apple trees. They were building a barn and making improvements in the house that summer. Son Per went to work on the railroad and came back home during Christmas week after an absence of six months.[38]

The next few years were especially difficult for the Lobeck family. Grasshoppers showed up in their fields in August 1874, toward the end of the growing season. Rain damaged their corn and tobacco crop. In November four of their sheep fell through the ice and drowned in the nearby slough.[39]

April 1875 brought a terrible tragedy to the family. Son Per, now 22, who had been confirmed, along with his sister Kari, by Pastor Wahlin the previous November, was accidentally killed by a gunshot wound on an errand to collect the pastor's salary.

A minister's salary at that time was usually negotiated with a dollar amount, perhaps about $150 [$3,600], and donations of food products from the parishioners. For Pastor Wahlin, the agreement included a sack of oats per year from each family.[40]

Per and Pastor Wahlin got along well together. On the morning of April 16 Per and the pastor left early for the store of A. G. Solbergs in order to haul the Solbergses' promised yearly load of oats to Wahlin's farm where he lived with his parents, near Kensington.

Per usually had his gun with him as he was a good hunter, often bringing home game for the dinner table. This day his gun was lying on top of the sacks of grain in the wagon. When some prairie chickens flew up in a nearby field, Per reached for his gun. As he picked it up by the muzzle, the hammer caught and discharged. The shot struck him under the ear. He died instantly.

Embret Persen wrote in his journal, struggling to accept what tragedy had been given him.

> He did come home the same evening – but stiff and dead. Neither he nor we had any thought when he left in the morning healthy and happy to be in company with our dear Pastor Wahlin. Yes – strange are God's ways.
>
> April 20. We took him to his last resting place in the grave and before we left home Pastor Wahlin talked to us about 2 Corinthians 5:9. O Merciful God, help me to a blessed death.[41]

In March 1876 Embret P hurt his arm badly while plastering the well, and "was lame for a long time." On July 9 "there came a frightful swarm of grasshoppers that almost took possession of field and meadow."[42]

And on July 13 young Embret saw a boy on horseback galloping so fast he broke through the fence-gate. "The Indians are coming!" At first young Embret laughed, but then remembered stories he had heard of settlers being killed by Indians. He ran to tell his mother. His father heard the news while out draining a bog, and commented, "Ja, this will probably be worse than the grasshoppers." Rumors were flying that Fergus Falls was burning and people were murdered. Some neighbors prepared to flee to Alexandria or Morris for protection. Others let their cattle out to roam free and carried furniture and possessions to the woods and buried them to protect them from theft. Embret Persen remained calm, putting an extra load in the old shotgun and a pitchfork by the head of the bed.[43]

All proved to be a false alarm. Nothing but rumors. The *Alexandria Post* stated the facts in the next issue.

> Several weeks ago a party of Chippewa Indians went over to the vicinity of Big Stone Lake and bought a lot of ponies of the Sioux. In returning through Elizabeth City in Otter Tail County they got some bad whiskey. Crazed by its influence, they were emboldened to help themselves freely to provisions and to graze their ponies in the grain fields. The story was circulated over the country; and by the time it had traveled to eastern Otter Tail and to Grant and Douglas Counties had become distorted into a massacre which soon brought on a panic and flight. ... In about twenty-four hours the scare was over and all took up the homeward march.[44]

Two days later, a heavy wind and rainstorm came up about midnight –
three inches of rain in about thirty minutes. Buildings rocked on their
foundations and some were "slightly deflected from the perpendicular." A
building in Alexandria was knocked "two inches to the east" and was
righted again with a combination of ropes, pulleys, and a capstan.[45] Two
weeks later, more rain came, accompanied by significant hail.

In May Embret Persen had taken out an insurance policy issued by the
Mutual Hail Insurance Co. of Wisconsin. For the premium of $6.15
[$150] he was insured against loss or damage by hail up to $410
[$10,100] on twenty-five acres of wheat and six acres of oats. Wisconsin
Mutual had to pay out over ninety losses in the area.

In August "the grasshoppers came again and overtook the fields and the
air was so full of them that it looked like a big snowstorm, and those of
us who had to be out on the land had to wade and step on them
wherever we went."[46]

The yield that devastating year was only 101 bushels of wheat and sixty
bushels of oats after planting a promising thirty-three acres in the spring.
The year before, in 1875, Embret had harvested 584 bushels of wheat
and 187 bushels of oats.[47]

Young Embret years later remembered the grasshoppers.

> The first summer they laid their eggs and they lay so thick in the road that
> when we drove with the wagons it stuck under the wheels as though we
> drove on wet roads. They made a small hole where they laid their eggs and
> the field's surface looked like a sieve. Next spring the eggs hatched, a
> wriggling, unending, teeming mass. It was as though the dust itself had life.
> We killed them by the barrels, dragged big boxes with open fronts and
> smeared coal tar on the inside. The pests jumped into the boxes by the
> hundred thousands. We also dug long trenches and when they were half
> full of grasshoppers we covered the trenches and filled them with straw
> and set fire to it. It was no use. When fall came there was nothing left but
> dry sticks.[48]

Some farmers, in their desperation, used strychnine to kill the pests.
Later, as the pests departed, piles of grasshopper poison were bulldozed
into pits across western Minnesota, creating hazardous waste sites into
the twentieth century.[49]

What's the government to do?

The ravages of the grasshopper plague brought the debate concerning government's involvement in public assistance to the fore. The same arguments were expressed then as now.

The stricken farmers and their families were desperate. Nearly all were new immigrants, so they had no accumulated wealth to see them through difficult times.

During the span of the plague, Minnesota had three governors: Cushman Davis, Henry Sibley, and John Pillsbury. They recognized a need but differed in their responses.

Davis appealed for funds – unsuccessfully – to the U.S. War Department, "asking that the quota of arms due the State of Minnesota for two years, the worth of which will be about $8,000 [$200,000], be turned over in the shape of supplies."

Davis advocated helping the needy as "the victims of a calamity no vigilance can guard against." Appealing to the legislature, he said that "the government, acting through counties and cities, has from the beginning extended a liberal charity towards individual sufferers. Here, however, is an instance where the sufferers and inhabitants of entire communities are identical. They cannot as communities help themselves."[50]

Henry Sibley also appealed to the legislature, even though he was not governor at this time. He had been at the forefront in organizing disaster aid after the devastating blizzard in January 1873 that killed hundreds on the prairies. The legislature allocated funds up to $30,000 [$745,000] to be disbursed at Governor Davis's discretion. No more than $35 [$870] should be disbursed to any one family. Davis worried that he would be criticized for mismanagement if there were problems regarding distribution, so he required exceptionally many "dos and don'ts," making the task needlessly cumbersome.

Davis also began collecting information from residents about grasshoppers and their habits, in hopes of learning what could be done to stave off so much destruction in a subsequent attack. And he appealed to those who were better off to look into their hearts and help the needy with private donations. This call largely fell on deaf ears.

The legislators were slow to respond to requests. They were suspicious of the recipients' integrity, suggesting that further aid would be bad for their character and tempt them to do nothing but wait for aid. The legislature demanded that any recipient must provide a "verified petition showing necessity of such relief," making it all but impossible for a destitute farmer to claim relief.

Sibley, by then governor, in an address in August 1876 stated that the "poor should not expect relief as a right. To protect the poor from their own weak natures, the state should discourage dependence." Sibley believed that aid should only be given to those willing to help themselves. And those would be the ones who had such strong moral fiber that they would not ask for help.[51]

In May, the grasshoppers were back, covering the ground. In early July they began to leave and the air was black with them. At month's end, there were no grasshoppers to be seen. They had gone as mysteriously as they had arrived. But the damage had been done again. Lobecks had no yield that year except eighty loads of hay and some potatoes. All the corn and oats were taken by the grasshoppers. Embret Persen had debts to pay. In September 1874, just before the start of the first grasshopper plague, he had taken out a bank loan for $250 [$7,000]. He had to stake all his land for collateral plus a note for $300 [$8400]. And now there had been three miserable harvests since.

June 1877 brought destructive weather again, with tragic results for the neighborhood. About two miles south of Lobecks, Halvor H. Engemoen and his wife, Kristina, had just built a new frame house. Only the youngest son, thirteen-year-old Olaf, happened to be home with his parents on Friday afternoon, June 29, when the wind came up from the east, swung to the north with pelting rain and force, then switched to the west and evolved into a tornado. The frame house overturned. Olaf and his mother ran for the cellar. When her husband was not behind her, Kristina stuck her head out of the cellar to call for him. Just then the house blew away and her head was crushed.[52]

Halvor "was thrown two or three rods and was left lying between the floor and ceiling upside down with all the furnishings and the rest of the house broken in small pieces." He was pulled out of the wreckage with a dislocated thigh and head injuries. Within six months, he, too, died.[53]

The next few years were not so dramatic. The Lobecks cut logs from the woods to build their granary. Marriages and deaths occurred. Church activities were attended. Crops were planted in the spring and harvested in the fall with help from the neighbors. Ola found work driving cattle or building railroads, but would be home six months of the year. Inger carded and spun wool, constantly knitting thick warm clothing and mittens that Embret would brag about. Included on the charge list at the local store in March 1878 were two spools of thread, seven yards of quilting, and five yards of sheeting at nine cents [$2.50] a yard.

1878 was the year after the grasshoppers disappeared. The Lobecks' harvest was encouraging: 348 bushels of wheat, 244 bushels of oats, fifty-two bushels of rye, and five gallons of maple syrup.[54]

Summing up

On September 29, 1878, Embret posted his semi-annual letter to his sister, Johanne Viken, in Trysil, Norway, recounting events of the year and revealing his thoughts on church and reasons for leaving the State Church in Norway. Scattered throughout the letter are echoes of Scripture.[55]

> Though it is not so long since I last wrote to you, we have however reached another season of the year where the vegetation fades, especially the leaves and the grass with its flowering beauty and delight. This reminds us of the fleeting of time, life's instability, and our own perishing and the futility of all flesh. Even if we are old and have lived many days and years in this world, it is not even a finger's width of time. Yes, we must work while it is day for when the night comes no one can work anymore. May we never lack for oil in our lamps. …

> I know and see that one after another from our youthful days are dying, and this reminds us too, that this is the way for all of us … the old must die and the young ones can also die and nothing in life is certain. …

> I still have so much to thank the Good Lord for … that I have health, even though I get tired. I still do not have any weakness or pain in any of my limbs. My only problem is that I do not sleep peacefully at night … thoughts and worries, outward and inward … and I am all too often very unwilling to cast all my cares on the Lord. His Fatherly counsel is that I struggle with them until I understand that I am not capable to handle them alone. So sister, it is an art to be able to see one's wretchedness.

We see from this that God still keeps what he has given us so generously, this hourly sojourn for a time. May our dear Savior give us a true hunger and thirst after the heavenly manna and pure wine. …

You will most likely be happy that I, rather we, have regained our senses, now that we are letting our children be confirmed … but in the Swedish church where we have been, and are now, the children do not have to take any thoughtless oath, or give the prest their hand and repeat that they have, and will continue in the Lutheran Christian teaching solely in agreement with the Bible, and by public confession of this before God and the Church they become members of the Church. Likewise in Baptism, the godparents do not renounce the devil for the child. This and other matters are what drove me and many others away from the State Church. I will not insist that we acted wisely in everything, but there was no middle road, so we had to part ways.

Six months later, on March 24. 1879, he wrote again to his sister.

It is strange how the tooth of time gnaws so relentlessly, and how it reminds us more and more about our mortality and the disintegration of our body, would we then be able to grow and increase in our inner being day by day, as we decrease in our outer being, then our God by Jesus Christ would have won his purpose with us, to his glory and our eternal bliss. …

It is so interesting to hear about our old home place and the acquaintances of our youth, be they alive or passed away, even if I think that if I could visit now, I would get to see much that is not in compliance with Christianity and a godly way of life. I can see how it goes here, there is more effort put into pleasing the world and in worldly things, than in pleasing God and loving his commandments, especially with the poor youth that pursue all new fashions, without true godliness.

There is no shortage here of schools both in English and Norwegian and Swedish, and Christian preachers, and quite a lot have reverence of the word of God, but the majority does not feel they have time, etc.

When it comes to worldly things, there is no shortage here of provisions, but a common complaint that money is short, and most of us are getting deeper and deeper in debt, and now for two years there has been no crop to sell, and most of us have had to buy both food and seed, so we are in a tight spot in these matters, even if we, this fall, got a decent crop measured in bulk, but the density was too light, so we had to sell it as No. 2 and 3 and even partly as No. 4, and this fall we got only 55 cents [$16] per bushel, and those most in trouble had to sell what they had at that price. Now for a time the price has been 75 to 80 cents [$22-$24] per bushel, and the rich ones have been selling. …

Ola came home shortly before Christmas after having been away for one and a half years, so we are having good help, but there is enough to do with cutting and bringing home both fence materials, timber and firewood. We have also bought horses this winter for timber and a couple of oxen, as it is almost impossible to drive with oxen when the field is bare and frozen. The horses cost 275 dollars [$8200]. …

The only income we have is freighting cord wood to Morris for 4 dollars 75 cents [$140] per cord, but as we cannot take more than 3/4 cord per load, and the distance is 22 miles, the profit is not very great.

Ingerinus finally got married last New Year. The other children were wondering, I think. He took a Swedish girl, our closest neighbor.

There has been a lot of illness here, especially colds and throat inflammation. E Haugen's three children died in a short span of time.

New immigrants are already coming here from Wisconsin and other American states, to buy land, and many are going to Red River and Dakota, and also to Nebraska, because now it is starting to get crowded in the eastern states, and they are going farther west. One from Wisconsin came the other day and bought a farm for 2,000 dollars [$60,000] in cash. …

I must start ending this letter with a sincere thanks to God for health and wholesomeness and the daily bread, and that we are not experiencing the same troubles that we read about in the papers, striking other places and nations. We see how Hungary suffers from floods, and China from hunger, and it's all a Fatherly penalty and punishment, that we have deserved as well as the others. …

I hope that if you live and are in good health you will write so I can hear from you soon. It will be very bleak if you can't write any more, or if you have passed away forever, but that time will come to all of us, maybe to me first. God alone knows. May he in his grace and mercy help us to a true and living faith until the end comes. Amen!

Embert's reflections on death, a "time that will come to us all," were fueled not only by his theology but also by repeated encounters with death's suddenness.

February 1, 1881, Trysil Ladies Aid was held at the Lobeck home. Guri Aasen was there but not feeling well. She asked if she could lie down for a while. Almost at once she gave birth to a stillborn baby boy. Hardly anyone attending even knew what was happening, as Guri didn't cry out.

Guri stayed overnight at the Lobecks'. The following morning a severe blizzard had closed them in (the winter became known as the "snow winter"). Six days later, the snow and blizzard subsided enough for Embret to retrieve some fence posts from the farmyard and make skis so he could get to the store. He made nine pairs of skis before he was done. With the aid of several men and sled and skis, they were able to take Guri home.[56]

"Pondering on progress"

On April 18, 1881, Embret writes to his sister.

> Where the snow lay still, it was three feet deep, and that was unusually much here. We have not had so much snow any winter since we came here. …

> We are now wondering whether our acquaintances from Trysil have started their journey here. … Maybe the ice around the coast of Norway is stopping them from going away as early as they meant to. May the Lord be with them on their journey.

> Here they are now beginning to talk about traveling to Montana, about six to eight hundred miles west of here, but that will be a long trip from Trysil. Maybe, if they have some money, they can buy from us who came first, and then we can move again.

> They are now constructing the railroad westwards as fast as they can, to meet the one that comes eastwards from the Pacific Ocean, and then go by the Iron Horse from Duluth to Puget Sound across America at the northern end, too. Yes, God alone knows how long the world can keep on like this. It looks like the end days is at hand, if it isn't already here, as all nations and all people and almost every single person is pondering on progress, so they can become rich without a sweat on their forehead.

Our task this spring has been bringing timber to build a stable that we started building last year; now it is ready for roofing. We have also built a roof over the door and the windows on the south side and boarded some of the walls on the outside. Inside there are also many things lacking, but if God gives us a good year this summer and I am allowed good health, I have good hope to catch up with what's lacking in the house. …

When I now look out into the realm of Nature, everything is black, dark and dim, both forest and fields, but then I can hear and see so many kinds of birds that sing so merrily, flying happily around and reminding me that it is still spring, and the summer is approaching. There are yet no buds on the trees, but still everything heralds that the summer is near. It is often like that for me in the land of Grace. Many a time everything looks dark and cold, but in a little while God is sending an exhilarating ray of light, so we can both see the road and gather strength to walk it, and that way our faith and hope that the Eternal Summer is near is strengthened, when all tired wanderers may come to the right Sabbath rest. Yes, may God help us to get there, amen.

We are all in this home in fair health, praise the Lord, and the same goes for all the Tryslingers around here, even if during the winter there were a lot of minor illnesses, especially among the young ones, with coughing and throat inflammation. I have not heard anything from Red River for a couple of weeks. Last time we heard from them they feared floods, but the worst floods, both in America and Europe, I believe to be the pride that shows itself through the infinite fashions of clothes and behavior, in gestures and speaking, especially among those who in the Scriptures are named virgins or young girls. This annoys and torments my mind quite a lot, and it looks like a cataclysm which no one can save them from. Maybe it is equally bad in poor Trysil, especially in the more distinguished weddings. It sounds jokingly ghastly, but maybe I am wrong, maybe they have washed their hands white in the blood of the Lamb.

The Lobecks, as well as most of the Tryslingers, thought education and learning very important. In 1881 Embret subscribed to a newspaper and recorded various international and national news items in his journal (including the inauguration of Garfield as president on March 4, the assassination of Tsar Alexander II on March 13, and the shooting of Garfield on July 2). He also felt it important that his sons receive further schooling.

Young Embret took part in the Reading Society, the Holmes City Læseforening. Members paid one dollar [$29] for books. Young Embret claimed he "dug on the farm in the day and read literature in the night."

Reading societies were generally "located in areas heavily populated by Norwegian-American immigrants and all were organizationally embedded in church-centered, Norwegian Lutheran communities. Most of them did not have a formal connection to the local church, its governing board or its pastor."[57]

However, Holmes City Læseforening differed. Organized by Pastor Christian Saugstad in 1877, the society had a constitution that excluded those who "denied faith in the Holy Scriptures as God's Word." Later, the wording was changed to a more positive note and "limited membership to those who professed the Christian faith."[58] Though many reading societies did not allow membership to women, the Holmes City society included several women – as long as they were Christian – but they were not allowed to speak or vote.

With the passage of time (and the arrival of rural post delivery, which made access to books much easier), interest in the Holmes City Reading Society waned.

The Holmes City Læseforening met on December 30, 1905, twenty-eight years after its founding, to consider whether to continue or disband. The group decided it should not continue because "no one bothers himself to work, read, or pay their dues." Any income from the sale of remaining books was to be given to the Ladies Aid.[59]

On June 24, 1882, Embret writes again to his sister, this time with wedding news.

> We are in relatively good health, God be praised, but both Inger and I are experiencing more and more illnesses, amongst which the common toothache is a faithful companion, bringing headache and many other unpleasantnesses along. And lately I also have been both faint and bad at both eating and working, but I have the freedom that I can stop when I can take no more, as all three boys are at home this summer.
>
> Inger is certainly more busy, having to accommodate and attend on so many, and has only little Inger for help. Kari is also home now, and has been since about fourteen days before Whitsun, and you can imagine how it helps mother with her in charge, and we are all set in motion preparing

the wedding that will be held here the coming Saturday, July 1, and it would be fun, and not unreasonable, if the old ones at Viken came here to spend a day with us. … Oh, now I remember it is a long distance, and you would not make it in time.

Embret P's Journal records that more friends and relatives began to arrive from Trysil. Lobecks often had the new immigrants stay with them for a time. Nils, Oline, and Johanne Viken, grandchildren of Embret's sister in Norway, arrived separately. Embret felt responsible for watching over them, though none of them lived long lives after immigrating. Nils eventually went to Canada and died in a cave-in while digging a well. Oline died in Fargo of typhoid fever in March 1884. Johanne married Svan Tockselius, a Swedish tailor in Fargo, gave birth to a baby girl, Agnes Henrietta, and died November 1886, when Agnes was six months old.

Young Embret and Nils went to find work in northern Minnesota and the Red River Valley for six months in 1883. On June 4 Embret Persen wrote to them, encouraging them to enjoy their high spirits but to remember to stay on the right path.

Thank you so much for the letter I received in the last mail delivery. We are so happy to hear that you are in good health and have been earning some money, perhaps not so much, but you have the very good fortune of living with good people, and even better that they are godly people, who have a reverence for God's Word and lead a good Christian life. My most fervent wish is that they set good examples for you and teach you not to work for man alone but for God. I think of you so often, and especially both morning and evening during our private devotions, and I wonder then if you thank our Father and pray to him, either alone in your rooms or with the family. Keep Joseph's example in mind. He was a young man who was sold as a slave, but because he had God looking out for him, things turned out well for him.

In summer 1885 the Per Nordby family with nine children arrived from Trysil. It had been eighteen years since Mrs. Nordby had seen her parents and siblings leave for America. Martha Persdatter Nordby was eleven years old. According to family lore, when twenty-one-year-old young Embret E saw her, he declared he would wait for her to grow up and then he would marry her. Eleven years later, on June 3, 1896, he did.

Martha and E.E., June 3, 1896

January 1886 began with cold and drifting snow making it very difficult to get to the Ladies Aid auction at Trysil Church, across the road to the east of the Lobecks. In February the Holmes City store owned by Sodergren and Wagenius burned down, taking the life of Sodergren. Kari and her husband, Carl Alfred Petterson, had a little boy, Oscar, in late February. In early April Carl Alfred was arrested and taken to Alexandria, probably for unpaid debts.[60]

Temperance Society

In an event with huge consequences for the rest of this story, in December 1886 Trysil and Oscar Lake congregations came together to organize a Temperance Society. A month later they met again to draw up a constitution. Among the officers was twenty-two-year-old E.E. Lobeck.

Between the organization in January and the first regular meeting in March, a huge sadness came to the Lobecks.

In early February 1887 Ola was sent to summon Dr. McIver. Mother Inger was very ill. A few days later, John quickly came home from his studies at Minneapolis Academy. The rest of February she continued very ill, deteriorating even more the first week in March. The minister came to visit and then on March 12 Embret Persen wrote, "My dear wife Inger died at 7 o'clock in the evening." She had died of dyspepsia. Four days later, the family made the lonely procession up the road one mile to the north to bury their beloved wife and mother in the Oscar Lake cemetery. Nearly 100 people attended the funeral.

At the Temperance Society's first regular meeting, held on a Sunday afternoon in March at Oscar Lake Church, the membership list numbered 282, comprised primarily of members of Trysil and Oscar Lake congregations.

By 1888 Temperance and Prohibition issues were dominating public conversation. In January and April, lectures were given in Trysil Church by Hans Petter Rud, a shoe salesman from Fergus Falls who had immigrated from Norway in 1880. Trysil Church hosted a conference to talk about alcoholism, with speakers Pastors Anders Melland of the Conference and Vinbor from Minneapolis. In late June Rev. Professor Theodor Reimestad of the Conference and Augsburg Seminary came to the community with some of his students and held Prohibition lectures.

Reimestad was also a musician and authored many Temperance songs, greatly influencing young Embret.

In early March 1889, Kari and Carl Alfred (who the previous April had been arrested; he eventually paid off the debt – it took three years) and their two children moved in with Embret. This was a big help for companionship and household help. E.E.'s brother John married Emma Linden from neighboring Hoffman in May.

Kari and Carl Alfred had another little girl, Ellen Camilla, in late August. In September, John and Embret had gone back to school, studying at Augsburg Seminary in Minneapolis. Young Inger was also in Minneapolis working in the dining room at Augsburg.

John and young Embret had often been away at school in Minneapolis during the 1880s, interspersed with work on the railroad in the summers and trips home to help with farm work. John had begun his studies in 1881 at Augsburg Seminary, followed with studies at Minneapolis Academy and Valparaiso University, and finally at the University of Minnesota in 1890. Young Embret attended high school at Willmar Seminary, which probably gave impetus to the Temperance leanings which later became his life's cause. Willmar Seminary's "president, Hans S. Hilleboe, was considered one of the best school men in the state. He was … often called on to lecture on educational and Temperance subjects. He was a fine orator and a dangerous enemy of the saloon."[61]

Young Embret also attended Augsburg Seminary, Wraaman's Academy, and for a brief period studied literature at the University of Minnesota. Wraaman's Academy, in existence only a short time (1890-97), owed its success largely to the teaching skills of the founder, Wilhelm Wraaman, who had himself been educated at Augsburg Seminary.

How John and Embret paid for their schooling is not known. Both spent periods of time working on the railroad; they had probably done occasional odd jobs for hire. While in Minneapolis, young Embret and John did some singing, for which their father hoped they were receiving some remuneration. The city of Minneapolis employed young Embret as a street lamplighter in the University area.

"Branches that have grown are now exposed to the wind"

Embret wrote to his sons on October 21, 1889.

It didn't rain a drop the three weeks I was out in the cornfield, and during that time, in my solitude, I thought a lot about the past and present, and the future. Well, less about the future, I guess, for my days can soon come to an end. But the branches that have grown are now exposed to the wind, especially those standing on high. There is nothing I can do but pray for you and for myself, and thank God that he has sustained and protected us until now.

Kari's husband, Carl Alfred, had been having problems for some time, resulting in an alarming incident as told by Embret in a letter dated February 21, 1890, to John, Embret, and Inger.

I can almost say that we do enjoy an abundant life. We have food and drink, milk, and meat, and pork, as well as our good health.

Alfred is, of course, the exception. We don't know where he is, or whether he is alive or dead. He was home last Sunday, and he left Monday morning in time for his job. On Wednesday evening, the fellow in charge of the grain elevator came to our place and asked for him, as no one in Hofman had seen him since Saturday evening. Well, of course, all of us were very astonished. And because he had said before he left that he thought the shortest route was via Berns, Ola went there in the evening and asked around. But no one had seen him there. Then he hurried to Kensington to send a telegram inquiring whether he had arrived there (I mean Hofman), but no one had seen him. Now thirty to forty men have been searching the entire week without finding a trace of him. It is a mystery to everyone. Wherever we go we must remain aware of how near death is. We cannot fathom that he could be lying dead somewhere along the route he has always taken. The wells have been checked too. So there seems to be no explanation. Some folks had seen a couple of men (not together) from a distance, so now others are trying to find out if he could have been one of them.

Today, the 24th, three men – J. Aas, O. Andersen, and our hired boy – left from here, but they found no trace. So it seems everyone will just have to stop worrying and leave it in God's hands.

I see from your letter that you have no money and possibly will have to wait to receive something from Alfred. This isn't so strange. God is mysterious in his ways, and he can turn water into wine. As usual, I don't have a cent to my name. It seems so hard to lay my hands on a few dollars which I ought to have at my disposal by now.

Life had changed for Embret after Inger's death. The children were grown and living their own lives. Carl Alfred's mental illness persisted. No report has surfaced for how, when, and where he was discovered after his disappearance, but he does reappear in the family story until 1898, when he was admitted to a mental hospital in Fergus Falls. Serious-minded John was married. Young Embret was away at school. Ola helped with the farm work but had thoughts of moving elsewhere.

Embret often felt lonely. He wrote to his "dear children in Minneapolis," March 25, 1890.

> I often have no one to talk to here in the house; "yes" and "no" is usually the extent of it. I miss heart-to-heart conversations, and would that I spent more time communicating with my dear Lord, who alone can hear my supplications and provide me with that which best serves me.

He did the tasks he could do and rested when he could. Eyesight was waning, his back ached, and handwriting became more of a task – though he always gave thanks that his health was good. Cold feet are mentioned most often in his writing.

In the fall of 1890 John and Emma were living at Farwell where John began teaching at the public school. They built a small house, and were adding a room for Embret. Ola had started a business in Farwell. Kari and Carl Alfred had built a small house just east of her father. When he wrote to son Embret in April 1892, Embret commented that "they don't often have any real conversations that interest me" at John and Emma's.

> Ola is not often home during the day. I am often over at John and Emma's puttering with something, but I sleep at home.

> I guess Ola will help John add on to the house, so I'll have a room there. It is going to be awful moving from a place where I have felt so at home. I've always wanted to end my days in peace. But in God's Word we read: Believe in the Lord with all your heart, trusting not in your reason.

> Time steals away slowly; the hourglass runs out rapidly; death is at our heels; eternity before us.

Always interested in the newspaper, keeping up with church affairs, and reading about political events, in November 1892 he sleighed into Holmes City to vote for the first time on the Prohibitionist ticket.

> We read in the paper today that there are 240,797 saloons in the United States. Isn't that shocking.

> April 14, 1893. Friday. This was moving day for me.

Old neighbors came to help with unfinished tasks at the house in Farwell, including hanging the door on the room Embret would occupy.[62]

The wedding of Inger and Olav Refsdal took place in late June at the old farm. They moved shortly thereafter to Escanaba, Michigan, where Olav had been called as a pastor.

Young Embret finished his schooling and decided to make Prohibition his life's cause. He gave Temperance lectures in Minneapolis, Wisconsin, and Michigan, where he also visited Inger. But by September he was back to help with the threshing before leaving for his lecture circuit in October.

Embret Persen now had time to reflect on his life. His family and his God were what his life had been about. He had tended his faith, his family, and his fields with love, care, strength, and resolute humble belief in God. His optimistic outlook had seen the family through many hardships. Many times Embret had surveyed his fields and remarked about the beauty as he gazed out over his land, smelled the apple trees in blossom and observed the abundant plum blossoms, trusted in God through all adversities, and thanked God for an abundant harvest.

Engebret Persen Lobeck died April 19, 1896 at Ola's house in Farwell.[63] His son E.E. wrote:

> Now we close our old father's eyes. He has moved beyond, he went in peace. It is a good blessing to know that there is a haven of peace in Heaven that poor tired sinners go to when earth no more has room for them. God give us siblings, once again, the same haven of peace where father and mother now are so eternally in safekeeping. At 12 o'clock today (Sunday) he got the message to lay down his walking staff – he did not need it in the beyond – and he was glad to lay it down. He has been more or less in a coma these last two weeks, but his whole way of thinking turned to the one necessity and therefore we could hear him both night and day at his bed:

O, Jesus, vær du Jesus min,
O, Jesus lad mig være din
Bær du, o Jesus, min Tillid
Saa har jeg nok til evig Tid.

og

Hjertens Jesus, i dit Hjerte
Er saa godt at gjemme sig,
Uden dig er idel Smerte,
Ingen Ting fornøier mig.

O Jesus, be thou my Jesus,
Oh Jesus, let me be yours.
Bear thou, O Jesus, my Trust,
Then I have enough for eternity.

and

Jesus of the heart, in your heart
It is so good to hide,
Without you is much pain,
Nothing brings me joy.

Three days ago he woke up out of his daze and told me that he had not been on earth for several days.[64]

Once more the funeral procession plodded up the road to the north, to his waiting grave in Oscar Lake Cemetery beside his wife, Inger. He was eighty-three years old.

An affectionate smile, a friendly word,
Gladdens the heart, and lightens the soul,
And life does not grow weary of the day.
Takk for alt. [Thanks for everything]

Chapter 3

Temperance Lecturer

The year 1892 was an election year. By summer's end, political discussions about Prohibition were heating up in the Holmes City community, as evidenced by a letter E.E. wrote to *The Reform* newspaper

in Eau Claire, Wisconsin, a leading forum for Temperance and Prohibition advocates. His letter has the tone of one who enjoys being in the middle of a political fight, perhaps even helping to provoke it.

> The political situation is lively here. Abstinence meetings are quite well attended, and we have more time to discuss which political party to support at the next election. The Republicans complain; it is almost too hot for them. At a discussion meeting they all went out, the tension taut, and slammed the door after them when the Prohibitionists gave them a beating for their lack of Temperance sympathies. The most radical of Republicans, nevertheless, stay at home. They cannot stand to hear anything about Prohibition; it raises their temper to the boiling point.[65]

The Reform would quickly come to play a central role in E.E.'s life. The beginning of the connection is recounted in a memorial note written at the time of E.E.'s death in 1922 by Waldemar Ager, the paper's then editor.

Editor Ole Br. Olson found him out in a small town in Minnesota. Olson had come back from a lecture tour. Tired, he leaned himself back in his chair and looked up to the ceiling with his dimmed, mournful eyes: "There is an energy out in the country, if we could only get it out." And so he began to tell of a young man who had been with him recently, of his enthusiasm, his remarkable singing voice and fervent zeal to come out and work for Prohibition.[66]

In 1905 *The Reform* told of its engagement of E.E. to go to the Pacific coast, praised his popularity and eloquence, and asked readers to help him on his travels.

> What makes his lectures apt and mighty is the poetry of his highly colored language, reminiscent of the ancient prophets. ... Many a home beyond the prairies or among the hills of Wisconsin remembers Lobeck as an agent in the hands of God to bring peace and happiness to their hearth.[67]

The paper wished him happiness, and declared, "You are at your strongest now and the saloons are at their highest peak." A little over a decade later, the 18th Amendment to the U.S. Constitution, passed in December 1917 and ratified in January 1919 – "After one year from the ratification of this article the manufacture, sale, or transportation of intoxicating liquors within, the importation thereof into, or the exportation thereof from the United States and all territory subject to the jurisdiction thereof for beverage purposes is hereby prohibited" – shoved the saloons to their lowest valley.

For thirty years, from 1892 to his relatively early death at age 58 in 1922, E.E. was an indefatigable advocate for Temperance and Prohibition. (Indefatigable is something of an understatement. At one point he recounts a day in which "I held a speech in Kendota at 11:00, in Little Sauk at 1:30, at Nils Berg's at 4:00, and in Gordon Church at 7:30."[68]) According to the Minnesota Legislative Reference Library, on its web page recounting his service in the State House of Representatives (1907-10) and State Senate (1915-18), E.E.'s "Occupation (when first elected)" was "Temperance Lecturer."

Of course, the context changed dramatically for the last three years of his life, but in 1906 he had written, "Some have been asking what we shall do once drinking has been defeated. Do not fear, there is no danger that there will be so much sense in the world that reformers will be without work."[69]

"Across Minnesota in all directions"

E.E. kept up his efforts during the periods when he served in the Minnesota House and Senate, and when he ran for governor and for the U.S. Congress. He covered Minnesota, Wisconsin, North Dakota, South Dakota, Illinois, Michigan, New York, the Pacific Northwest, and even Manitoba, Saskatchewan, and British Columbia. In one colorful account of a previous few months, "I have cut across Minnesota in all directions, like a woman cutting a cake. I have crossed Wisconsin, haunted Michigan, and stormed North Dakota in rain, snow, cold, and heat, sandstorms and snowstorms."[70]

Reminiscing in later years, his children remarked that "Papa was never home." In 1911 he wrote in his newspaper column that not long after returning home from "a lengthy tour of North Dakota," he got a letter from a Temperance group in Michigan inviting him to "say a few words" at their upcoming New Year celebration. "My wife said 'Stay at home!' The children said 'Don't go!' But I was not so good with that. The bags were packed and by the door."[71]

To take simply one year's summing up, E.E. notes that between March 1, 1894, and January 30, 1895, when his work was almost exclusively in Wisconsin, he had given 176 lectures, organized nine associations, and 486 had signed Temperance pledges. His meetings had been well attended with a minimum of 100 people at each. He had covered the northern part of Wisconsin twice; twice he had gone east as far as Lake Michigan; once as far south as Dane County, but most of his work had been in the central part of the state.[72]

One feature of this account seems exaggerated – "minimum of 100 people each." Over and over again in his periodic reports to *The Reform*, titled "Under the Pencil," he acknowledges disappointing attendance. There were certainly occasions when several hundred showed up, but there were others when the audience was scant. Indeed, E.E. displays a kind of disarming honesty that isn't always characteristic of proselytizers.

Weather was often the culprit, but poor planning was sometimes to blame. Harvest time was not auspicious; people had to bring in the crops. There were locations where there was simply little or no enthusiasm for the cause, or actually derision for it. Leaders didn't always step up. Occasionally even pastors were lukewarm.

- I was in Lincoln County four days but was not able to get people together more than two times. The message was sent around and I went around myself without results.

- The 1st of October I was to be in Cottonwood, but nothing came of that meeting.

- The 10th I traveled to Morris to have a meeting the same evening but was informed that the meeting, by mistake, was scheduled for the 11th.

- The 12th the Temperance folk held a conference in Starbuck, but few people were present as harvest work was now in full swing.

- The 13th I was to be in Langhei but the man I wrote to there three weeks ago had not even announced the meeting to his closest neighbors.

- In Curtiss everyone was present for the meeting for the most part. There is also substance enough for a society, but no one could be pointed out as fit to lead it.

- Many people attended and among the crowd were German and Irish young people who made remarks that showed they were uneducated. I was glad to hear that no Scandinavians were part of the mob.

- The 12th there was a meeting in Chimney Rock's schoolhouse which was filled to congestion with people, mostly young, and many of them were not mother's best-behaved children. It is disgusting to see boys sneer at the most serious things, but the Temperance cause is such a ridiculous cause for many that they can hardly keep from laughing when anyone joins.

- The leaders of the people must wake up. It is sad but true that there are ministers also in La Crosse who are, even now, so enclosed in their own shells, they cannot publicize an abstinence meeting.

- The other night the meeting was well attended, and it would have been better if a lot of people had not gathered in another place because of some misunderstanding.

- The reason was, said one, that it was an inopportune time of day for a meeting; it was only two o'clock.

- Three joined the society there but many could not join now because it was too close to Christmas and they must have a little amusement, and Temperance people could not do that.

- In Bloomingdale, it lacks leaders. Three, four times the society was founded there but nothing sticks. For this reason, it is not worthwhile to organize anew.

- The work in Soldiers Grove labors under much resistance. They must find a location in the town since the schoolhouse, not to mention the church, is closed to them.

- In Clear Lake, I met no one who knew anything about meeting and was thus forced to leave town without saying a few words about the Temperance cause.

- The society I founded has progressed so slowly, it has gone backwards.

- It is sad that the association gives itself the final death blow. I dare to believe that no association has been stifled by opposition from without, but it is the members themselves who destroy it.

- Now, there is too much laziness among us humans, weaklings who at the first breath of a storm crawl into their snail houses, waiting for annihilation. The right thing to do for us is, at the first trumpet sound from our enemy, to bare our breast to all flying arrows and blinking swords, either to fall like men or fight to clarity and peace.[73]

There are certainly more accounts of success than of frustration or failure. They tend to sound pretty much the same.

- Sunday the 9th of October I was in Hanley Falls in the evening. It was so dark out to begin with, the schoolhouse was locked and a few of the town girls who sat on the stairs had heard nothing about the meeting. Pastor Thorstensen's son and a few others went through the town and finally got the key, lit light in the schoolhouse, rang the schoolhouse bell and soon the house was filled.

- In Glenwood, it was really a mass meeting. When people just do their duty to advertise the meetings, it gets people out. Young and old were present and listened with anxious attention.

- There was a youth society that had a meeting that evening. A burning desire grips me when I see a bunch of young people, a burning urge to show them the right way. I feel great responsibility when I speak to a young audience, since I know that they all bear an immortal soul and there is a responsibility on those who speak.

- The pastor let people know how he stood on the issue straight away when he came because either the beer kegs and other things will be done away for funerals and other acts or the pastor will be gone, because, he added "they do not fit together."

- What a meeting it was. A Temperance society was formed. The sail has been hoisted! Good luck!

- One attendee said he would drive over 20 miles to hear Lobeck.

- Woodville's society has shaken the sleep off themselves and started to work again.

- In Ogema, the Swedish Pastor Ander formed a sort of Temperance association and the work goes pretty well. Ander said that no Christian can be indifferent about the saloon and its curse and he seriously doubted that one who goes into the saloon to have a dram is a Christian.

- Anderson is a very reasonable man whom I would recommend to all Temperance folk because besides driving me these 30 miles, he paid for my dinner too.

- A storm came up and turnout for the meeting was small. Seventeen people came to the meeting, but the unusual thing was that all 17 signed the Temperance pledge and a society was established that was given the name – well, I do not know if I shall like it – but they called it the Lobecks Total Abstinence Society.

- It is good to see that there are some strong ones who are faithful until their bark wrinkles and their days end.

- There was no dinner that night, but an old, nice woman gave me an apple, that I kind of laid as a foundation for my speech.

- In spite of terrible weather, the meeting in the evening had a fair audience. And I got acquainted with some real dedicated teetotalers – some of whom followed me from place to place every evening for two weeks. They worked at day and travelled with me at night. We rarely got to bed before 12:00 o'clock – at times not until 2:00 or 3:00. And these people – Iversen, Olsen, and Christensen – had to get up again at 5:00

o'clock to go to work. There were others, too, who followed much of the time, but these three gentlemen were the most stubborn and tenacious of them all.

- [In the town of Somers, Montana, aid came from an unexpected source.] O'Brien, a Catholic, had asked to introduce me. He had at one time also been a Temperance speaker – a very warm-hearted man he is. He had asked Pastor Skindlov if he could greet the Norwegians in the city, and if they did not quit drinking and if they did not belong to the Norwegian Lutheran congregation, then he, O'Brien, would dismiss them from work. And when O'Brien owns the whole town, his words carry weight. There are nice Catholics too.[74]

Once in a while E.E. recounts the free-will offering that would help pay his expenses. Sometimes the sums were very small, only a dollar or two (though in his time, a dollar was worth about $30 of ours). But in Lily, South Dakota in 1908 there was one astonishing surprise.

At 2 o'clock a handful of people shuffled through the mud to the church. It was sluggish to begin with, but after a while the assembly thawed, the ice melted and young and old sat attentively. "Give up!" was given and received. At the high point, souls embraced each other. But, I think, should I ask this small gathering for support for the Committee? They are so, so few and it looks so poor in the report – but let it go. I also am looking out for the Committee and must do what they command. Passed the hat. The sound of coins and promises were made. When I had counted it, and I did three times, I could hardly believe my eyes. $47 dollars [$1,600] lay in the hat. Since that time a lonely, ashamed man has walked over the South Dakota Prairie.[75]

In mid-April 1894 *The Reform* advertised E.E.'s strenuous schedule, and included this admonition:

Friends, give these meetings good publicity! If possible, announce it in the local newspaper. Ministers in the town can do a big service for the cause if they publicize the meetings. Lobeck has his guitar with him and will sing, play and talk for the good cause. So go yourself to hear him and try to get both friends and enemies of the cause to go. That therefore it will be a successful meeting for the friends of the cause in the town. Try to rent a large roomy location for the meetings that will be held in your neighborhood. It is important to give the meetings good publicity so the place can be filled.[76]

The reference to music highlights a feature of the Temperance mission that played a crucial role in its success. E.E. himself was celebrated for his singing voice. His presentations often included songs.

Musical groups, especially a quartet from Augsburg Seminary, were major drawing cards for Temperance events. "All the singers love the cause of Temperance. Most of them – maybe all – have given themselves to the Cross and been saved. God bless you, singers!" Sometimes the singing outlasted the meeting: "Afterwards ten to twelve Temperance people gathered in the front of the church and then we sat there in a cluster and sang from 'Forglemmigei' until 11 o'clock. Then we parted with 'Come again soon.'" And it wasn't always just voices. "A male voice choir attended and sang during one of the meetings, and then they have three musicians: a violinist, a flute player, and a clarinet player, and then a lady who played the guitar."[77]

On at least one journey there was a moment of levity.

> I traveled back down to Minneapolis again but on the way I stopped a bit in Hinckley to make inquiries. "Are there many Scandinavians here?" I asked the hotel proprietor. "No, there are only a few Scandinavians, but there are lots of Swedes." No meeting there.[78]

On another trip there was a dialogue worthy of inclusion in a comedy stage play.

> In transit I stopped one night in Davenport. Came in by midnight, and in the hotel office I found a man, stirring the ashes, that burnt poorly.

> "Who are you?" the man said, turning a face red as a pumpkin towards me.

> "I am a traveler."

> "And where are you going?"

> "Westwards."

And then he started talking about this and that, and in one, two, three, he entered the topic of Prohibition, and could tell me that comforting knowledge that the State would go bankrupt if the saloons were not immediately allowed again.

That was strange, I offered, and ventured to say that I just came from Fargo and Moorhead, and apparently Fargo stood out a lot better than Moorhead; but then, believe me, the ashes started flying.

He stabbed and rummaged in the oven so it crackled, and sparks flew, and roared that Fargo soon would be sold at a mortgage auction.

"There is no life in Fargo now, compared to when I was running a saloon there."

"So, you have been a saloon proprietor?"

"Yes, I was, and I had a lot of customers."

Then he poked in the ashes, and simmered and swore at the Prohibition.

"Say, how much did you make on an average a day, the year through?"

"60 dollars [$2,000] a day."

My eyes widened. "60 dollars a day, – and how much did you pay out?"

"10 [$340] dollars a day."

"Are you telling me that you made 50 dollars [$1,700] a day as an average all through the year?"

"Yes, I did. A lot of good customers."

"For how long did you run the saloon?"

"Ten years."

"Fifty dollars a day for ten years – what kind of business are you running now?"

"Oh, I paint, and put up wallpaper."

"But where is all the money you made when running the saloon?"

"The gods know where it went," he said, "I don't know – I have nothing left."

I went to bed, and knew that if the Prohibition has done nothing else, it has gotten this man into honest work, where he has to use his muscles to earn his daily bread.[79]

There could be peril.

E.E. went down to the train depot with a couple of friends. After farewells, he was pelted with eggs by an angry mob. An innocent bystander boarding the train was also hit. Leaving the depot and making his way back to the hotel, E.E. was pursued with hollering and eggs almost all the way. A man walking beside E.E. was hit in the neck with a stone and sank to his knees, holding on to Lobeck. The editor of *The Reform*, concluding this story, remarked, "For shame that such can be carried on by and among Norwegians!"[80]

Trains were sites of intermingling, sometimes hazardous.

- On board the train were people of different standing and habits: drinkers, card players, politicians, pastors, Temperance speakers.

- A couple of my fellow passengers were drinking, shouting, and swearing so it was terrible to witness. After a while a Bohemian pulled his knife in order to slaughter the man next to me, as he became convinced that he was Satan.[81]

But on trains E.E. often became reflective. Here he is on the way to Montana in 1905.

The night falls silently. Good night, friends! You will not hear much of what I speak with. [This seems to mean that he is about to fall asleep and his mind is wandering.] It is something invisible that comes visiting to cool the mind, that has worked itself hot today. And then the introverted ponderings of Life, Existence, the Soul, the Transformation, Death and all these things that rise like shadows in the yearning blue half-sphere in myself. The great birds of thoughts with shining swan wings sail past me, – to fathom the depths of the spirit was not my calling, – to inquire into the depths of secrets was entrusted to others. Only small fireflies of thoughts are circling my spiritual sphere, but it moves towards greater lights – life is not without destination.

Then I remembered the bunch of lefse my wife had put into my bag. These are things I can understand. There is taste and distinction – a need that is satisfied – and blessed be the hands that made these.

Then I rolled myself up like a big lefse, fell asleep and woke up when someone shouted: "Great Falls!"[82]

The automobile

Partway through E.E.'s career, a change that would reshape America was beginning. In 1902 the Prohibitionists purchased an automobile to expedite travel between cities, to carry people faster and allow more speeches in less time. (A recent study has shown that "in 1909, there were two million horse-drawn carriages manufactured in the United States and eighty thousand automobiles. By 1923, there were ten thousand carriages manufactured and four million cars."[83]) E.E. did not like the idea.

> The election campaign of the Prohibitionists this fall unfortunately got a setback because of this automobile madness. It may be all right of me to say something about that now. I could not do so earlier, because then it was interpreted as if I were jealous because I was not allowed to participate.
>
> No, that was not the reason that I criticized the plan. I have gotten so many handshakes with a "God bless you," "Come on," and "It was the best we ever heard," so I can well stand that others are praised. The first thing I opposed was the bragging before the machine had had a truly thorough and tough test.
>
> When I came to Minneapolis and saw the machine, I had to smile at the thought of fully grown men – some of them overgrown – dreaming of traveling all around the country in such a monstrosity, and at the speed which they had calculated. We well know that Americans can fill their plans with great measures of fantasy, but that a Norwegian brain could get into such a dissolved condition is "Nota Bene" way past my imagination.
>
> That's why I told Sneve and Eide, when they were climbing into the wagon to go to Stillwater, that this would be the last time we saw them. I received a mild reproach from them, which was not so very strange, but I know much about moving a heavy wagon on our roads, and I knew what I was talking about.[84]

After this article appeared, there were letters to the editor that harshly criticized E.E. for his disdain and attitude about the automobile bought by the Prohibitionists. He was accused of being mean spirited and not following the precepts he continuously spoke about in dealing with people and pulling together for the cause.

One letter explained in clear terms that the committee who had purchased the automobile had used a great deal of their own money, even up to $300 [$10,000]. Three exemplary men had traveled to Chicago to try out a car similar to what they eventually purchased, and gave it a thorough trial, driving it in deep mud and over piles of lumber to check its performance. The fact that the purchased automobile did not live up to expectations was because the engine did not have the twenty-five horsepower that had been guaranteed by the company. The letter writer then added that if Lobeck as a farmer had ordered a "binder" he had seen work well but did not get what was promised, then he should be called a "madman" just as Lobeck was calling the automobile madness. If Lobeck did not know the facts, he should not be writing about it and should not be talking about dreamers and follies.[85]

Though much of E.E.'s work was in small midwestern towns and rural areas, he also had occasion to visit – and evaluate – huge cities.

> Then we started for Chicago, the metropolis of the West, and one of America's places of sodomy. The city was black of smoke, the weather was bad, the meetings small, the streets dirty – and a lot of people got sooty both outside and inside. Both body and soul get cramped when you walk the overcrowded streets. Humpbacked workers cleaned the streets. The elite, with upturned noses, passed proudly by in shiny carriages. The streetcars on the ground and in the air made a lot of noise, the drivers shouted. One couldn't hear a thing, and it was a relief when Pastor Halvorsen took me to Dearborn Station, and I rolled eastwards towards New York in one of the beautiful trains of the Erie Railway.[86]

At least one of Chicago's features – the El, those "streetcars in the air" – amused and delighted this Norwegian. "It is told that an adventurer by name of Peer Gynt rode through the air on reindeer, but in Chicago one rides through the air in trolleys – on many occasions so high that you may lift your hat to the people living on the second floor."[87]

Return to home church

The most poignant moment for E.E. in all these travels occurred in 1910. His reminiscence begins and ends with a characteristic reverie on the surrounding scene.

Responding to a call from Ole Mauseth to speak at Oscar Lake Church, E.E. took a nostalgic, emotional stroll into his memory-filled past on a beautiful spring Sunday morning in May.

On old stomping grounds

Burrrr! rang the telephone on Friday afternoon. I put the microphone up to my ear. "Hallo!" – "Hallo," it said so far away. "Is this Lobeck?" it sounded as though through a fog. "Ja!" "This is Ole Mauseth – we are having a Temperance meeting next Sunday evening. Can you come and speak?" "Ja!"

Sunday the 22nd of May 1910 dawned fine and brilliant. The clear sun radiated warmth over the fields and into every corner. The wind also was still – not one little breeze was allowed to tumble about. Some playful little gusts tried to make a little disturbance out on the lake but retreated and the lake lay like a large mirror with a green frame around it and Heaven in its arms. We have not had such a day like that in a long time. "Jennie" took over. She walked over the trails, bobbed her head sideways and enjoyed the overwhelming glory of the Lord. From the eastern sky the sun streamed its rays down over the fields and there I was sitting in the buggy completely moved by the great Master's kingdom, for all this glory of life and healing to both body and soul. There were prayers in my heart. Songs sprang from my heart like waters from a spring. That a poor one such as I should be in the midst of this blessedness – yes, even me – God's goodness is great.

There lies Lake Latoka like a glistening fairyland, between fairylike forests mirrored in the water. And there is Lake Mary, broad and bright as a peaceful kingdom, where love and peace are the guiding spirits. The birds twittered, sang and whistled, flitted from twig to twig in love with a blazing sun above them that instills warmth into the enchantment of life. A pair of cranes sailed high up in the blue and announced with shrill tones that they too were awakened this blessed day. Some crows sat away up in a tree and talked together, jumping from one branch to another, raised their wings, moving their whole bodies upright to call their "CawCawCaw."

Between the trees shadows crept about in a secret kingdom under a foliage roof. Some glimmers of sunlight shone down through the leaves and down the field as if looking to give small joys to a soul in great sorrow.

The beautiful farms pushed the forest back, punctuating the land like independent powers. Everywhere there was sun and song and heartfelt harmony.

Flower dust and a cool, pleasing aroma from the green grass lifted themselves up as an offering from the earth, and leaves and flowers served as tangents where all grace from lake and woods and plains assembled and went as a powerful song up towards the light and peace. In this splendor, in the afterglow of eternity, my soul can take wing … . Such days I have not had many of. Days of being spiritually regenerated are few.

Now Mill Lake twinkles between the tree trunks. The road meanders its way like a band with verdant green on both sides. The Holmes City church tower rises up through the forest, pointing the weary pilgrim to the country where there are no shadows. The church doors are open; the organ music rolls out. Men's and women's voices come after and fade out. I lingered on the way, tied the horse, and then Bishop Johan Oluf Wallin's familiar refreshing hymn of new birth roared out to me. Yes, it fit. Now it brought new birth through the whole countryside. The hymn came to strengthen the faith, enliven hope, and increase the infinite sense of well-being that surrounded my soul.

> *Välsignad vare Gud, som har*
> *Oss födt på nytt till lifvet,*
> *Och oss en evigt mildrik far*
> *I Jesu Christo blifvet!*
> *Med honom vi*
> *Och skola bli*
> *Medarfvingar i hoppet,*
> *Til himlens ro,*
> *När i sann tro*
> *Vi här fullbörda loppet.*

> *Blessed be God,*
> * an eternally gentle Father*
> *Who has given us life through*
> * his son, Jesus Christ.*
> *We are his children.*
> *With him we will be co-heirs in hope*
> * to the tranquility of Heaven*

When in true faith
  We here complete the race.

The strong organ tones welled up in me from a devout congregation in powerful song. The tones went out, into the flowers and leaves, and was laid to rest. The sermon was forceful, borne out of a strong mind and a sincere faith.

Well, "Jennie", we have to be moving along. There is Grant Lake as in peaceful contemplation. The little village, Holmes City, is doing exceedingly well at the end of the lake. Two giant trees stand again in town to show the kings who reigned in the forest's heyday before the immigrant's ax was laid to the roots. No interference now. Just life, sun and song. Is it really possible to live through an entire day without a single sharp arrow that will come and hurt: "Each happy moment you have on earth must be paid with sorrow." Yes, let the arrows come. After such a cleansing for both body and soul in the sunlight, birdsong and flower dust – a whole blessed Lord's Day – dazzlingly bright and invigorating, one must endure a bit of everything.

There is Blackwell Lake, bright as molten silver in a setting of promontories and points of land, kissing green beaches and lending peace to the entire surroundings. The road crept along the beach hugging near the water and echoes of:

Med en drømmende sjæl jeg i væven her staar
Paa den friske og kjølige strand.
Tanken vugges saa født og den kommer og gaar
Som smaabølger gaar til og fra land.

With a dreamy soul I stand here trembling
On the fresh and cool beach.
Thoughts are born and come and go
As small waves go to and from the land.[88]

It changed to meadows, forest groves, and shiny ponds. Hills and valleys took each other's hands and slopes in between – all in sparkling sunshine. "No, Jennie, now you must take leave. You must stir yourself a little. We must get to Oscar Lake Church by 3 o'clock." Again, I came into a richness, beautiful as in a bright dream. Holmes Lake and Oscar Lake are neighbors and between them goes the road. The water was so mirrorlike that you could see the fish far away. Everything stretched toward the sun.

The warm lifegiving wealth of flowers, trees, and shrubs. Even the fish tossed and romped near the water's surface. The sun pulls us.

High up with a broad view on all sides stands Oscar Lake Church. I was the church singer (klokker) there for eight years over twenty years back. Ja, it also happens to be where the meeting is. All things are organized for today. I came into the church, went to my usual place, but where are the people? Where is the youth? Where is the singing? So gray the people have become. Time pulls us along and wears on us. The grave mounds outside have increased lately. There also are father and mother side by side. Memories come swarming forward and fill the soul with inexpressible sweet sadness, the kind of sadness you wish to hide.

The sun moved to the west, the meeting was ended. There were handshakes – you can believe – and lingering glances over these dear places that shaped themselves in my soul in childhood years. For miles around lay lakes, forest groves, and plains. Peace and quiet over all. I hitched the horse to the buggy and in half an hour I was at the home of Ole Mauseth, who now lives on my father's old place.

"You go in and have a seat," said Mauseth, but it was not so easy. It was like I saw father and mother everywhere – heard their voices. I nosed around the farm. It was like it cried out to me everywhere. There is the little slough where we small children made little channels and built waterfalls when the snow was melting in the spring. Over there was where half the village's young men gathered to wrestle with me. There is where Peder Grambo and I one evening wrestled (took the boss's grip). The grass was damaged that evening. There is the little grove where I sneaked to practice wheeling leaps like in a Halling dance. The pine where I scraped the bark with the heels of my shoes at one time has now grown pinecones on its twigs. They were high up then. Now I cannot reach it with fingertips.

I noticed an ant hill, where it was thirty-five years ago, breaking the little pieces in the bog to get building material. Ever busy in their nest. Slothfulness has not attacked the colony. During these many years, they have paved a beaten path about twenty feet long out from the nest and there was traffic on it. Small bits of wood, insects, and all sorts of possible fragments carried to the nest. It was not an eight-hour day. It was now quarter to eight in the evening, but they were just as busy. Go to the ant hill and watch them.[89]

After an hour the sun's rays went out of the valley, gathering them home for the evening. Sent a farewell glance over the large slough. Ja, it is now dried out. Where we went in a boat in the old days, Mauseth now sails about with his swatter machine in the summer. Everything changes. The schoolhouse bell rang in the distance. Every foot of the trail through the woods I knew again. People came from all of the community, near and far, for miles around, known and unknown. A splendid meeting.

"Now I close my eyes". But before they close I must still look back on the day. I sit on the edge of the bed and call forth everything glorious that I have seen and met. Taking it all into me and living it again in big, shining dreams.

The life of spring teems outside, stars burn high above, memories come to visit and among them I see father's and mother's faces. The birds' songs are silenced. "Now I close my eyes."[90]

Chapter 4

Interlude: The Context

The focus of the rest of this book will be the Prohibitionist political career of E.E. Lobeck. However, alcohol was not his only concern – though he often declared that it was the root of nearly every significant problem. It is instructive to take a brief side trip here to get a larger sense of the context in which he was a major player.

Maintaining Norwegian identity

It is likely that closest to E.E.'s heart was the challenge known to every immigrant group – holding on to the ancestral tradition while assimilating to the new culture. As time went on, more and more – and especially after he was elected to office, though at least as early as 1897 – E.E. lectured in English as well as in Norwegian, but his ancestral tenacity never waned.

> I have travelled through some regions where the Norwegians have become extremely Americanized. A strange "grand air" grips some of our fellow countrymen. And then they put on some American varnish to hide their Norwegian heritage, but then the basic color is too strong, and they appear quite pitiful.

> I heard about a Hillesø somewhere, who strove to forget the Norwegian – then he became Mr. Hill, though the poor whelp could speak nothing but Norwegian. Such a person isn't worthy to serve as a floor mat, onto which an honest Norwegian man and woman can swipe their shoes.

> There is also the story in the new saga about a man called Halvor Høyenes – he, too, got the American sickness, and immediately his name was Howard Hawkins. Maybe this is a little strong, but really, such people should go to jail.

When a person like Washington wasn't ashamed of his Norwegian ancestry, then these, from vanity-narrowed souls, shouldn't either be ashamed of the Norwegian. [William Jennings] Bryan seems to be proud of his mother's Norwegian heritage, and ex-governor Van Sant [1901-05] does not shy away from letting people know that he descends from a man who came from Sande in Jarlsberg. Let us preserve the Norwegian, if possible, until the last of days.[91]

Eight years before he published these words in *The Reform*, E.E. had made what was considered, at least in the circles in which he moved, a triumphal return to Norway.

In April 1900 *The Reform* reported that in the summer E.E. Lobeck would travel to Norway to visit his childhood home – "I will love to see the midnight sun" – and to speak about Prohibition. The Temperance organizations in Norway were planning to hold "demonstration days" all over Norway on June 17. E.E. was not alone. In early May the newspaper declared that two special trains from Minneapolis to New York were required to carry the number who had signed up for the trip. A songbook, "Viking Train Songs for the Norway Tour 1900," had been printed. Nearly 2,000 people arrived at the railway station in Minneapolis to see the Viking Train leave. "There were excellent speeches and strong singing voices among the Vikings. But everything went very quiet and subdued at departure. Even those who were filled with enthusiasm for the Temperance cause were somber."[92] Martha, five and a half months pregnant, remained home with two small children.

The Reform singled E.E. out.

E.E. Lobeck has over seven years worked as Temperance missionary among his countrymen in the northwestern states. ... Few readers have any idea how much dedication, energy, power, and genius the Norwegian Temperance people have had to exert to prevent our Norwegian people from making themselves contemptible in other nations' eyes because of drink. Anyone who knows our national character when it lets loose from the conventional will understand it.[93]

Upon arrival in Kristiania, the group dispersed to friends and relatives throughout Norway, though E.E. and B. B. Haugen spent some time together that first evening wandering about Kristiania. With "tongue in cheek," Haugen wrote to *The Reform*:

The citizens enjoyed the sight of two conspicuous, artistic looking persons wandering up one street and down another, who joked and gestured like professional speakers. One was a major figure with long raven black hair, musical, and the other one was also very tall, had light curly hair and sharp, intelligent, well-defined features.

Here in the city every night in tourist time many famous artists are incognito, and at any rate, somewhere I heard people guess that one was a famous foreign musician and the second one probably a great foreign actor. If they had known that the two gentlemen were just two useless Norwegian Temperance speakers from Minnesota, they would certainly not have taken them so seriously.[94]

The travelers eagerly returned to the homes of their birth – E.E. to Løvbekksetra. Shortly after his return to Minnesota, E.E. reminisced.

Strange to see the marshes father had made into land and the ditches he had dug. I came to my childhood home 12:30 at night – peaceful everywhere – Løvbækken rippled – the birch woods stood light against the dark, half-gone night and spoke to me of bygone days. The spruce forest seemed to me a phonograph where I heard father's and mother's voices. My cheek became wet and warm. Not tears of pain; it was something soft, gentle, and grateful that flowed out. Anyone will cry without pain if they go thither where the spruce forest echoes the beloved departed voices.[95]

At a meeting in Støa on June 16, "E. Lobeck from America said, amongst other things, that the Temperance Movement created good patriots. Moderate drinking can by no means gather the people to something whole." At the end of the meeting, it was agreed that the crowd should gather at 10:00 the next morning and march to meet the Swedish Temperance people at the border.

The next day, with the musicians in the lead and banners and flags waving, they formed a procession along the road eastwards towards the border. At a bend in the road they saw their Swedish brothers and sisters. In tones of music both processions met and Norwegians and Swedes, 1,500 in all, were together.

A speaker reminded the crowd that it was Temperance Demonstration Day, and they should remember the thousands who were gathered under its banners to rally against liquor trafficking.

Newspapers carried excerpts of Lobeck' speech.

Lobeck was happy that he could participate this day and stand on the same ground as his forefathers. The times were different now from when his grandfather was sitting up a whole night, making bullets to shoot into the breasts of the Swedes. He felt elated to face so many people. He said that to him it seemed that God had created Dovre [a Norwegian mountain range] as a barricade of freedom for the Norwegian people. "It seems that God has lowered the valleys and turned them into cradles for free men."

"Let us then as free men and women send a redeeming and freeing cry up Ljøra [the river where the rally was held], the Trysil River, Glommen, Lågen og Nidelven [these are all major or well-known Norwegian rivers], and then we will, from The Seven Sisters, Torghatten, Skagastølstinderne, Romsdalshornet, Galdhøpiggen , Trysilfjellet, Fulufjell, Faxen, and Støten [Norwegian mountains, the four last situated in Trysil and the neighboring Swedish municipalities] get this answer: Down with all that stops the progress of man, and let the teachings of Jesus of Nazareth shine through your lives.

Remember – that the all-powerful God shines before those who fight for the truth. For God's true warriors on earth there is no retreat, no stagnation, no death, and no bad year – only God, Eternity, and Victory. This is where we will stand until the battle has come to an end and victory is ours."[96]

A little over a decade later, in 1911, E.E. responded eagerly to news of a publication project undertaken in Trysil, Norway, that was to include information about Trysil immigrants to the U.S. and Canada. Would E.E. encourage them to send information about their experience? E.E. put a notice in *The Reform*,[97] and noted also that he had been asked to write a chapter. Would the readers send information to him as soon as possible and include stories of their struggles and reason for leaving Norway? To include pictures of their family, house, or farm would cost 10 kroner [730 kroner] each.

As noted previously in Chapter 2, E.E. wrote "Tryslinger i Amerika" which he finished in 1912, and included "Trysil Bygden Ved Red River og Sheyenne River, Nord Dakota," the settlement at Winger, Thief River Falls, the west coast Tryslingers, and pastors who came from Trysil.

In the first difficult years after their arrival, new immigrants tended to settle near each other for moral, emotional, social, and even financial support. They organized their churches, established organizations, and lived within walking or horse and wagon distance from each other, sharing letters from home, tools, food, and conversation in their native dialect. They helped each other with planting and harvesting, and with childbirth. All these features of their life preserved traditions from Norway.

In the early 1900s the idea of forming bygdelags (organizations of descendants of immigrants from Norway) took root, and many developed, each with a regional focus. Organizers hoped a bygdelag would preserve the connections between Norwegian Americans and a national romantic or idealized view of the old Norway of childhood memories. A main purpose would be to hold a stevne (reunion) each year, usually in the summer after crops were planted or in the fall after harvest, since Norwegian immigrants were primarily farmers. It would fulfill a longing to strengthen family ties and friendship, converse in the native dialect about their struggles, indulge in foods remembered with fondness from their childhood days in Norway. Add in music and singing, fiddle-playing, folk dancing, tours, church services, and speakers, and three days of festivities passed quickly.

To keep the ties to Trysil strong, E.E. helped organize the Østerdalslaget bygdelag (Østerdalen, on the eastern edge of Norway, includes Trysil), that held its fledgling stevne in Fergus Falls, Minnesota, June 17-18, 1910, with about 135 in attendance. E.E. was elected secretary, and in 1912 became vice president.

The Østerdalslaget had over a thousand members by 1923, but began to diminish as a new generation grew up and wanted to just be Americans. World War II interrupted and disbanded several lags. The last Østerdalslaget was held in Fergus Falls in 1950. Some other bygdelags are still functioning.

Amidst all the immigrants' concerns about what it meant to still be Norwegian, the home country itself gained a new identity.

In early June 1905, Norway and Sweden dissolved their union and Norway became independent. E.E. was in Fargo attending a song festival when the news came. Writing about it, E.E. suggests that nature itself was celebrating.

That afternoon, when the family waved "goodbye" and I went to Fargo, it was exceedingly bright sunshine and beautiful. Rain had just washed the earth and it was, as it is said, bursting in its green garb.

The "Flyer" sped westward over the fullness, through intersections – shiny lakes off in the distance and green kissed beaches. The forest stood with branches stretching toward the sky, seagulls moved in silence with a quiet roof overhead, flower and leaf served as the tangents from the gentle summer afternoon rising up in worship to God in pianissimo.

Douglas and Ottertail counties had donned their best clothing, and when the train snaked out from between the folds of their robes, one could hear us shout: "Oh, how beautiful." "Just look at that lake, will you!" When we rolled out into the flat lands further west, they seemed to lie waiting for something to come.

"Fargo!" screamed the dry brakes. I snatched my bags, rose and fell straight into the arms of E. Christiansen from Appleton. Down the street, people surged along in a wave. "Hello!" sounded on all sides. The flags swung to and fro and certainly in American and Norwegian colors. One or two tasseled Norwegian student caps from Kristiania flapped in the crowd. The whole city was in celebration.

The Student Choir had taken the city by storm. They also were singing that evening. Their minds were stirring when a cablegram just announced that the Norwegians had dissolved their union with Sweden. They stood in groups and argued and, naturally, the Swedes lost and with flying colors.
…

A lot of Norwegians who came to town to celebrate the festival, of course had to go to Moorhead and sully themselves – a perpetual shame [Fargo, North Dakota was dry; Moorhead, Minnesota, right across the Red River, wasn't]. If they want to make a mess of themselves, they should binge at home and not come to these meetings to show off. They wore tricolors on their chests when they stepped over to Moorhead and when they staggered back, they had received the "red in our flag" on the nose – and many of them would go head over heels to Norway and beat up the Swedes if it came to war.

For my part, it has been difficult to sleep since the 7th June. Should it succeed for Norway to become a republic? I do not know why they are looking for a king. It may be desirous for the small rocky country to get some recognition from other powers, but certainly one should go towards a republic.

War – no. They have better sense, I should think. Should the matter be decided by force, I propose that Norway seek out a man for president with steel in him, for example, [Fridthof] Nansen [1861-1930; explorer, diplomat, 1922 Nobel Peace laureate for his work as the League of Nations High Commissioner for Refugees], who could amble towards the border and meet Gustav from Sweden. And then these two gentlemen at once engage in a Norwegian back-wrestle with twisting, wrestling, lifting, and tripping. And if Nansen takes the victory, Norway must become a republic, but this would probably not be recognized by the international powers.

Seems like nothing weighs in the people and the eyes of power without blood, and God alone knows how long it will be before people get passports to justice and war for eternity becomes extinct. The blood could freeze to ice in the heart at the thought of the horrible human slaughterhouses in East Asia.

Down with the firearms, and God bless Norway's land![98]

Poverty and squalor

With E.E. we are in what is known as the Gilded Age, when muckraking journalists called attention to the appalling conditions in which too many Americans lived. The January 1903 issue of McClure's Magazine carried "The Shame of Minneapolis" by Lincoln Steffens, exposing the city administrators' complicity in criminal activity. In "The History of Standard Oil," Ida M. Tarbell exposed capitalism gone awry. In "The Right to Work," Ray Stannard Baker exposed the battle between unions and management. Most famous of all is a novel whose title makes its point: *The Jungle*, by Upton Sinclair, published in 1906.

E.E was, in his own way, a muckraker.

As early as 1894 he was highlighting social blights, especially as they affected children.

> [I was shown] around the state fruit farm [near Sparta, Wisconsin], where a home for orphans and neglected children is also operated. The total number of children there is 240 or 250 of them and 75% of them are

there because of drink. And then we hear that they are, together with the drinkers, the ones who get to take the consequences of drunkenness.[99]

In 1903 he called Plato to witness.

Plato, the great Greek thinker and philosopher, had a sense that the Earth was an enormous creature with life – and that animals and humans were some kind of bugs.

I have been pondering about this lately. I think the old man was partly right about this. Then our cities become abscesses filled with bacteria, the ocean and the lakes are the blood – whales, sharks, sea lions, and all other swarms are microbes, the volcanoes are open abscesses, the lava stream is pus that flows out of the body – and, should I judge by the statements I have heard and the sights that I have seen at a hotel – then the people – a part of it – be some ugly bugs – lice.

What follows is a tale of his going outdoors to what he thought was a North Dakota hotel's outhouse but was apparently a gathering place for gay sex.

My attention was caught by seeing people hurry to the back yard. At first I could not understand what they went there for. It is not usual that a lot of men have to go at the same time, but maybe they had taken a laxative? A bit later I had to go to the loo, and when I saw a door going to "a certain place" and opened it, I began to understand. I did not hit the right place. There stood a whole lot of men, drinking, and it smelt more sour than sour and more disgusting than disgusting. But how upset they became. After a while one dared ask me what I wanted. I told him my errand with no uncertainty, and added that I seemed to have come to a worse place than what I sought. I could feel how their eyes stabbed me in the back when I left. Fie! How can people sully themselves by such unnatural sin and bestial debasement.[100]

In 1902 E.E and has family had moved to Alexandria. Three years later he wrote about the city.

Reform has, as far as I know, never had anything worth mentioning from Alexandria, and being an inhabitant of that town, I take the liberty to inform *Reform's* readers with the following:

The town is known across the country, especially for two things: Knute Nelson [who will become an implacable political enemy of E.E.] has in his bright career brought the name with him, and lately streams of tourists have come to this place – rich people, lying drowsily by the lakes when the summer sun gets hot – and their virtues follow along. …

It is not boasting, when one declares Alexandria as one of the most beautiful towns in the state. At the coming census one expects to find about 1,500 citizens [the 1910 census counted 3,001 residents of the city of Alexandria].[101] …

Alexandria has many shops, two factories, mechanical workshops (garages) etc. The spiritual need can be satisfied in thirteen churches, and the bestial in thirteen saloons. The thirteen saloons have most followers – the beast is worshiped there seven days a week, the spiritual need is satisfied once a week in the churches.

A lot of the people go several times a day, seven days a week, to the saloon and one day to the church. A very few never go to the saloon. From this, one can learn that the moral of the town is miserable.

The salt is losing its strength more and more, and the light is put under the bench, – salt and light are purifiers, and everything rots where they are not used.

Some time ago a new pastor came and took over the duties at the Congregational Church in town. He was new in Alexandria and new in his outlook – he was, it is said, broad minded and liberal. A broad spiritual view is not to be despised, so I went to his church the 5th March to enlighten myself. A lot of new thoughts held house in his "top floor," and his wisdom hardly knew any bounds. His teaching was like a constructed road, big and wide, where one easily could bypass both reconciliation and salvation – and there was no need to stop at the old crusader's halts – Calvary and Sinai.

His congregation members are great and rich. They must not be burdened, – for the rich there must be laid a broader way to Heaven, so they buy automobiles and speed trains, and with their fine ball suits, decks of cards and shot glasses can drive homewards.

During the night they had kind of participated in a local celebration of the president's Inauguration Ball in Washington, as presumably [Theodore] Roosevelt could not be inaugurated properly, unless a few humming tops in Alexandria could spin round in a dance.

Here the pastor had a great opportunity to chastise them for their sins; but no – Roosevelt was the one that most of his sermon was about – he became big and Jesus small.

The President was lifted up as a Christian and an example worthy to follow, – and then the newspapers on Monday came with sensational articles about the great, bright Inauguration Ball, where the costumes shone, the pearls glittered, and how many hundred dollars Mrs. Roosevelt's bodice was worth, – and to alleviate those who might have a tender spot in their conscience, they told that the President and his wife opened the ball with a dance, and participated in the party during the night.

One should maybe not say anything about the big ones, but I know this: Should I participate in such balls, I would be denounced of all Christianity. Is it then like this, that Our Lord is so glad to have the bigwigs on his side, that he allows them into Heaven with their sins, but keeps us poor people outside? Is it so?

I set out to write about Alexandria, but it went straight to Washington. Now then. At the behest of the new pastor, there has been installed a bowling alley into the basement of the church, in order to, as he said, drag the youth into the house of God. Poor blinded man! If he preached the gospel of Christ in its rich, warm fullness, he would not need to roll them into Heaven on a bowling alley.

For Lent the pastor had acquired a spiritual doctrine, containing the newest of the new in the area of Faith – and he asked his congregation to make use of and take advantage of his teaching during Advent.

Oh yes, indeed there is need for "New Thoughts," spiritual broadness, liberalism and bowling alleys for the Heavenly Wanderer under our circumstances.

An evangelist is expected in Alexandria in June. May his work be a blessing to the town! It is certain that if God's spirit gripped the people, the town would soon be cleansed of saloons. One would see that it was wrong to let evil stay, just because it pays well. And may all pastors in the town blow their trumpet loudly.[102]

About the same time he was writing this, E.E. heard a speaker he hoped would reverse this tide, but he was disappointed.

I have heard William Jennings Bryan. He honored Alexandria with a visit and spoke in the Congregational Church about "The value of an Ideal."

The ticket cost one dollar [$34]; but a man who has gained world fame as an orator and made millions listen to his ideas, should be worth one dollar.

…

Slowly and dignified he spoke, it sounded beautiful, his voice was beautiful, the man was beautiful – the snide, cutting remarks were masterly aimed – the materialists were dismembered, the rotten politicians cut up, he knew how to employ satire in an appallingly brutal way.

Christianity, the true one, he defended supremely.

When will this slow murmur fade away and give way for the mighty storm? Is he not supposed to turn us upside down – will he not shake us with his eloquence – shall he not, with his spiritual power, speak to us so we'll feel the cold go down our spine? Personally I feel the cold down my spine when I hear something awesome and good – when one is shaken through and through, one remembers.

"Thank you for listening." he said, before I felt the cold. Me, I had expected more. Beautiful the speech was, like a big bowl filled with cream, but if this is Bryan's best, he is no match to Oliver Stewart from Chicago; still, he is too good to be a Democrat.[103]

E.E. judges his contemporary America against what he knows and believes about its past. He recalls riding the train along the Hudson River toward New York in 1903.

The Hudson River has borne witness to a lot of occurrences, both good and evil.

Washington crisscrossed it during the troublesome days of the Revolutionary War. Here, Cornwallis's boats have seen themselves in a mirror, and along the shores rifles have banged, cannons thundered, and precious human blood has run in rivulets.

"Peekskill!" the brakeman shouted. The name sounded familiar, and by rummaging around inside my skull I remembered that Gen. Howe of the British army sent a fleet up to this place to destroy the arsenal of the patriots. But when the commanding officer there saw that he was unable to defend the place, he lit the fuse – bombilibum – and the arsenal blew up with a thundering noise. …

Times have changed. Washington, Lee, Schuyler, and Lafayette have turned into dust. Howe, Cornwallis, and Burgoyne, their enemies, have gone into the silence.

The blood that ran where their banners billowed fertilizes the mustard seed of freedom, and it has become a huge tree. Up through the valley, where the roar of the cannons rolled at the time, you can now hear the beautiful sound of song and captivating music – where sabers clanged and the rifles barked then, you now hear the laughter of the festive crowd, dancing upon the graves.

Then we were approaching the outskirts of the city. The outer rim seemed threadbare. Further in, the tenement houses appeared. Children's faces could be seen up to the fourth floor. The rooms on the north side never see the blessed sun. The children never get out during the first years of their life. No backyard to play in. When they grow up they are relegated to the street.

Alas, what a fate!

Jacob Riis [1849-1914, American social reformer], the well-known Dane, has done a lot to improve the living conditions of these paupers, but the tenement houses still show marks of being planned by the Money Devil. The slaves of the Mammon worshipers built them, and the blessed sunlight of our Lord never shines in there. In a single room without sun, but with a lot of dirt, one can find father and mother and up to six children.

When I saw these pale faces pressing against the window panes to look down, I wondered whether it would be possible to build gigantic reflectors high up in the air, so they could reflect the sun's rays into these poor homes, in order to clean the air and bring health.

These millions have to live somewhere. The speculators have had their antennas out in good time, and large sums are sucked into the pockets of the rich ones from these houses where the poor masses live. But above the earthly courts, above the apartments of the poor, above the castles of the rich and the palaces of the bloodsuckers, is the court of Justice of Almighty God.

When the people live in such conditions that the heart grows hard and the brain grows soft, the Bells of Doom will soon sound their knell over the nation.

Awoke from my dreams about the bad conditions by somebody shouting: "Grand Central Station!"[104]

Three years later, in 1906, once more in New York, he is even more pointed and circumstantial in his judgment.

New York is one of the big cities of the world. The impression of the big cities is the same – a boundless hunt for the almighty Dollar and a business life going for full speed. The people are rushing in the streets like they were possessed – shouts, bellows and cries from the drivers – a multitude of newspaper sellers and shoe shiners.

The magnificent carriages of the rich people are sparkling everywhere, and so are the two-wheeled carts of the Persians in which they are moving their rag bags.

Beautiful costumes, through which one can glimpse a lining of silk, are worn by "The Upper Tens," while dirty rags, through which one can see dirty skin, are worn by the poor people. Beautiful churches and brilliant saloons, dark Midnight Mission houses where a blessed salvation work is done – and right by its side stinking opium dens and Chinese "Josshouses," where souls are sent to Hades wholesale. …

The Italians are narrowing their eyes, as if they have spotted a victim. The Germans put their fat bellies out through the saloon door to get some fresh air, while the business-minded Yankee, whose pointed face ends in a long nose, is speculating in people's gullibility.

I felt unsafe – the air felt sultry, as if a storm was coming – and when I see the limitless sin and indecency that rule here – lives are lost, souls are ripped asunder like rags and are slung into the Lost World – then I know that eventually there will come a storm, a terrible one, out of the hand of Almighty God.

The human spirit is haughty – the tall buildings mirroring it – buildings more than 20 stories high stick up like fingers, pointing mockingly at God. Tenement houses, planned by the money-greedy Devil, are housing thousands, who get no sun, and in these shadows crime sprouts forth like fungus.

Poor children, growing up without fresh air and sun.

Shiny palaces surround others, who in their riches stuff themselves in a godforsaken idleness, until they perish like morally rotten cadavers. A woman in this city [Giulia Pertinax Morosini, 1864-1932, daughter of a partner of the banker Jay Gould] spends 200,000 dollars [$6,000,000] a year on clothes alone. The newspapers print her picture and her words as if they were wisdom, when she explains that 200,000 dollars is in no way too much for clothing. If she could be dragged into the parts of the city where poverty and vice sit on the throne, and where souls are traded like merchandise, where destitute children lie in the streets at night and tramps are reeling around in their drunkenness towards depravity, maybe she would need a little less for clothes.

Small and big are lying in the nights, cold as it is, on the iron grilles of the ventilation pipes from cellars, where a little warm air is coming up, to avoid the cold. The small mouths are wailing, and in time the sighs of death from these little ones will shake Heaven itself and loosen the thunderbolts of judgment. The adults curse their destiny, and the cause of this despairing condition can be ascribed to the saloons and the consequent unemployment.

One evening a letter was stuck into my hand. There I found a Socialist tract where they were mocking the claim that poverty is a result of drinking. It is the money that lies at the root of it all. I will not exonerate the capitalists. God knows that they have a lot on their conscience – and God's words say that the rich eventually will howl – but when I have been at the Midnight Missions here and heard the confessions of those who have been converted and from those who are on the road to conversion, this is in absolute opposition to the claims of the Socialists.

Everyone, without exception, could tell that it was the drinking, not the capital, that had caused their fall. Some of them have once had money, but the drinking has also taken that. When this gathering of human wrecks were singing, you could hear voices that were trained, and which undoubtedly once had gladdened human ears, and when you turned around, and saw the singer, dirty, in rags and awful, your heart became all sorrow.

Maybe they don't know the root to their debasement themselves, and maybe we neither, seeing this mass of misery and poverty, can see the cause. But is it possible, that we who are fighting drinking, are just stumbling around in the fog, beating the air against an imaginary danger – is that possible?

The Chinatown Mission is led by a reformed drinker.

He still carries the imprint of his former life. He is red in the face, and his gestures, when he speaks, are those of a drunk. In his Mission he has sung the songs until the lowest ruffians knew them by heart – and the refrain goes like a storm. Therein even the most depraved of the Children of the Streets seek a little rest and get a little warmth. In the middle of the speech some of them fall asleep, snoring like a small thunder. Never in my life have I seen so many wrecks in one place, and it was maybe this sight that the following night caused me to dream that the angel Gabriel was expelled from Heaven because of excessive drinking.

And then you have the famous Bread Line over at the Bowery Mission. Half past twelve in the night we were there, and found about 300 men, young, old, lame, straight, healthy, sick, the majority without a coat, red cheeks, running eyes, vice and its children, waiting for the clock to toll one in the night so they could get a piece of bread. Staggering abyss, how many you encompass! When they had gotten their bread they just curled up like dogs in stairwells and similar places to rest for a while – and freeze.

With such pictures in my soul, how can I have a Happy Christmas? And then there is this, that the institutions that cause such unlimited human torment are protected by the laws of this country.

I have visited hospitals, and the nurses have told me that even 10-year-old boys are admitted, raging in delirium tremens. The sharks in human bodies, who deliberately present these little ones, body and soul, with eternal death, usually go free. And why not? After all, they pay 25 dollars [$800] annually into the Governmental Treasury to run their trade.

One day I was visiting "The Society for the Prevention of Cruelty to Children," and that did not ease my mind. It is well that there exists such a society, that can pick up the helpless little ones from the street after they have been abused and abandoned by their parents. But is it not enough to set your mind reeling, to see an exhibition of the tools that drunken parents have used to murder their little ones? There are axes, clubs, iron rods, wooden shafts, iron chains, and more, spattered with the blood of the innocents.

This society has through its 26-year existence picked up about 100,000 little children from the streets – and drinking, the supervisor said, was the cause of 95 percent of this staggering misery.

God, when will this slumbering, lethargic, indifferent, and narrow-hearted people wake up!!![105]

A few weeks after writing this, E.E left for St. Paul to take up his duties as a newly elected member of the Minnesota House of Representatives.

Four years later, after completing two terms as Rep. Lobeck, he wrote both more generally and more scathingly about the state of society, with a sidelong – and sarcastic – glance at the simmering controversy initiated by Darwin.

There is not a single redeeming feature in connection with those institutions [saloons], they cannot be amended, they cannot be defended, and hence they ought to be ended. Men are getting whiskey, minors get tipsy – where do they get it? Who is giving it to them? One poor woman in Alexandria came to me and told me what she had to contend with during Christmas days. A drunken husband filled her life with horror, oaths, and blasphemies instead of songs and praise, ill-treatment and filth in place of caresses and love. Christmas Day, this beautiful day, the saloonkeepers had the brazen audacity to have their saloons open, filled up poor whiskey-craving men, sent them reeling home after eleven o'clock in the evening, to drive the Christmas joys away from wife, children, and home. Clean out the whole business!

I have been pondering of late what position the planets occupy in the firmament. So many curious things are coming to pass that a person is almost led to believe that the people of old were right in holding that the heavenly bodies had something to do with the destiny of man. And why not? We are told that the moon has such an influence upon mother earth that it is drawing the mighty tidal wave across the sea – and now the scientists tell us that the sun raises the surface of the land several feet. Forces of that kind may be able to play football with man. Good many are of the opinion that when the planets occupy a certain position to each other, they cause storms, downpours, havocs, earthquakes, pestilences, and wars – and in changing position they may be the cause of good times, fine weather, peace, and good will among men.

As I have no chart of the heavenly bodies with me, and as the sun, moon, and stars have been hidden behind clouds for the last six or eight weeks, I know nothing of the relative position which they now have – but I know that something must be the matter. Quarrels and strife, ill-feeling and envy among the great political leaders as well as among the smallest and humblest of the human family. Frauds and falsehood in governmental and private affairs, deception and untrue testimonies before the courts, deduction of truth, when truth ought to be heard, a damnable greed for money and an everlasting desire to gain popularity, no matter in what manner it is acquired. Men forget their God-given mission in worshiping "self" – women who are so refined that they cannot raise children are raising dogs, cats, and monkeys. Scientists, in order to get talked about, are getting funny in their ways and funny in their words. A host of our papers and periodicals are digging up the most sensational things, dishing it out to a shallow public. Well, there must be something the matter, whether it is caused by the planets or not.

Listen to this, will you!

A scientist has recently discovered, for sure, that the apes are our ancestors. Darwin is to be vindicated because a chimpanzee had the intelligence to kiss fervently a picture of a stuffed monkey of the same tribe while she refused to kiss the picture of a gorilla. There is no mistake about it, says the learned man, that this act is suggestive of man's monkey ancestry. This great ape can demonstrate with other conducts too, that she belongs to our forefathers. She can shake hands like an old politician, scratch a match just as skillfully as Speaker Cannon and smoke cigarettes. Well, if the last stunt is to be an indication of her ancestry of man, she has many relatives in our country. But then, as [William Jennings] Bryan says, it is quite a difference whether we go towards or away from monkeydom. A learned professor gives out a statement that pigs are the best playmates for children. There you have it, but it seems to me that too many of our men choose rather to be hogs than human beings, even if they don't get the training among pigs, from the time they are small. Scientists and professors ought to devote their time in search of some better things than to try to lead humanity back to monkeys and pigs.[106]

A dozen years later, on October 19, 1922 – and less than two weeks before he died – E.E. admonished his son in a letter: "See by the paper that Bryan talks next Sunday in Minneapolis on 'Evolution.' Go and hear him. I am afraid you are apt to take too much stock in the flimsy argument of the Evolutionists."

Dancing

The issue of dancing in the community had already been noted by E.E.'s father, Embret Persen, in his reminiscences about P. Irgens Dybdal who, not long into the 19th century back in Norway, had encouraged people to "avoid drinking and dancing and the bad behavior that would result." [See page 20.] The question was discussed at length in news articles during March 1905. The Lowry Board of Education resolved that dancing was not in the best interests of pupils attending public schools. They went so far as to disapprove of any pupil attending dances whether public or private.

High school pupils disagreed. They challenged the school board, stating that if they couldn't have the Junior Ball then they would not participate in a scheduled debate. The newspaper continued: "the existence of a spirit in the high school that would make such a remark possible, shows to what extent dances and balls have come to engross the interest of the high school pupils."[107]

A particularly imaginative protest was given by Minnie Lobeck, daughter of Ingerinus (E.E.'s half-brother) and his wife Sigrid, hence a niece of E.E., and a friend of hers, also called Minnie. The newspaper told the story.

Girls Seek Fame

Take Ten-mile Walk and Dance for an Hour – Will Walk to Minnesota State Fair

Claims for the championship walker's belt are made by two Lowry young ladies this week. They are Miss Minnie Lobeck and Minnie Negaard who established claims to the championship by walking to an entertainment ten miles in the country. The walk was undertaken just before sun-down and they reached their destination in time for refreshments. After that the young ladies danced for an hour and declared they were not "tired a bit." They spent the next day at the home of Miss Negaard's parents and were taken back to Lowry in a farm wagon. They enjoyed their experience immensely and have announced their intentions of walking to Minneapolis to see the state fair next fall. Perhaps there is not another young lady in Minnesota who would undertake to duplicate the experiences of these two Lowry young ladies.[108]

The issue of dancing resurfaced even more virulently at an Alexandria school board meeting in March 1917.

Five churches and the Alexandria Woman's Christian Temperance Union (WCTU) were vociferously anti-dancing anywhere. An evangelist summarized the views often expressed by the WCTU:

> It is a sad comment ... on the part of some fathers and mothers, and often professors of the Christian religion, for a practice which from time immemorial has been looked upon by the best people of any land as a prolific source of immorality. ... In an age of looseness of morals, with from five to six hundred thousand fallen women and girls in the United States, we should not go into the business ... of learning our girls and boys a science which will make a demand for them in the halls of brothels as soon as they become experts.[109]

According to their undocumented claims, the majority of "fallen girls come from dance halls."

Fifty to seventy-five interested parents showed up for the school board meeting to argue, quite heatedly, their own views. The more moderate group argued that students will dance anyway, so their elders should provide a suitable place for them to dance – the school gymnasium. Also, boys and girls from the farms could have the advantage of "better culture and social training." They also thought the churches had no business interfering.

The WCTU and committees from the churches raised countless objections. Schools, they said, are entrusted with the moral and social training of boys and girls along with their education, and schools are supported by state aid. Therefore, they must act responsibly. Dancing would require chaperones, most likely teachers, which would give the message that the adults accepted dancing.

After these arguments and more, the Board of Education ruled against using the school gymnasium for dancing. The farmers, especially, expressed their appreciation for the decision. The comment about "better culture and social training," however, irked the farmers, who thought the town people felt superior to them.[110]

If dancing was a distraction carrying the risk of perdition, it was not alone. In 1916 Minnesota State Senator E.E. Lobeck was commencement speaker at Alexandria High School, where his eldest daughter, Evangeline, and her cousin, George Daly, were graduating. The Ministerial Association of St. Paul had recently engaged E.E. to head a campaign against Sunday moving picture theaters.[111] It is a safe conjecture that the subject was included in E.E.'s address that day.

Football

Dancing. Sunday movies. And football.

In 1906 E.E. was on a train in Wisconsin.

> Players entered with insane barks, infernal howls. … If we were not used to the most shocking things in our great, civilized country, we should have thought that our college youths went by full steam towards the madhouse – a sport so raw and brutal has gained national approval, and is seen as a necessity for the cultural development of the young.

> At each station we passed they howled, they shrieked so their backs were bent and their noses lay flat in their faces, and their eyes were halfway out of their sockets.

> This is our youth, with culture, enlightenment, and knowledge.[112]

Just a year earlier, the brutality of football had been given national prominence when President Theodore Roosevelt (who had been elected in 1904 with 56 percent of the popular vote while the Prohibitionist candidate, Silas Swallow, received 259,103 votes nationwide, less than two percent) called to the White House football representatives from the three largest programs in the country – Harvard, Yale, and Princeton – and declared that football must be reformed.[113]

In 1905 alone, 18 people died and more than 150 were injured playing football. At least 45 football players died from 1900 to October 1905, many from internal injuries, broken necks, concussions, or broken backs. According to the October 15 *Washington Post* (just six days after the White House meeting), "Nearly every death may be traced to 'unnecessary roughness.' Picked up unconscious from beneath a mass of other players, it was generally found that the victim had been kicked in the head or stomach, so as to cause internal injuries or concussion of the brain, which, sooner or later, ended life."

Roosevelt got attention. By December, 62 colleges agreed on a set of innovations that significantly changed the game. Yardage for a first down was changed from five to 10; a neutral zone was established between opposing lines; and the time of the game was reduced from 70 to 60 minutes. The year also saw the legalization of the forward pass.[114]

In 1901 Roosevelt had become president following the assassination of William McKinley just six months into his second term. Two years later E.E. had occasion to see Roosevelt in person, during the president's eight-week, 14,000 mile, 25-state tour. E.E.'s account conveys a vivid impression.

> I was scheduled to speak in Østerdalen, Fargo, and Moorhead, the 5th and 6th April. Then came the newspapers, informing that President Roosevelt would be in Fargo on the 7th. Such things can be called fortunate.
>
> Sunday the 5th was held sacred to decorate the city. Flags, red, white, and blue streamers billowed in the wind. Many people participated. On Monday there would not be time: but Monday came with devilish weather from the north, first rain and then snow. About an hour later the hanging flags, streamers and ribbons were withered and ruined as a Mark Hanna Policy [U.S. Senator from Ohio from 1897 to 1904, when he died].
>
> I awoke on the 7th to sunshine, clear skies and mild temperatures. Out of bed and got myself ready!
>
> I strode up the street with giant strides. One way or another one must step out in this world. If one cannot do it with his mind, one can do it with his legs, I thought, and stepped out one leg after another.
>
> A stream of people were moving forward on the way to the train: small and large, lame and crooked. They hobbled and bumped along. Ladies and gentlemen, talking and laughing in different pitches. All wanted to see the President.
>
> The Northern Pacific depot was the gathering place, where it was simply quite packed. Reportedly, the train arrived and there were many who were prattling and excited in anticipation of what was to come.
>
> Some jumped up on the window recesses, while we, who have quite a physical length, stood and stretched our necks.

The door of the train compartment opened. "Here he comes," cried a lady. No, it was certainly one of the Secret Service. "Der kjem'n" ["Here they come!"] said one in Norwegian. No, it was also one of the Secret Service.

Then came some of the city's tycoons pushing through the crowd and were ushered into the President and came back with happiness on their faces.

A face overgrown with a dazzling white beard and lined with hair pale as linen, looked out the window. It was the scientist that Roosevelt has with him on the trip. His face was keen and his nose sharp. It was very well suited to smell with, and it is most probable that that man sticks his nose into many things. [This was John Muir, with whom Roosevelt would be making a three-day visit to Yosemite.]

"Hip, hip," and then the crowd broke loose. Roosevelt came out on the platform wearing a fur coat, but since the sun was gentle, he jumped in again and came back with only an overcoat on, lifted his hat, greeted us and showed his grin, which is known all over the country. He went through the depot, ascended his carriage and drove through the town, spoke a moment in the opera house, came back to the depot, boarded the train, talked a little from the platform, but although I was just 30 feet from him, I did not hear a word, as I happened to be surrounded by a bunch of women, and they also had something to say then.

Incidentally, there are a lot of people who get mad under such circumstances: yell, scream, push, and shove and get angry because they do not get to be first and foremost.

One can easily see in the president's bearing that he is "envis" (stubborn), and I was so glad that he was. He appears to be independent, and does not run after the tycoon's bagpipe music.

When he opens his mouth to speak, he laughs quite dreadfully, almost like a "bulldog" when it is ready to bite. However, one must love him, and I say: God protect our country's President!

So, I came, saw, and did not hear him.[115]

Nonetheless, even with the reforms instigated by the powerful intervention of Teddy Roosevelt, concern about the violence of football persisted. In 1909 E.E. was on another train, this one in North Dakota.

Into the train swarmed the high school football team from Wahpeton, North Dakota. They had been in Fergus Falls, and I believe that a good many of them ought to have remained there – upon the hill. They had their lady rooters (some called them roosters) with them. You ought to have heard their yells and infernal screams. Megaphones, those hideous voice magnifiers, were used to the limit. Silly talking, silly laughing, idiotic actions, and gum chewing were a few of the characteristics presented by these cultured, learned, high school boys and girls from Wahpeton.

It is hoped this brutal sport will be done away with. Congress shall tackle it. Some of the congressmen have said that a sport that will destroy the life of some 30 or 40 boys in one year ought to die. Amen! It ought to. But then, what will the same men do to the saloon that kills 30 people every half-hour in this country? They will not exert themselves along these lines.[116]

For E.E., football and dancing (and maybe even gum chewing) were linked as social menaces.

When the school year began in 1913, E.E. and two pastors appeared before the school board, protesting a dance rumored to be held by the high school football team to entertain a visiting team. "Mr. Lobeck said he will not permit his children under any circumstances to attend dances. His children know it and will not do so, but it embarrasses them. They cannot under such conditions enter into the spirit of the school and take part in the social functions. He desired to know if it is not possible to prohibit dancing in connection with football teams."[117]

The board passed a motion that no dances would be given under the auspices of the school and none for visiting athletic teams.

Chapter 5
Beginning of Political Career

In early March 1906 the Minneapolis Auditorium, festooned with flags and bunting and a large banner screaming "PROHIBITION," and with mottoes and catchwords decorating the walls, was the site of the state Prohibition Convention. E.E. was one of the prominent speakers. By the end of the summer his prominence would escalate.

During the intervening months, family matters occasionally took priority.

Mama and Papa slept in cabin; rest of family in tents. Partial view of one tent in back.

A daughter, Ida Genevieve, was born into the busy Lobeck household on May 27. It wasn't long, however, before E.E. was on tour again.

He and Martha bought a cabin on Lake Darling, which was so small, the children remembered – it became part of family lore – that "Mama and Papa could sleep in the cabin and everyone else had to sleep in tents outside." The cooking was done outside and there were plenty of fish caught and subsequently cooked on the outdoor stove.

E.E.'s brother, Ingerinus, and his family were moving west that summer, lured by the great expanses of land in northwestern North Dakota.

In early August, Martha's brother Olaf P. Nordby died of tuberculosis at his home near Harwood, North Dakota. Olaf was a "Free Thinker" and not a believer in church affairs or sacraments. E.E. wrote a letter to him in his last days, begging him to accept Jesus. The telegram announcing Olaf's death was tardy, because the family was at the cabin. Martha missed the train to attend her brother's funeral.

From 1,175 vote loss to victory by 335

In late August 1906 E.E. filed for representative in the Minnesota state legislature on the Prohibition ticket. Mid-September's primaries did not show well for Lobeck. Matched against his opponent, Republican one-term incumbent – and a Swede – J. F. Landeen, Lobeck had 23 votes to Landeen's 1,198. Then citing his belief that "traffic in alcoholic beverages is a curse to the state, a foe to humanity, a crime against society, and a sin against God," he asked for the people's vote to pass a law for the "County Option."[118]

This County Option – the right for a county to decide for itself whether to go "wet" or "dry" – proved hugely significant for Lobeck. Voters did not necessarily vote the party line. Many who voted yes for County Option also voted for Lobeck, the Prohibitionist candidate.

Here is what E.E. wrote, less than a month later, about the election. In the interim he had made a lecture tour to Chicago and New York. The account includes reference to Senator Knute Nelson. As noted earlier, the antipathy between Nelson and Lobeck will loom large in the rest of this story. (In 1902 E.E. had referred to Nelson derisively. "Knute Nelson had been [in Sauk Centre] a few days earlier – and the audience was carried away in such a manner that quite a number had a boozing session afterwards, which led to one poor man amongst the drinkers falling into the water and drowning, and another one died in his bed. Knute did not ask them to do this, but there lies some responsibility with a party that has 'License' on its banner.")[119]

> The election campaign in Douglas County. is over, and the county has never experienced such a crossfire ever.

> Some of the state's most magnificent fiery mountains have let their light shine, but the people sat on their tussocks, unperturbed as ever.

> The County Option Movement came on the scene – and the man that filed the Republican ticket didn't bother to promise his voters to give this cause his support.

> He did not need the support of the Temperance people. Such men he could do without. And why not? First, he had Senator Nelson to support his back – besides the political machine, the prestige of the party, and in addition a doorkeeper and spittoon-washer from Washington. He did not need the help from the Temperance people.

> So it happened that the Temperance people came and asked me to run as a counter candidate, and after long deliberation, I went to file as Prohibitionist, without endorsing Knute Nelson's re-election.

> The "Barflies" laughed, the political petty kings shrugged their shoulders, and the primary election gave me 23 votes.

> The political bosses comforted me that I would get more votes at the fall election, others tapped their skulls to indicate that a person that would run as Prohibitionist in an overwhelmingly Republican county, where the senator has his home, and even ran for re-election – that man must have a brain that mainly consisted of moonlight.

> The people came in step. The politicians stared and gaped. Was anyone really stupid enough to support the Prohibitionists?

> A Mr. Youngdahl, working for the Anti Saloon League, started to play havoc in the county – and I wandered a little amongst the locals, and at last the movement went like a storm over water. ...

It's worth a brief pause here to call attention to this "Mr. Youngdahl" who "started to play havoc in the county."

P. J. Youngdahl (1883-1960; older brother of Luther Youngdahl, 1896-1978, governor of Minnesota 1947-1951), who on occasion appeared with E.E. on the lecture circuit, was superintendent of the Minnesota Anti-Saloon League. At some point in this era he delivered an address that was published as a 15-page pamphlet, "'A Birthright Restored' or County Option – What It Is and How It Will Work."[120]

The address demonstrates well-honed rhetorical skills. Youngdahl begins:

> The opposition to County Option comes from two classes of people. Those who know what County Option is, but who for selfish reasons are opposed to letting the people rule in the saloon question, and those who do not know what County Option is.

> The first class we cannot hope to convince. We must overcome them by ballots. The second class we are anxious to reach because we believe that when they fully understand what County Option is, how fair, how simple, and how American it is, they will not only favor, they will demand it.

By a quirk of Minnesota law, small villages were allowed to vote wet or dry, but cities and rural areas weren't.

> In the license question Minnesota law classes the farmer and the city man with idiots, Indians, and criminals. In demanding County Option we are asking for the enfranchisement of the four-fifths of Minnesota's voters who today thru political trickery and legislative treachery are bereft of this American birthright.

To provide context for his argument, Youngdahl then makes an appeal to an impressive source, the U.S. Supreme Court – quoting from Justice Stephen Johnson Field's opinion in Crowley v. Christensen 137 U.S. 86 (1890):

> By the general concurrence of opinion of every civilized and Christian community, there are few sources of crime and misery to society equal to the dram shop, where intoxicating liquors, in small quantities, to be drunk at the time, are sold indiscriminately to all parties applying. The statistics of every State show a greater amount of crime and misery attributable to the use of ardent spirits obtained at these retail liquor saloons than to any other source.[121]

Youngdahl follows with a careful and nuanced argument for County Option in terms of an ancient American principle – no taxation without representation, a principle that is breached when county residents who oppose liquor are required to pay taxes for the consequences of havoc wrought in a "wet" village ("Today four-fifths of Minnesota is powerless to protect itself against such a situation").

And in a move that might not have elicited approval from E.E., Youngdahl calls to witness a stage play, based on Lew Wallace's 1880 novel, *Ben-Hur: A Tale of the Christ*. Youngdahl recounts his excitement as he watched the chariot race – and then he suddenly turns to Minnesota politics:

> And then how disgusted I was when from the gallery I beheld this magnificent scene. I was disgusted because I wanted the best team to win, and because sitting from my point of vantage I could see how the horses were running on rollers for it was only a stage scene. They were moved forward and backward not by their own speed but by machinery beneath the stage moved by the hand and will of the director in back of the scenes, who decides how and when and by whom the race should be won.

> There you have Minnesota's politics over again. We have our runs for office, our races, with flare of torches, rattle of drums, shouts, hand shakes, cigars and speeches but after all it is only a stage play. For down beneath is a machine which has been planned and put in operation months and months before. It is the hand of this oligarchy of selfish interests which through its well built, well oiled machine of corruption and bribery dictates the nomination of candidates, some to be elected and some to be slaughtered.

And Youngdahl leaves no doubt where the blame lies.

> The strongest and most powerful, because of its organization among these selfish interests is the liquor traffic. Without its help the railroad and steel trust and other corporations would be practically helpless in the hands of the people. The men who are bought and owned and controlled by the liquor traffic not only are unable to represent their people upon the liquor question, but upon every other question of any importance. ... We find that every important bill that came up for consideration [in the last legislature] in which the interests of the people and the interests of the trust oligarchy conflicted the liquor controlled gang voted practically as a unit.

In a concluding peroration, Youngdahl urges his hearers/readers to action.

> Do you want your birthright as an American citizen restored? If so join your protest with ours, and let us move forward in a mighty, organized, powerful, growing sentiment, that shall result in the election of a legislature which is willing to trust its own constituents in this matter.

Now we return to E.E.'s account of 1906. The machine didn't get broken, but in Douglas County it suffered a surprising setback.

> Governor Johnson's shares were rising, and then one had to meet at the battlefield with the forces – Congressman Steenerson fired a round over Evansville, J. J. Jacobsen from Lac qui Parle shelled Brandon and Alexandria, Lindbergh invaded Holmes City, Kensington and a couple of other places, while Senator Clapp directed his efforts towards Osakis.[122]

> The civil servants of the county put their work aside for a few days, and the chorus of the political song was: "Vote the ticket straight! Be loyal to your party! Stick to your party! Don't go back on your candidates!" etc. The people smiled cunningly and contemplated.

> The Prohibitionists' Tally-Ho carriage with Dorsett and Oliver Stewart also came to the county, and they made speeches (especially Stewart) as if their tongues were on fire – and then Election Day came – and when the counting was done, the old Machine lay with its feet in the air. Johnson won in the county, and the people pushed me into the legislature with a majority of 335 votes more [1,292 to 957] than my opponent [Republican one-term incumbent J. F. Landeen].

> From this day on the candidates will need the support of the Temperance people if they want to be elected.[123]

The Minnesota Capitol in St. Paul, designed by renowned architect, Cass Gilbert, was completed in 1905. Most striking was the gilded quadriga on the front – "the four horses representing the power of nature: earth, wind, fire, and water; the women leading the horses symbolizing civilization, and the man on the chariot representing prosperity."[124]

Inside, the unsupported marble dome, inspired by Michelangelo's vault in St. Peter's Basilica in Rome; the marble walls interspersed with Minnesota's native Kasota stone and pipestone; and spacious views gave the interior a warm glow and imparted confidence and pride to the people and legislature of Minnesota that they were established on solid ground and looking toward the future. Surely, great things must take place in this building.

E.E. arrived here the first week of January 1907.

It was extremely cold. Temperatures dropped quickly from 32 degrees above zero to 25 below in a few hours. Swirling snow drifted in some places to 18 inches. Trains derailed or were just stuck and unable to move. People who had driven horse and buggy to town on a relatively warm day were trapped, unable to return home. Mail was undelivered because horses were unable to make their way. And the temperatures continued to hover between 20 and 30 below zero.

Selecting a U.S. Senator

Nevertheless, things were already heating up in the House of Representatives. One of the first tasks was to select Minnesota's U.S. Senator. An obvious, uncontested choice would be Knute Nelson from Alexandria. He had already served in the U.S. Senate as well as the Minnesota legislature and as governor of Minnesota.

E.E. had his own choice in mind – W. J. Dean, who had three times run unsuccessfully for mayor of Minneapolis, as a Prohibitionist in 1888 and 1896, and as an independent in 1900.[125] Most freshman legislators stay in the background and rarely bring a bill or a speech to the floor. Not Lobeck. Nominating Dean, he made an impassioned plea – ominous for his future elections and pursuits. He came into the crosshairs of a popular and powerful Republican skilled in the art of politics and winning.

The Reform, under the headline "Minnesota's legislature," published the speech, which was editorially introduced this way:

> The two houses of the legislature met Tuesday to elect a United States Senator. The Republicans had in the House of Representatives selected their best speaker to nominate Knute Nelson. He spoke both movingly and beautifully about the barefoot little boy from Norway. The Democrats didn't waste many words nominating their candidate, and then E.E. Lobeck was given the floor to nominate a candidate on behalf of the Prohibitionists.

Here is what E.E. said.

Mr. Speaker, I ask for the honor to nominate a Prohibitionist candidate for the United States Senate – the first time for this to happen in the state's history. I consider it a great honor that this privilege has been given to me – to be the first one to make such a nomination in our North Star State. I understand that it befits a speaker at such an occasion to explain his party's principles and why he nominates a candidate in full coherence with it.

Time will not give me the opportunity to an extensive explanation, but – allow me, Mr. Speaker, to engage yours and these gentlemen's attention to explain that the Prohibitionist Party was born of the uncountable wails from hungry children, pale mothers, heartbroken wives, ruined fathers and spouses, standing on the brink of destruction with the taunting Demon of Alcohol behind them – exactly the same way that the Republican Party came to life by the rattling of the slave chains, the crack of the slave whip, the howls of the bloodhounds, and the moans of the dying negroes, echoing all over the country.

And parties with such a beginning and such an origin have had and will have a God-given mission. Several times I have heard encouragement to join your party. But I say, hold on to your principles, and shun both men and parties that do not teach the principles that are in accordance with your conscience and tuned in harmony with the best in you. I know that you, too, have principles that you will not give up. I have myself such principles, that I cannot support anyone who is not in accordance with them. Principles that have developed in me through years of struggle, dark days, sleepless nights, and great suffering. It may cost me both sorrows and worry to hold on to them. It may not be "policy" to hold on to them. Principles, gentlemen, are important for a man who struggles to live a real life in the midst of a suffering humanity.

We should learn and understand that for all real men it isn't always what they rather would like to do, but what their honest conviction forces them to do, that determines their careers. It will cost them pain and sorrow, but it is impossible to serve the course of justice in this world without the cost of pain and sorrow. Abraham Lincoln was a man of principles, and he was a man of sorrow. He was faithful to his principles, but his soul was at times shrouded in darkness and despair. When something great is to be done, God calls upon certain men to do it. When slavery was to be exterminated from this country, God spoke to such men as Garrison, Lovejoy, and Wendell Philipps, but especially and foremost to Abraham

Lincoln, and this remarkable man stepped forth, tall and ungainly, knuckled hands and a face wrinkled as a walnut, but he was a mighty tool in God the Almighty's hands when slavery should be banned from the United States. He absolutely believed that slavery was wrong, and he said: "I find in the teachings of Jesus Christ, the simple Nazarene, that slavery cannot exist a day longer without sin, and if the enemy is driven back over Potomac, I will declare the slaves free."

But Lincoln had to receive the violations of his opponents. From November 1860 until April 1865 his horizon was covered by stormy clouds, but he stood like a rock in the middle of the upheaving sea, and got through the four black, desperate years of Purgatory, while God the Almighty absolved this nation's sins through blood and fire. He was true to his principles all the way until John Wilkes Booth sneaked up the stairs of Ford's Theatre in Washington the evening of 14th April 1865 and put a piece of lead into Abraham Lincoln's head, and his great heart trembled and stopped beating. The whole nation was hushed into silent weeping when his great heart stopped beating.

You will find, Mr. Chairman, that the principles of my party are, even if in a different form, covered by the famous words of this giant personality in world politics the last four hundred years, when he said: "A house in discord with itself cannot last. I do not think that this Government can continue to exist, half pro-slavery, half free. I do not expect to see the dissolution of the Union, I do not expect to see the house fall, but I do expect that the dissension must end. It has to be one or the other."

So much for President Lincoln. Here is what I mean: I do not believe that this nation can exist for ever, half drunk, half sober. Totally sober, and this nation will have a tremendous development. Totally drunk it will rot and die. This is the flaming conviction in my soul. These are the principles that I applaud and stand by. I believe that the alcohol trade is the most terrible curse of all humanity's curses, and my faith, founded on this fact, has been crystallized into a principle I cannot deviate from without being unfaithful. The man who sells his principles is the greatest fraud in the universe.

Therefore, Mr. Speaker, I asked for the floor to nominate a man who is in full harmony with this principle. We claim – and you know – that it is a fact that it is wrong to license a trade that generates idiots, paupers, criminals, and epileptics, and then throws them at the society to be kept by decent, honest, and industrious people. We claim that it is wrong to allow a trade that raises the taxes by filling up jails, charity establishments, madhouses, asylums, and hospitals, and increases the cost of police and courts. We claim that it is wrong to uphold a national quarantine against dependent and criminal classes from other countries, and at the same time allow 250,000 saloon keepers to produce dependents and criminals within our country.

That is why I nominate a candidate who both in heart and mind is in harmony with these our principles. I am honored to nominate a very good person. He has given a hundred dollars [$2,700] a year to Temperance work and the protection of homes against the saloon. He is a good businessman. He is a patriot and philanthropist and one of God's noblemen here on earth. I have the honor to nominate for the United States Senate W. J. Dean from Minneapolis, and will when the voting comes, throw my vote for him.[126]

Knute Nelson received 98 votes, Dean three. The hometown newspaper of both Nelson and Lobeck, *Alexandria Post News*, theorized that Lobeck had made a big mistake. Rejecting such a wonderful man as Nelson would hurt Lobeck's chances of advancing the Prohibition cause.

"The new members meant well, ... but alas ..."

The County Option bill, though advocated by the House, was "indefinitely postponed" by the Senate in March. Township options were still permitted. The Senate felt that County Option would give rural voters too much power, and would not generate enough revenue for police and fire protection. Instead, they proposed that the number of saloons be limited, and those saloons would pay a higher license fee. They hoped to appease the Temperance people with this proposal. It took until 1915 for County Option to become law.

On the last day of the session, April 24, the House disintegrated into disorder and merrymaking. After rushing through the passage of thirty bills and with 15 minutes to adjournment, "the chamber filled with flying paper, books, beans, and other miscellaneous objects that could be aimed at the heads of merrymaking lawmakers. From the galleries, showers of torn paper kept up an artificial snowstorm."[127]

Interviewed at the end of his first legislative session, E.E. stated he had enjoyed the work, but "the new members meant well, came down to do business, but alas, ... as the days went by, the stress of corporations and the political machine bore down upon them."[128]

Good news for Lobeck was that the towns of Kensington, Nelson, and Lowry had voted out saloons – but two months later, two "blind pigs" were discovered at Kensington.

Chapter 6

Back on the Lecture Trail

While the rest of 1907 included some family time, E.E. was frequently
off on the lecture tour. Here is his account of those months.

There could be said a lot about my extended tour in North Dakota
through the summer, especially through Williams County with nice sod
houses and heartwarm settlers, and it might have given material for a long
story. The wonderful climate, the unforested, endless plains with a brilliant
blue sky above, embraced my whole being. The far sights over the plains
gave peace and strengthened body and soul. No wonder that Jesus took his
disciples aside when he wanted to fasten the roots of hope for eternity in
them.

When I came home the bags were put away, the traveling clothes taken off,
and then I spent every other day fishing on the lake. When the lakes
around Alexandria lie like mirrors, the air is still and the sky is clear, then
you find yourself in a corner of the realm of nature, gracious and
beautiful, to which there is no comparison.

When the foliage took on the strong colors of autumn, there came a letter
from Calumet, Michigan, with an invitation from the marvelous
Temperance league there to participate in some meetings. I travelled by
"The Steamer" [train] to Buffalo, Minnesota, where the meeting that
evening became so hot that the depot caught on fire and burned down.
Then through Minneapolis to Bayfield, Wisconsin. A somewhat more than
six feet tall man towered on the platform of the depot and gave me a
warm welcome. That was Pastor Samuelsen, but he must remember that
he owes me a good fish cake. In Washburn I shook hands with a lot of
Temperance friends, among them Adelsten Berge – a really tough one in
the struggle. In Ashland I met the newly arrived Pastor Halvorsen – with a

warm heart for everything good, a mild presence, and devoted to God in his work.

I was supposed to be in Calumet at 8 o'clock. "I will come to an empty church," I thought. Who would sit waiting far into the evening for my sake? "You are late," a man said, meeting me at the station, grabbed one of my bags and strode away towards the church with long, rapid strides. Under the row of lights he reminded me of a pair of pincers. "Are we going in?" I asked as we came up to the door. "Yes, please", he said, and opened it – and I was greeted by a sea of hundreds of waving handkerchiefs. Had they seen my face they would have found me blushing as a virgin.

Had three marvelous meetings there – and I must say that it is comforting for both soul and mind to be among these friends. Pastor Russvold is doing a blessed work in Calumet.

In Ishpeming I dumped into the arms of Pastor Lillehei. The meeting was mainly attended by women, as their husbands are mine workers. In Escanaba I had two good meetings arranged by Pastor Berntzen – one in Norwegian and one in English. Berntzen was working on a plan to get the American pastors to participate in a nightly rally through the saloons, in order to, if possible, bring to terms some of these rough Goliaths, who kill the hopes of youths and snuff out the light of old age.

At the depot in Marinette I immediately discovered the benign face of Pastor E. D. Larsson. He had sent his wife to Minnesota, but his sister had made a stack of flatbread, and that was food for me. Two good meetings I had there. In Oconto and Peshtigo the meetings had a good attendance. All along the line one can trace a new

A Hard "Knocker."

From Evangeline's scrapbook: "Lobeck's punching bag"

interest. The opposition against the saloons is growing like a river in spring. One, two, three, and it takes on momentum, and the saloon with its staggering mass of sin and rot will die forever.

Under the auspices of the Prohibition Committee I worked 35 days in Minnesota. Started in the southeast county and took the lower row of counties to the Mississippi River, then westwards again along the third row until I was in the middle of the state, after which I rummaged around for a few days in the center of the state. What movement there is to be found in such places! The treatment the last legislature gave the County Option proposal woke rage all over the state. The Christian vice governor promised us a good Temperance Committee in the House, but the majority of the members of the committee were the most rednosed pets King Gambrinus could procure. Spite and shame! But just wait! A storm is coming, as the boy said, his mother took out the whip. Soon something unusual will go up and down on the mosquito bites of these weaklings, who trample the people's dearest interests underfoot.

The breweries own 92 percent of the saloons in Minnesota. A good sign of the time is that they have great trouble in selling their swill. They obviously have seen the handwriting on the wall, – seeing the coming judgment; they want to get rid of their saloons. The next election campaign will become the best the state ever has had – a struggle between Temperance friends and saloon friends – a struggle between God and Belial. Therefore: Everyone on deck!

Went for a quick trip in North Dakota. Spoke in Fargo, Portland, Mayville, Bethania, Hatton, Urdahls Church, and Northwood. An unusual interest in the cause was evident everywhere.

Am now at home. The children's songs are all around me, dolls' prams, little lambs and other children's stuff are lying all about on the floor. Flutes, games, "hooting horns," and other musical instruments fill the room with music – and even if the listeners are not too excited, the concert troupe seems to have great fun. It is Christmas.

1908 is now the number that shall be written on our deeds. At the change of the year the memories are gathering, to support the thought. The year we look back upon has been rich in events. Temperance and Prohibition have shone like a great torch over 1907 and lit it up. With renewed courage and great expectations we are standing on the threshold of 1908, lifting our eyes to Heaven, and trembling, watching the movements which, unfulfilled, streamed from the old into the new. What will become of these children?

Then you, my friends, be greeted in the warmest of ways! The last year has been my best since I, seventeen years ago, took to the road for the first time. I must say with David: "I am less than all your mercy." May God in the new year give us warmer hearts, more humble minds, and greater faith. Happy New Year![129]

"A picture of the pack of ogres"

Writing in May 1908, E.E. tells the tale of travels in the new year.

Like a swallow, rising toward the heavens in sunshine, the hopes of the soul are rising in springtime. Every fragrant leaf, every swaying stem, and every smiling flower is a message from God, the central point of love, about life, resurrection, and joy.

The Prohibition Committee in Wisconsin has arranged a month of meetings for Ben Blessum and me, starting in Milwaukee. On the fourth of May again a heavy bag was hanging from each hand. Small and big hands were waving farewell, and the same old lump pressed in the chest, the home disappeared, and I was again on the road.

Due to circumstances, I had to let Blessum rummage alone the first three days. I got to Minneapolis in the afternoon of the fourth. After having wandered aimlessly for a few hours I went to our common friend Ben Skørdalsvold. At present he has grown well into tomatoes, celery, carrots, and other plants.

As we were standing there, enjoying the budding glory, Student Hovland came and told that some German riffraff had tried to kill Prof. Nydahl. Skørdalsvold took off to the fighting site bareheaded – came back and told us that that spawn of German soil had thrown a rock about three or four pounds at the professor's head. It was a miracle that Nydahl hadn't been killed on the spot.

I arrived in Milton, Wisconsin, at 11 o'clock on May 5 in a pouring rain, a city full of water and Seventh Day Baptists. Blessum had already arrived. I had not seen him for about 11 years; he had changed significantly. He was carrying with him a big tray, a scaffold, and gigantic rolls of paper. He employs both his mouth and his hands. The evening arrived with downpour, darkness, and few people. "You start, Blessum."

"Ladies and gentlemen!" He seems slightly nervous, is unable to stand still in front of a gathering. Grabs a piece of chalk – now it really comes – makes a movement like washing the paper, and upon it appears something that looks like a lemon or a full moon, then some curves and turns, arches, a question mark, and everything has a name. There are faces, some beautiful, others of a character that would make even a crow take to the woods. Barrels with hoops around them take the form of humans, as a knot hole becomes an eye, a rip in the wood becomes a mouth, etc. At the very last the political Boss appears, a specimen to make you understand. Red nose, blue cheeks, fat as a well-fed pig, a cigar in the mouth, with a smug expression in every line, this is a picture of the pack of ogres who administer the political whip in our conventions and legislatures.

I must say, though, that Blessum does not bring on his best as a "chalk talker." He does not get the spirit. But I also must say that when he speaks free, without his drawings, he is a joy to listen to. With unbelievable ease he speaks both languages, with a clear logic – he has a beautiful, poetic language – and it is my sincerest conviction that he is one of the absolute best orators among us Norwegians. He has abandoned a well-paid job in Chicago, thrown himself into this work. Now the friends of the cause should encourage him as best they can. The friends will benefit from it, the cause will be strengthened, and Blessum himself will be inflamed and develop further.[130]

The sixth of May we went on foot through a buffeting westerly wind to Milton Junction. I see in the "Scandinavian" that a Haugen from Pigeon Falls, Wisconsin, has announced to the world that the Temperance speakers are just bread-and-butter politicians – then it was best that we walked between some stations to stir up an appetite.

In Stoughton you will really see something happen. A veritable host of Drink's enemies live there – the saloon was brushed out with an overwhelming majority in the spring election. Pastor Hegge and family and the Vea siblings took turns doing their best for us.

A terrible downpour kept many of the people away from the meeting.

We took a detour through Madison, where we visited Rasmus B. Andersen at his lodgings, and had a conversation with the man who has the courage to reprimand to the right and left, friend and foe. He was spitting in his hands – a heavy piece of work was to be carried out in the nearest future – and I surmise there will be blisters on the skin of quite a few who will feel the whiplash. In the position he has taken, the steel will get no time to rust.[131]

The Prohibitionist Convention

In June E.E. writes, and coins a witty phrase that could have a place in the 21st-century Twitterverse: "thin as a Republican platform, thin as a Democratic cause."

In a beautiful, pouring rain, whose droplets seemed like pearls because of the electric lamps, my brother John and I went to the depot 15 minutes before 3 in the morning.

Minnesota's Prohibitionists were meeting together in the third convention at 10 o'clock in the morning. We looked neither to the right or left, tied ourselves in a knot in our seats and went to sleep. It went well for me.

The Winnipeg-Flyer clattered through the darkness and small towns and rolled into the station in Minneapolis at 7:15 in the morning. We rubbed the sleep from our eyes, got our limbs in the right places, grabbed our bags and went.

At 10 o'clock we gathered in the Courthouse Hall and Higgins grabbed a chair and banged the meeting to order. And so it went for awhile, with singing, speaking, and discussions. Participants from four corners of the state, side, and center were present. A youth of 87 years, Judge Burbank from Fergus Falls, was also there, excited, full of life and fighting spirit, high-pitched voice and back straight as a rod. A half-blood Negro, 72 years old, went around with a grin on his face beaming with happiness to be with us. A 17-year-old from Willmar with a body of 225 pounds came to the meeting happy to be with us in the dry element.

"The first president I voted for was Lincoln," said one. "I was active four years before," remembered another. "I helped Grant." Thus the old bearded men sat talking. They told of the time when they became Prohibitionists. "I voted for Blake," said one. "My goodness, you were really early," said another. "I sat with the Republicans until Garfield was out and when I thought the movement stopped. I got off and now I am here." Old men amuse themselves superbly.

The First Baptist Church was filled to overflowing in the evening. A man emerged who at first sight seemed like he had come from a factory a little too soon – not really finished. Looked like they should have started with the head but reduced the shoulders and side due to lack of material and set up under the body a pair of thin little legs. This was Clinton Howard, one of the country's utmost speakers. A veritable electric battery. The man weighs 110 pounds and Sam Jones said that Howard has 109 pounds body and a pound of skin and hair. Out of this little scrap of a man and this big head came a great voice, and after a while we were in the heart of events of wit, humor, sarcasm, anecdotes, tall tales, facts, mighty doomsday bells tolling, and a heavy salting of dusty church people still sitting so far behind that through old political parties they keep embracing the Devil Drink.

A power and stamina he had that borders on the unbelievable. A warm smile lit up his handsome face and sparkling dark eyes gave the impression that the man borrows his fighting strength from a source no mortal can see.

Howard talked for three hours and it was, for him, as if he had rested in a rocking chair.[132]

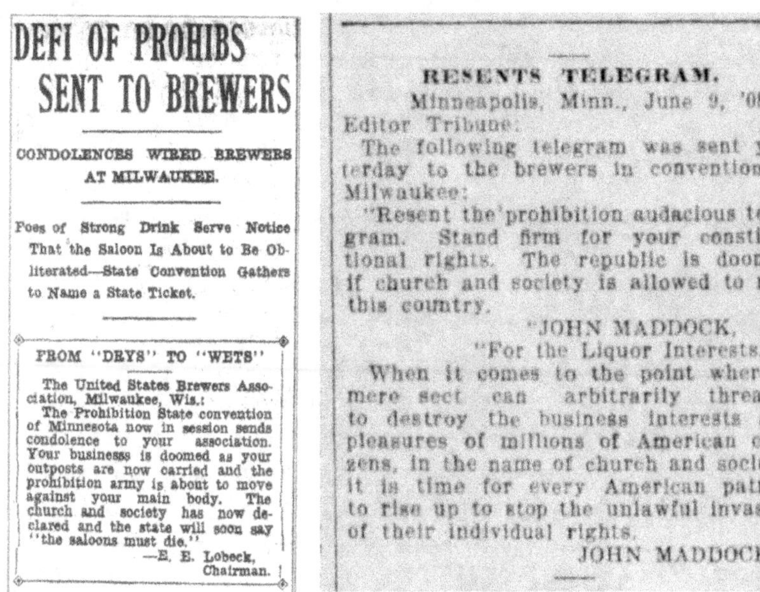

DEFI OF PROHIBS SENT TO BREWERS

CONDOLENCES WIRED BREWERS AT MILWAUKEE.

Foes of Strong Drink Serve Notice That the Saloon Is About to Be Obliterated—State Convention Gathers to Name a State Ticket.

FROM "DRYS" TO "WETS"

The United States Brewers Association, Milwaukee, Wis.:
The Prohibition State convention of Minnesota now in session sends condolence to your association. Your business is doomed as your outposts are now carried and the prohibition army is about to move against your main body. The church and society has now declared and the state will soon say "the saloons must die."
—E. E. Lobeck, Chairman.

RESENTS TELEGRAM.
Minneapolis, Minn., June 9, '08.
Editor Tribune:
The following telegram was sent yesterday to the brewers in convention in Milwaukee:
"Resent the prohibition audacious telegram. Stand firm for your constitutional rights. The republic is doomed if church and society is allowed to rule this country.
"JOHN MADDOCK,
"For the Liquor Interests."
When it comes to the point where a mere sect can arbitrarily threaten to destroy the business interests and pleasures of millions of American citizens, in the name of church and society, it is time for every American patriot to rise up to stop the unlawful invasion of their individual rights.
JOHN MADDOCK.

Minneapolis Journal, June 8, 1908   *Minneapolis Tribune,* June 10, 1908

The *Minneapolis Tribune*, in a front-page story on June 9, 1908, reported at length on Howard's speech ("teeming with epigrammatic and caustic witticisms") and noted: "In conclusion, Mr. Howard said that the saloon would die in every state if the voter balloted in the name of Christ, with the baptism of the Holy Ghost upon him, and that the saloon would go to a place where Judas Iscariot could tend bar without changing his residence."

E.E., who was chairman of the convention, continued his account.

The last day of the convention was choosing the party's standard bearers. A Doctor Haggard for candidate for governor and the renowned sharp businessman, T. J. Anderson from Belgrade as vice-governor.[133]

The convention ended with prayer and words of encouragement, handshakes and promises to faithfully work for our great cause. Then everyone went their separate ways, some to their farms, others to their businesses. One thing that pleased this writer was that so many Norwegians were with us. Several of the Free Church ministers were there and took a keen part in the discussions. It was reported by an American whose work was with schools that Augsburg College in relation to its size has sent out more Temperance workers than any other school in the world. God bless Augsburg for that.

Had to take a hasty farewell of my friends to go to South Dakota where I had promised to hold meetings for twenty days. I flung myself in a St. Louis train in the evening and headed westward.

A monster shrew of a man lay in one of the back-tilting chairs and gloated. Another man took the seat in front of this monster and did not know any better, thinking that he too was allowed to sit with his chair tilted back but that got the shrew kicking like a mule. It was a real skeleton of a man, tall, and thin as a Republican platform, thin as a Democratic cause, and his face was adorned with a horny snoot that gave evidence of defiance and self-righteousness.

Four o'clock in the morning I got off the train in Revillo, South Dakota, and was surprised to find the town white with frost, 10th June. Had two meetings there where I got the opportunity to talk about the troops of the Temperance movement in South Dakota.

A few years ago one of our abstinence friends by the name of Seim had died and I walked around heavy in my mind that I would not meet him. Then, I rubbed my eyes twice and he was alive in front of me, the one I thought was dead and the reader must know, I was both surprised and pleased. It was another Seim who had died.

The next day I went to Altomont, a German town where beer is a necessary commodity. Ignorance among these people is big and I had the thought of Bismarck's words: "Beer makes stupid."[134] We went to a small group of trees where I spoke to a gathering of mixed content. A few Norwegians, lots of Americans, and some fiery Irishmen.

In the evening I took the train to Watertown; but the town should be named Whiskytown. I do not know that I ever have seen so many red-nosed, bloated pets of King Drink as I did there – and how they swore.

The evening was so lovely. Why then, this deformed, obnoxious sight in the middle of such glory – yes, why? Once I saw an advertisement that if you drank a lot of "Beer" you would not swear, that "Beer" would calm the nerves.

They had perchance not drunk enough yet in Watertown. Ugh, for bad judgment! The fact that so many men prefer to be pigs than people.

Friends, with God in mind, let's put life into abstinence work.[135]

Now it is a month later, July, in South Dakota.

Never should you let your courage fail. "If you show yourself discouraged in the day of trouble, then your strength is small." In an overwhelming downpour, I came to Lily. The rain drove like nails into the ground. "Now the meeting will be over for today," said the old Adam, or even worse, perhaps.

At 11 o'clock the clouds parted and the sun broke through.

[The immediately subsequent paragraph, about the passing of the hat in Lily, with the astonishing collection of $47 [$1,600]), was previously quoted in chapter 3, p. 63.]

I came to Summit in a blowing west wind. Up stepped Pastor Swenson. I was supposed to speak out on the street, but it was suspected that the weather would be mischievous. Pastor and I went out on the town. We got hold of an empty store. Simonsen cleaned it. The "prest" and others carried in planks and after a while everything was in order. A couple of small boys each got a cymbal, clashing it around the city and called the people together. There was quite a friendly gathering.

The primary elections are just over in South Dakota and the people have not gotten their breath yet. There has been a heated battle between insurgents and stalwarts, two factions of the Republican Party. A house divided against itself cannot stand, Jesus said, and it does indeed look like the old good party is going to crack open by latitude and longitude.

I try to think through the differences between these factions, but I can't see it. "Tell me you, stalwart, what do you stand for?" "For Reform!" "And the Insurgents?" "Oh, never mind, they are some layabouts who only seek office."

"Tell me you, insurgent, what do you stand for?" "For Reform!" "And Stalwarts?" "They are just after the offices."

That is all I have gotten out of all of it yet. There may come more light on the subject. But I know these two factions wave their arms like a windmill in a storm and yet there are many waddling around like a duck on both sides.

If you just get the people to fight for a great, noble cause, something that is for the people's temporal and eternal well-being, soon there would be a dawn in this country.

Hill after hill north from Webster was adorned with Norwegian homes. The life-giving sun rose higher and higher, showering blessings in the fullness of light and strength.

Roslyn Park lay in the middle of this peaceful sunny Sunday. People came en masse. Dots appeared on the horizon. They came closer until they took the form of a long trail filled with gaily dressed men and women. Songs and speeches came after each other for five hours.

The people were very attentive, but then we must also bear in mind that within a circumference of 15 miles lives a human race that is the backbone of the South Dakota Prohibition Party. Pastor Hammer had canceled worship in Fron and came himself to the meeting and brought many with him. God let such seed grow.

"Hamms Beer" stood over the door of a house and outside the door stood a young boy with an overwhelming stomach out of proportion to what is human. The hotel was even closed. I scurried down to the depot again. Then came a young man named Langager. "I am a bachelor," he said, "but if you want to make do with my place, then come." Langager is the town's butcher and leading abstinence man. He cooks for four other bachelors.

Langager need not marry for the sake of his stomach. He is a forthright fellow but has built himself a magnificent house so don't tell me that it won't soon happen.

A good meeting in the afternoon

A freight train went in the ditch west of Bristol. Tore up 16 rail lengths of track. After a wait of eight hours we departed.

Sisseton seemed deserted. I did not come before half past eight in the evening. But the people were sitting there, patiently, as Norwegians are.

Met a bunch of willing people in Sisseton. Pastor Fosse sang some solos, and his voice was of good quality. Pastor Rudie was out on a journey and came home when the meeting was almost over.

Had two meetings in Roberts County. The cause moves forward and the old politicians who constantly stirred the political pot are beginning to be apprehensive about the coming days.

So the national Republican Convention has come to an end. It was stormy. The police had to come in order to keep the members in check. Taft is the candidate for president. He is heavy enough to hold the chair down. The case seems to be simplified for those who hate the saloons.

No one has been more eager than Taft. Taft put his fat, huge body and influence against Oklahoma to prevent it from being integrated in the union as a Prohibitionist state. Taft presented to the United States Congress a proposal to pay $30,000 [$970,000] to saloon keepers and brewers in San Francisco for the beer and brandy that ran into the streets and served as nourishment for the fire that broke out in the earthquake. The matter is simple. Those who hate the saloons cannot vote for Taft or the Republican Party.

Very nice sheep without ever seeing. Many a "prest" and others hate the saloon from the depths of their soul. And from the depths of the same soul loves the political organization that has given us saloon laws, the saloon and the curse of saloons.

Go home and write "Hypocrite" on your forehead.

Bryan has set his foot down and refused to take a Prohibitionist plank in his platform. It is sad that great men must be so miserably small when they come up against King Gambrinus.

"God give us men that flattery can buy."[136]

Chapter 7
The 1908 Contested Election

Alexandria had two newspapers, the Republican *Alexandria Post News* and the Democratic *Alexandria Citizen*. The Temperance folk thought this was not enough. They urged Carl Wold, owner and editor of the *Brandon Echo*, to move his paper from Brandon to Alexandria.

Wold, a committed Temperance man, never accepted advertising by the liquor interests and ran a "dry" paper. (One Prohibitionist blind spot: Patent Medicine, which contained as much as 80 percent alcohol, and many of the tonics used cocaine and morphine. Newspapers owed their survival to advertising dollars. Nearly every Prohibitionist newspaper, including *The Reform* and the *Echo*, ran ads for Lydia Pinkham's Vegetable Compound and Peruna patent medicines, especially favored by Temperance folk. "A dessertspoonful, four to six times a day, in water, and a tablespoonful on going to bed." E.E. railed against alcohol and its ills, but never wrote about patent medicines.)

E.E. was running for re-election in the autumn of 1908 and needed the support of Wold's paper. Wold needed a larger pool of subscribers.

With the backing of Lobeck, Rev. Floreen of Evansville, Rev. Lindberg of Ida township, and C. H. Larson of Nelson, the *Park Region Echo* – the "out-and-out Prohibition paper" – was incorporated in August with a capital stock of $3,000 [$97,000], with the first publication on September 3, in good time for the campaign. The incorporators were listed as Rev. B. A. Benson, president; John Anderson, vice president; E.E. Lobeck, treasurer; Carl Wold, secretary and editor.[137]

The campaign battle began in full swing. Knute Nelson, with his connections and influence, now had a chance to make things difficult for Lobeck as payback for not voting for his selection for U.S. Senate in the last Minnesota House session. Because the election was on Nelson's home turf (both he and Lobeck resided in Alexandria), he had been affronted by Lobeck's successful 1906 election by a healthy margin.

"Down with Lobeck, cost what it may"

According to the *Echo*, Senator Nelson handpicked the candidate, O. F. Olson, president of Brandon State Bank and a prominent businessman, to oppose Lobeck, and strong Nelson influence discouraged any other Republicans from filing. The Republican cry was "Down with Lobeck, cost what it may." The contentious County Option issue favored by the Temperance folk was vigorously fought in the papers with accusations, emotionally charged words, and passion. Candidates did the same. Because County Option was the hot issue, the Republicans at their county convention declared they were in favor of it.

In late September a special train rolled into the new Great Northern depot with Senators Nelson and Taft. Another special train rolled into the Soo depot from Glenwood and Starbuck, accompanied by two brass bands. Hundreds of people marched to the Great Northern Depot where an enormous crowd had gathered. Taft spoke first and claimed that intelligent men vote the Republican ticket and all reforms come through the Republican Party. All would be lost if people voted for a party without experience (a direct hit at Lobeck). Nelson spoke next, echoing Taft. Nelson spoke interminably. Carl Wold, who often referred to the "Republican machine," noted that "the train pulled out while the Senator was speaking."[138]

The following Friday evening Lobeck spoke to an appreciative audience in the Urness township hall. They asked him to return on Sunday evening. The house was packed, standing room only. The same Sunday the congregations in Ida township listened to appeals from the Republican Party to help elect O. F. Olson. Lobeck spoke to a secular crowd, Olson to a religious one. This was not the norm, however.

The *Echo* drew a sharp contrast. "While E.E. Lobeck is advocating his principles from churches and schoolhouses, O. F. Olson's cause is being championed from the saloons – all of which will conveniently serve as branch headquarters for his campaign. Thoughtful and conscientious voters will mark the difference."[139]

Lobeck announced his candidacy.

> More and more convinced that the drink traffic is the greatest barrier to
> the advancement of Christ's Kingdom; and believing it to be the greatest
> source of crime, immorality, lawbreaking, and political corruption; and
> believing in self-government by the people, I declare for County Option
> and pledge myself, if elected, to the best of my ability, to work and vote for
> such a measure.[140]

In late October Nelson, before a packed Alexandria opera house, called
Lobeck "a man of only one hobby, a political freak."[141] The local Taft-
Nelson club orchestrated a torch-light procession, marching through the
main streets of Alexandria, accompanied by a band and carrying
transparencies. Such a display, used by both parties, was a throwback to
the political campaigns of the 1860s, when political clubs were organized
to mobilize their base and keep them in line. Lots of noise, commotion
and torches with transparencies attached generated excitement and
interest, resulting, partisans hoped, in votes for their candidate.[142]

The *Echo* contended that Nelson's machine arrayed their forces against
Lobeck in the last few days of the campaign, sending personal letters to
anyone and everyone of influence in the county and making deals with
those who had previously supported Lobeck. The effect was obvious, as
measured by the variation in the vote tally from the previous election.

A 12-vote majority

Election day dawned. Voters spoke. Lobeck was elected. "Hon. E.E.
Lobeck, the valiant Prohibition legislator, won out over his Republican
opponent in Senator Knute Nelson's county (Douglas) by a majority of
twelve votes. Every license village went against him and nearly every
township gave him a majority. Good for Douglas County!"[143]

A majority of twelve votes. The defeated Olson and Nelson backers
immediately challenged the results. Along with several other townships,
the Holmes City township election board was irate at having their
honesty questioned. They, however, were singled out for being Lobeck's
home neighborhood.

Olson and Nelson hoped the contested election would be resolved by the
House legislators, comprised mostly of Republicans who could be easily
influenced to seat Olson.

Rumors abounded of election improprieties on both sides: accusations
that the Holmes City election board had kept the doors open past 5

o'clock and seven people supposedly voted for Lobeck in that time; accusations that potential Republican candidates had been offered backing of up to $2,500 [$80,000] to run for the legislature and defeat the County Option issue. It probably is true that much money was flowing liberally to provide victory for personal interests, but it is also true that the Republicans could well outspend the Prohibitionists.

On November 16 the sheriff served Lobeck a notice of contest to the election.[144]

A growing outcry of protest against the contesting of the election resulted in a large meeting a week later of 200-300 influential men of the county. They hoped to convince the district judge that no recount was necessary – Lobeck won and that should be the end of it. Someone suggested that a petition be sent to Olson to withdraw the contest proceedings. This was emphatically rejected. The election boards and the people claimed they won in a fair and honest election and the outcome should be respected.[145]

The recount began November 27. Lobeck still won.

Row in Douglas County

The issues of the late election are still being discussed in Douglas County. The Republican candidate for the legislature, O.F. Olson, who was defeated by Hon. E.E. Lobeck, that undaunted champion of Prohibition, by a small margin, refused to acquiesce in the result of the vote and a recount being futile, now is trying to collect evidence that will give the Republican majority of the House an excuse for seating him in place of the man who received a majority of the votes. The proceedings instituted to secure such evidence are scandalous to say the least. Men whose right to vote have been questioned by reason of any technicality whatever are brought before some creature of the machine who happens to be a justice and the lawyers and judge try to browbeat the witnesses into committing themselves as to how they voted for the legislative seat. Most of the witnesses know their rights and refuse to give up their constitutional right to a secret ballot. Such disreputable methods are reacting on the instigators in the county, and it is said that scores of voters who voted against Mr. Lobeck in the late election are flocking to his banner, and some of them are even talking of promoting him to the senatorship two years hence. The most significant fact in regard to the result in Douglas

County was that the fight against Lobeck was actively headed by no less a personage than U.S. Senator Knute Nelson himself, whose home county it is. It is said that this eminent statesman so far forgot the dignity of his high office as to go on the stump and appeal to his home people to down Lobeck because the latter had even dared to vote against Knute in the last session. Even Taft, the candidate for president, was brought into the county to try to re-awaken that "party loyalty" which has been the chief stock in trade of venal politicians for many years back.

But Lobeck is a fighter, who would rather fight whiskey politicians than eat any day, and is losing no sleep over the outcome. He will win out in the end, no matter what jobs the old ring politicians put up.[146]

Finally, after two months of consideration, with the community in aggravated suspense, the final decision was announced by the election committee. Lobeck was seated in the House on January 19, 1909, two weeks into the session. Olson dropped the contest.[147]

In order to protect himself from further attack by the Nelson "machine," E.E. presented to the legislature a huge petition, signed by the voters of Douglas County, that he was now the chosen representative and there must be no further dispute.

The *Minneapolis Tribune* on March 31 reported as follows:

Only Successful in Contested Elections Reimbursed

Precedent in the matter of payment of expenses of parties to contests involving a seat in the Minnesota House of Representatives was set yesterday when that body voted down a bill to reimburse O. F. Olson of Alexandria for expenses incurred in contesting the election of E.E Lobeck and of a bill to reimburse William Foreman, who contested the election of James A. Carley. Legislatures in the past have been prone to recognize claims which, upon investigation, have been found to be invalid, but the House yesterday went on record as, while willing to reimburse members, being opposed to reimburse unsuccessful contestants.

Representative Campbell of Hennepin inveighed against the practice of former years, saying it simply encouraged contests and would be an inducement for unscrupulous lawyers looking for fat fees to solicit suits. After killing the Olson and Foreman bills, the House proceeded almost unanimously to pass the bills to reimburse Representatives Lobeck and Carley, the contestees.

Lobeck got $304.11 [$9,800]. Olson had asked for $1,800 [$58,000]. [148]

Reporting back to Norway

Now, officially seated in the legislature, E.E. wrote to his friend Per Olaf Torgals in Trysil, Norway.

> I can now tell that I have again been elected to the legislature, but my, oh my, what a battle. I came into Senator Knute Nelson's disfavor two years ago and this fall he set himself across my path to hinder my re-election. And you can understand how I felt when I saw what great might was against me. I took hold the best I could, and the battle raged on for several weeks with crushing blows, in all seriousness. I am, as you know, a Prohibitionist of political faith, and it is already a thorn in the side of the "big men" who set to get their help from the liquor traffic. So, besides Knute Nelson, I had the whole state's liquor league against me. And then the United States Steel Trust came forward onto the battle ground and laid a barrage against me because I dared to vote that they should put a tax of five cents a ton [$1.60] on the iron that was taken from the mine.
>
> Then we had Taft who now is elected president and at Knute Nelson's urging came to beg the voters not to shift from the Republican Party. Nelson himself held a meeting where I was presented as a fanatic, a fool, a legislative monster, and a political anomaly, etc.
>
> They imported some politicians to hold people in line; but it did them no good. I was elected, but only by a small majority. Now they have set another agitation in motion to throw me out of the legislative assembly. If I leave, it will be a fantasy. They don't know what one may do in such a circumstance. I don't think they will dare to do this since the state's newspaper, without respect for political color, is swinging more and more in my favor. I am also elected for a two-year term. Both friend and foe agree that there has never before been such a furious battle in this district. There could be much more said about this election, but you are no doubt tired of it already.
>
> Nevertheless, let me tell you that Knute Nelson sent in his own handwriting a letter to the voters in his district three days before election

telling them they must strike me from the ticket. It almost makes me a little proud to be the first to be in a position to ruin his plan.

In this past year I have longed so sorely for Norway. If God grants me health I may once more see the rocky coast.[149]

Lobeck as legislator

Lobeck began the 1909 legislative session with a bill to reinstate a former law against charivaris, gatherings "of three or more persons, assembling near a dwelling house to make a noise or disturbance, by shooting firearms, beating drums, shouting or other means." In an article headlined "Ridicule kills several bills," the Minneapolis Journal noted that "When the representatives realized that the author intended to make it an offense t0o serenade a newly-married couple with an orchestra composed of horse-fiddles and tin pans, it struck them as a huge joke and they never got over it."[150]

Next he attempted to bring a bill toward the goal of a state-wide constitutional amendment for Prohibition. It was killed in the House by a vote of 61-38. County Option was also defeated in this session.

The Princeton Union noted the friction between Lobeck and his legislative colleagues.

> Lobeck unfortunately is of that severe type. It is the straight and narrow with him always and the measures introduced by him, generally covering some infraction of the moral law that he regards as an evil, are drastic in the extreme as to penalty. He never temporizes. It is the electric chair or nothing. Naturally, the relations between him and the balance of the House are strained.[151]

A very different assessment was offered by Lynn Haines, a prominent commentator on the political scene – he was editor of "Searchlight on Congress," a publication of the National Voters' League – who offered this evaluation of "Lobeck and His Labors" in the 1909 session.

> E.E. Lobeck of Alexandria, was elected to the legislature as a Prohibitionist. I am not interested in his legislative life and influence because of that fact. He was one of the broadest and the best members of either branch, which is my reason for suggesting some phases of his record.

Mr. Lobeck's point of view is indicated in the character of the bills he introduced and championed. He was the author of measures providing for the Initiative and Referendum, State Wide Prohibition, an increase in the age of Consent, and the Abolition of the White Slave Traffic. The two last named were enacted into law.

Among the reform measures for which he fought were these:

(1) Changes in the rules restoring the rights of the House as a deliberative body. He sought to remove the Cannonistic conditions which make the standing committee the all-powerful element in legislation.

(2) The Initiative and Referendum which would give the people an authority over legislation superior to the present power of special privilege interests.

(1) The J. N. Johnson bill to free the public from further watering of railroad securities.

(2) County Option which would enfranchise the great agricultural element that now has no voice in the regulation of the liquor traffic.

(3) A tonnage tax on iron ore which was intended as a means of compelling the steel trust to pay nearer its share of the tax burden of the state.

(4) State-wide Prohibition.

(5) The anti-cigarette bill.

He Opposed With Voice and Vote:

(1) The Alderman-White brewery bill which, tho masked as a Temperance move, gives to big breweries an easier and more profitable monopoly of the saloon business.

(2) The legalizing of Sunday base ball.

(3) The Cass Lake normal bill which was the result of wholesale log rolling and barter.

(4) The club bill which sought to enable social and commercial organizations to sell liquor without a license.

(5) The repeal of the corrupt practices act.

(6) The members' salary bill thru which representatives and senators broke an implied contract with the state and voted themselves salary in advance.

A Strong Speaker. His Arguments Feared by The Brewers.

Mr. Lobeck was one of the strongest orators in the legislature and it was a great tribute to his forensic ability and that of other members that the brewery controlled majority of the House shut off all debate on the County Option bill by moving and carrying "the previous question." They did not dare to face the speeches that had been prepared and the Lobeck arguments were feared most of all.[152]

Haines's encomium concludes with a quotation from his own book, *The Minnesota legislature of 1909: A History of the Session, with an Inside View of Men and Measures*:

> Insurgent leader; strong for rules reform, and took an active part in the fight for direct legislation; voted consistently against the pool, and was aggressively opposed to all special interest legislation; one of the authors of an initiative and referendum bill, and championed three measures to improve social evils; author of a state wide Prohibition bill. Lobeck was a strong and able champion of the people.[153]

"The pool" is Haines's term for what he calls "the predatory interests that are merged for the political control of Minnesota."[154] His own political sympathies are revealed by the dedication of his subsequent account of the 1911 session: "To the Progressives of Minnesota."

As Haines reported, Lobeck had brought to the floor a bill raising the age of consent to eighteen years. This involved changing only the words "age of sixteen" to "age of eighteen" in Minnesota 1905 Laws 4927 and 4930, "relating to the Carnal Knowledge of Children and Abduction."

> Every person who shall carnally know and abuse any female child under the age of eighteen years shall be punished as follows: [summarizing] child under 10, life in state prison; 10 to 14, seven to 30 years in state prison; 14 to 18, state prison not more than seven years or county jail not more than one year.[155]

He was successful in securing its passage on March 24 without one dissenting vote in the House. The issue had long been a struggle; Lobeck was able to accomplish this in a couple of weeks. The hometown newspaper congratulated him on this victory.

The session ended in April. "With gifts and speeches, Minnesota's legislature adjourned today. Led by E.E. Lobeck, Prohibitionist, in the singing of 'America,' the House dispersed at 1:15 p.m. ... The House indulged in much ceremony and leave-taking and was in session three

From "The State House Guide's Last Spiel," *Minneapolis Sunday Tribune*, May 2, 1909

hours. ... Later in the day each member drew $500 pay [$16,000] and set his face homeward."[156]

After the session

Summer days spent at the lake were a beehive of activity. The family, including Uncle Ola, went to the lake the first of June, kids in tow, carting the piano, and staying until summer's end. With extended family and friends dropping in, always meals to prepare and young ones to care for, Martha's days were filled with necessary work while the children and their cousins filled their days making mudpies, climbing trees, weaving wildflower necklaces, playing games and dolls. Ola tended the garden, including his crop of ginseng. E.E., now a man of some importance, acquired a big fishing raft, akin in size to today's pontoons, so he could entertain those who came to call. Lake Darling, teeming with fish, never disappointed when the family shoved off to wet their lines. Evenings were filled with music. They were idyllic summer days that instilled in his children a lifelong love of music, nature, and fishing.

Speaking engagements took E.E. to northern Minnesota and west into the Dakotas in late summer. Newspapers gave him high praise for his ability to hold audiences captive. Campaigning for the Prohibitionist cause, his speaking was concentrated among the Scandinavians, but increasingly his speeches were in English as well as Norwegian.

The legislature, with its propositions, votings, staying up late, bartering of votes, and political fuss is over; but it also went into history as the most corrupt, not to say the most insignificant of all of the state's legislatures. The greater part of the legislators were, though, excellent tools in the hands of the combined corporate lobbyists.[157]

When these powers are unable to get influential members to do their bidding, they seek to get the district's greatest "tools" in there. And it would be a vast exaggeration to claim that the legislature consists of only "great talents."

"Such vermin would be well worth to exterminate," as a Swedish man said, and I shook his hand on that. Should we not expect, once and for all, that the people would take these, who always trample on the rights of the common people, and put them on stakes as a warning to others? But there are still too many amongst the voters who do not bother to think, to read, to hear, but go backwards through the world, and stare with awe at things that the people of progress long ago left behind.

Still, along the outposts of the political lines there are now heard clear trumpet sounds, warnings of a new day. Other lines will soon be established, and they will march straight to the goal, and then there will be a devil of a row among the corrupt leaders and a ripping hullabaloo amongst the old political pirates. Just wait a while, until the masses awaken – wait until they see how the politicians barter their rights – and wait until Aldrich's 32-feet-high Tariff giant, with the most necessary things for the common people at the top, has gone through the country a few times – then, yes then – there will be a terrible revolution, a sea-salted Armageddon.[158]

So good that we have small people in the world. They are the first to detect dangerous undercurrents. They are the first to give a warning cry, the first to call all men on deck. The great moguls in their high positions cannot see along these lines, until the trumpet sounds from the common majority, and scares the devil out of them – and now the great ones in this country are starting to speak out to both Congress and Senate for these houses' nameless panderings with the people's interests.

It is also high time for an awakening along the whole line, before the worms have eaten the skull totally empty.

So it happened that I was going to Cloquet – a lively town west of Duluth. It was the first Sunday in May – a charming day with a high sky and a bright sun, but what an amount of slush in the streets. The snow was fast melting. It was as if the winter was crying, and it really had a reason; it had been harsh.

Pastor Høstager is determined that the saloons are an evil. So he started to stir the pot – and the more one stirs in such matters, I am sorry to say, the more it stinks. The pastor was to be expelled – "he had abandoned his calling" – the riff-raff said. "He ought to preach the gospel," these red-nosed big tummies, the servants of King Alcohol, opinionated. The pastor felt, though, that these gentlemen needed a bit of law, and that they got. They are now left, forgotten like the sticks from fired fireworks in a back alley.

"Can you come here for a turn?" I heard from Goodhue County. I almost felt the cold go down my spine when I heard that some 26 Prohibitionists' clubs had been started lately in that county. The local little politicians are running (aimlessly) around. People who get lost are always going in circles – maybe one day they get out of the fog. It is clearing up in Goodhue County now.

Came to Zumbrota one Saturday at noon, and found my friend Hammer with his head down an ice cream freezer. He looked up, and smiled as always. That day he had kneaded together more than 5,000 pounds. He sold barrels of butter and ice cream. The man has grown both fat and prosperous, but his heart for the cause is as warm as before, and his wallet just as open. Seventeen years ago he drove me around the county, we were both young, and we were both poor, but we believed that the cause was God's. Looking back on these years we have to say that God has been very good to us.

If it continues in Goodhue County like it has started, this county will stand like a beacon in the heart of Minnesota and show the way to political reform.

Ed Hammer bought himself a new pair of shoes, and followed me to St. Paul. We shook hands with the governor and other of the state's servants, stayed for a while in the Dairy and Food

Commission, etc. Then we went and looked at Sageng's new threshing machine, that promises to revolutionize the threshing.[159]

On a totally still, warm sunny day I arrived at Dalton. As soon as I got off the train I received messages from Senator Sageng's and Mr. Brandvold's families to go straight to them.[160]

Almost there I came across Brandvold, riding a corn plow in a field. "Go up to the house," he said, "I will soon be there." Senator Sageng was gone to the big cities as a member of the Memorial Gift Committee.[161]

Personally, I am not satisfied with any of the different Memorial Gift propositions that have been offered. Should we really raise a memorial for the posterity, we ought to use our influence, money, and persuasion to reunite Iceland and the Faeroes with Norway. We would still the yearnings from thousands losses, steering from these islands towards Norway. I have read yearning psalms from Iceland and the Faeroes, through which they try to still their bleeding wounds, until both my heart and my eye have wept.

Iceland and the Faeroes should again be laid to their mother's bosom. ...

Everybody's eyes are now turned towards Washington, where the great men of the country are struggling with the Tariff. It is a true pandemonium with iron, lumber, cows, and hides. Just think how they quarreled about the hides – Taft wanted free hides – the future will show the result. We were promised a revision downwards, but so far it seems to go the way the chicken kicks [i.e., backwards]. A great hope gripped my innermost some days ago, when I learned from a New York newspaper that a 24-year-old man named John Curran was sentenced to two years and six months hard labor because he stole two cents [65 cents]. Imagine this wave of morality in Washington. Yes – we might even get rid of a whole bunch of Senators-for-life.[162]

Campaigning in Iowa, North Dakota, and Minnesota

Beginning in September, an aggressive campaign by the Prohibitionists was scheduled in Iowa, with a goal of continuous education and agitation until the 1910 elections. The WCTU and major Prohibitionists from throughout the country, Lobeck among them, descended on Iowa.

Thursday, September 23, I boarded the train in Alexandria for Iowa. Along the line down to Minneapolis the people were in mourning, the whole state seemed to be hushed into silent weeping when the casket containing the remains of Governor Johnson was lowered into its quiet and dark chamber at 3 p.m.[163] Our train stopped for five minutes and the conversation sank into a subdued whisper.

Saturday we went with the speed of Jehu.[164] We passed Shakopee, St. Peter, Mankato, Lake Crystal, Blue Earth, and Elmore, where we plunged into Iowa. I was not very much impressed with this state at that place. Sloughs, marshes, and lowlands took each other by the hand, spread themselves out in all directions, and shoved the settlers away so they resembled dots, few and far between.[165] This land is now being tilled, and in a few years will look like a garden.

At 4:44 p.m. I was dumped off in Story County, a real garden spot, beautified with artificial and natural groves, where a good and well-cultivated soil, large cornfields, thorough-bred stock, and herds of brown hogs gave the farmers something to do, a sunny face, a broad smile, and a well packed pocket book. Land is selling at $150.00 [$4,900] per acre. You ought to see the corn cobs – why you would almost think they were abnormal – they are of Taft dimensions, long and thick, worth 65 cents [$21] per bushel, and when you get them inside a hog they are worth still more, the farmers told me.

What success will I have down here? This is a new field – will these people receive the message? What kind of an undercurrent surges through the soul of the inhabitants of this place? Have they lost sight of the beams of the good guiding star? These are the thoughts that shot through my brain like rockets while I was spinning in a livery rig from Story City to Roland. I am glad though, that I, in life's struggles, have learned not to put faith in luck – if I had, I would have been a loafer like the others, who, having put faith in it, are walking with their hands in their pockets waiting for something to tip up.

No life is hopeless so long as it gives others happiness, and so I lifted my eyes up to him who, through my 19 years of public work, strife, and struggle, has spread a shield of mercy over me – and in this mood I faced for three nights in Roland an audience of 500 people.

President Taft is not considered very much of a man down here. His Winona speech seems to go like a ghost along this latitude. Senator Cummins has decorated himself with war paint, and the giant Dolliver has rolled around twice until he got a good anchorage and now he sides in with Cummins.[166]

The people here are asking me what Viking Knute Nelson and Moses Clapp are going to do. They have asked the wrong man as I don't know – but this I know, if they can swallow that Winona speech without setting their whole state afire with protest, they are not worth the confidence that the people in the North Star State have put in them. It is simply laughable that the president considers himself capable of ridding out of the Republican Party all those who did not bend their knees to the eastern Baal. We have heard from Tawney – now, what have the others to say? Some of the Minnesota papers think it will be best for the insurgents to keep quiet in order to have a harmonious party. Well, if they put party above principles that theory is good – but when the party goes back on the principles, the patriots will have to go back on the party.[167]

Parties are not made. They came into being of themselves, born in God's time, being evolved from the tremendous conditions – they are born out of the struggles of the human race, out of the people, and always from the bottom of the pile. Then they climb to the top where they are corrupted and finally stifled by evil forces they were born to fight – and so the patriots will have to leave, and some of them have left.

If the Iowa people could get hold of the 32-foot-tall Aldrich High Tariff bill, they would behead it at both ends, and yet, it is claimed by our president to be the best tariff bill that the Republican Party had framed and passed.

How many times has a sheriff to be called upon to go to church and arrest old Christians coming from prayer meeting under the influence of Christ's spirit to keep them from fighting? The sheriff of Story County had to go to a place near Roland the other day to arrest one coming from the saloon under the spirit of Gambrinus to keep him from fighting. He went over into a field and scared two men who were ditching, out of their wits. Bad words began to fly and the men began to fly, and the great "inspirator" had to be given a free ride to Nevada (Iowa).

My two meetings in McCallsburg were well attended and Iowa is heading for state-wide Prohibition.[168]

In November E.E. spoke in Buffalo, Minnesota.

I faced an audience of culture and refinement. I know this because the liquor faction had gotten up a dance at the same time and the unrefined were there. The governmental problems are getting uppermost in the minds of the people. They feel that something has got to be done. The good people begin to understand that they have too long been voting together with those who serve the corporations and bend their knees before the saloon devil in the land. Lincoln said: "All we want and all we ask is that those who believe slavery wrong shall quit voting with those who believe it right."[169] This is sound political doctrine, and all we ask today is that those who believe the drink traffic to be wrong should quit voting with those who believe the drink traffic to be right. Such actions will clear the political atmosphere and line the people up where they belong.

In remembering a trip earlier in the year to North Dakota, E.E. distills faith and his politics into a single question.

The question in the minds of the people is "What is God's will in regard to political questions? What does he want me to do?" The reform forces are seeking to find a common ground. … The old gods are not believed in as they were before. A revolution is brewing in the mind of the tiller of the soil. It is the man with the burden upon his back who thinks.[170]

E.E was home for Thanksgiving but left the next day for Iowa again. In relating his reminiscences of the next several weeks, written in January 1910, he categorizes them under headings.

Thanksgiving Day came and went. Great blessings have been showered upon us. How have they been received? In what way have we thanked the good giver for things given to us? Some came together in churches in thanksgiving, others stayed in their homes – some met in the dancing halls, others in saloons. Some were at their card tables, others at the family altar. What shall each and all of us answer our God because of the way we spent the day?

WEARING DRESSES TOO SHORT AT THE TOP AND TOO LONG AT THE BOTTOM

Another Iowa trip has been planned. The day after Thanksgiving I came
to Minneapolis on my way to that state. The papers told a pitiful story of
the effects of Thanksgiving Day. Scores were in bed sick because they had
gobbled down too many gobblers – especially ladies, so the story told, were
sick. Eating turkeys during the day, went to the ball in the evening in a
dress too short at the top and too long at the bottom – the weather was
damp, sidewalks wet, rubbers out of style, and so they took sick.
Gentlemen – an expression taken in vain – had to take the sick ones home.
Afterwards they met and smoked their coffin nails, drank their brandy,
parted their hair in the middle so as not to unbalance their brains – and
the day after Thanksgiving they were unfit to work. Well, the city of
Minneapolis had the "blues" the day I struck it. An Egyptian darkness
reigned over the city.[171] A fog so dense, damp, and thick that it made it
dangerous to travel. The lights had to be put on in the cars when we
started for Iowa, after nine o'clock in the morning. A very unpleasant day
it was, but the coaches were warm and nice so I spread out myself and the
Minneapolis Journal and read with delight a report from W. E. Johnson that
Becker, Hubbard, and other counties were wholly or partly dried up. The
darkest days have their bright moments. I hope that the same wave will
strike Douglas too. The saloons there have no more right to operate than
they have in Detroit. I met W. E. Johnson in Minneapolis, and he appears
to be a husky fellow, brown eyes, bald head, broad shoulders, and put
together just like a saloon smashing machine ought to be.[172]

THE CHERRY MINE DISASTER

The Cherry Mine disaster was a sickening affair.[173] Hundreds of young
wives and small children stood waiting for news from the pit. Now the
press all over the United States has taken it up. Strong articles calling for a
thorough investigation to find out where the responsibility for this
stupefying, heart-rending catastrophe rests, have been published.

THE AMERICAN SALOON

The *Indianapolis News* states the horrible fact that between 1900 and 1908,
23,539 persons were killed in American mines. Have we not in this
country great minds enough to devise plans that will protect human life in
a better way? Is it because of the greed of money that nothing has been
done? But now – shall I bring it forth? The drink traffic – the legalized
abominable American saloon – killed, not in eight years but in eight

months the same number of people. But along these lines the press of the land has been silent – and if they had anything to say, they would prattle about Prohibition does not prohibit. And so the wonderful things are seen that the papers, which have printed hot condemnations about that mine disaster to stir the people up in order to change things in the mines, are at the same time trying to pacify the people in regard to the saloons by telling them that high license is the right thing. Why not license the mines and let them run in the same old rut?

BAD WEATHER IN IOWA

For one solid week and a half I have had the worst kind of weather to buck. It rained and rained and rained until the roads were knee deep in slush and mud. The mail drivers had to give up their daily trips and stay at home except an old Viking down in Kensett, who walked it day after day – but then he was a young sprightly boy of 65 years. He is the hero in that section of the state. So it came a bitter frost and then you ought to have seen the roads – chunks as large as buckets filled the road bed and the farmers have crept into their dens like a bear and you cannot even smoke them out.

MUST REGAIN THE GOVERNMENT FROM THE LIQUOR TRAFFIC

There is a great awakening along Temperance lines in Iowa at present. People realize that something will have to be done to regain the government from the clutches of the liquor power. A lady sprang to her feet the other evening where I spoke and shouted, "I have gone through every stage in this awful, awful strife, and friends, we have to do something for this cause. I know what it means, as I have been a drunkard's wife for many, many years." This little speech had its effect upon the people. They only wished that a certain minister in the town had heard it, as he has been preaching for years that a man can be just as good a Christian if he gets drunk time and again. God take pity on such a preacher. Is there not misery enough, tears, heartaches, and woes enough without having this fearful doctrine preached to the people that it is no danger even to be drunk time and again – they can be Christians in spite of this.

HOW ARE WE PREPARED TO MEET THE PRINCE OF PEACE?

Christmas is drawing nigh – everything whispers about it, the snowflakes are reminding us about it, the children are singing about it, and I am turning my eyes towards home. A wonderful strange feeling creeps into my soul and directs my thoughts back to years gone by. We are reminded about the Prince of Peace, who came to do for us what we could not do for ourselves. But how many have tried to blot out this blessed name, erase it from their hearts and minds? Many would like to see it scraped from history – get it out of the world. Many would like to see the cross, this sign of victory, sunk into the grave, never again to be lifted up above the sorrows and pleasures of a struggling and suffering humanity. We don't know when he is to come – is today the highest wisdom – but Christmas comes again. That blessed name will again be before us.

What sayest thou about Jesus who is called Christ?

How will we receive him?[174]

Time home at Christmas was cut short by a trip to Chetek, Wisconsin, for the funeral of E.E.'s niece, Agnes Petterson, daughter of his sister Kari.

In early January E.E., tired and a bit churlish, returned to Iowa and bad weather. It was in this mood that he penned the skeptical, deprecating thoughts about Darwin noted in the previous chapter. And he had, as always, much more to say, including something about President Taft.

When One Meets Drunken Men in the Road

Iowa has more snow than it has had in 40 years. It is quite a serious thing to meet on the highway. When teams are to pass each other, they dive into the snow, and a man in a cutter or light sleigh goes under. You can see marks in the snow all along the way where hay loads and corn loads have rolled over, and in some places you can see the imprints of human form indicating that someone has been sitting down, standing on their head, or rolled over in a rude manner. The worst trip I have experienced in this state I had one evening going into Cylinder in Palo Alto County. This county has saloons, and going into Cylinder we met a string of men who had gone to town with full pocketbooks and empty heads, and now they came back with full heads and empty purses. They gave warning when they were half a mile away that if we did not dive out of the road they should help us out. They came with the speed of Jehu and shouted like demons. My driver had to watch his team and I had to serve as ballast to keep our sleigh right side down. You ought to have seen my operations, sometimes I slanted 45 degrees to leeward – and in the next moment I ducked into the other direction and we were able to keep on top. I have traveled in Iowa for 68 days, all the time in Temperance counties – and this, I will state most emphatically, that I have not seen so much of drunkenness in 68 days in Temperance counties, as I saw in one hour in Palo Alto County driving from St. John's Church and into Cylinder.

Closing Up the Saloons

But show me the pleasures of this life – like a thunderclap from a clear sky came the doomsday over the saloons in that county. The Temperance forces swooped down upon them, served an injunction, put locks on their doors, and Palo Alto County went dry. One saloonkeeper had his saloons two feet too close to a schoolhouse. He had gotten into his mind that he, for once, should comply with the law, so he started to build a partition in his place of business two feet inside of the wall, but the doomsday came too sudden. He was knocked out before he had finished his work of repentance.

Insurgency Strong in Iowa

When you come near to the borders of Nebraska, a wholesome spirit of insurgency is wafting over to you, loaded with indications that a change in political life is coming. Iowa seems to be the hotbed of insurgency. People are saying things now that would not have been tolerated 15 years ago. Let us hope for the betterment all along the line, and let us thank God that we have to fight hard for every inch of ground that we are acquiring. The old regime dies hard, but the reform people are beginning to live strong. Let us take hold with a firmer hand, stronger mind, and a more courageous heart than ever before, and the day of victory shall be ours.

Pres. Taft to Send a Delegation to the North Pole

If we shall take what our daily papers dish out, President Taft is to send a message to Congress asking for money to defray the expenses in connection with an expedition towards the North Pole and vicinity.

I move, Mr. President, that the expedition be headed by Aldrich as captain, Cannon as pilot, and the Standpatters[175] as mates and that the expedition shall not return within 15 years from the time it starts out.[176]

Returning home for only a few days in late February, E.E. was off again campaigning for County Option throughout eastern Minnesota, culminating with a big campaign in Duluth lasting two weeks. An enthusiastic crowd of 700 heard him speak one afternoon in both English and Swedish at the Swedish Bethany Lutheran Church. The *Duluth News-Tribune* reported it under the headline, "Rain of Dollars for 'Dry' Orator."

> When the speaker asked for subscriptions to carry on the work of Prohibition and County Option the responses were liberal. Someone in the gallery threw down a silver dollar on the altar and it was followed by a perfect shower of the coins, until the speaker signaled them to desist and asked the ushers to wait upon the audience with plates. The total contribution was over $132 [$4,300].[177]

A few days later, when he closed the Duluth campaign, E.E. was accompanied to Union Station by a band of 200-300 people with songs and a "general good cheer rally in his honor."[178]

In early March, the *Park Region Echo* carried a front-page article about prostitutes doing business in Alexandria and efforts to roust them out. The article is full of rumors and hearsay, but there were prostitutes in town. Most likely, they were brought to town by some of the saloon owners and given a "wink" by three aldermen: Mat Haberer, Joe Prodger, and C. J. Gunderson. As the story unfolded, the women were forced to leave town, assisted by Prodger who moved their furniture for them as stated in his own words. Then he denied any knowledge. Some of the Alexandria men thought the removal too extreme, believing that "it was a necessary evil and such houses should be provided but located in the country about a mile out of town."[179]

The County Option Convention

In February E.E. attended the County Option Convention in St. Paul. His account includes some deliciously vivid reminiscences of speakers, and concludes with what may be his finest poem.

> Such uprising you might never have heard before. Thousands of eyes shone with enthusiasm, so that they glowed in the dim light. If you have faith, in what was honestly meant by speeches and resolutions, I cannot see how there is to be found any shred left of the saloons or the Republican Party in the near future.

These known facts cannot go unrecognized: the Republican Party recording the County Option into its platform, the saloons packaging their paraphernalia together and getting into the Democrats – the last worse than the first – and if the party will not accept County Option – well, then there ought to be salt enough in the church people to leave – and if they don't leave, all the brilliant speeches and lightning sabre cuts against the saloons were not honest – and if so – yes, then God must judge.

A little bit about the program. The governor's [Adolph O. Eberhart, Republican – and a Swede – who as lieutenant governor had succeeded to the office following the death of Governor Johnson the previous September] speech was the usual politician's miseries without vigor and legs. Powerless, sappy, faded as a cotton rag. As soon as he was done, he went to Duluth.

Elias Rachie sprang up and blared like thunder. Youngdahl [see pp. 72-74] came forth like a cyclone.

J. F. Jacobsen raged like a tempest in bad weather. Senator Sageng swinging a halberd as if berserk. Prof. Magnusen struck with the sword like an adaptable fencer. Prof. Nelson thrashed the saloons excessively in a purely classic manner. E.T. Young did not touch the depths particularly.[180] A Catholic ecclesiastical sneezed outward at an extraordinarily beautiful speech. A Methodist minister from Minneapolis pulled some difficult thoughts out of his mind and shrieked violently, sending his forceful voice out over the audience.

Rep. Mattson spoke forcefully and with long strides stamped onto the platform as if stomping out alcohol out of grapes.[181]

Prof. McGuire with his short coat and long legs looked as if he would send the saloon out of this life with dynamite.

Seaborn Wright from Georgia went back and forth like a baited tiger, drew up his coat sleeve and pointed with a long pale finger towards the audience giving strong instructions.[182]

Have I forgotten anyone in this characterization, then hold me excused.

We surely believe this meeting will bring results.

For me it was like a celebration. All counties were represented with the exception of one. Kandiyohi County sent down a load of boisterous, loud, rich influential farmers with Mayor Bonde as leader. Songs sounded like a sonorous bell, ushering in a new era and a new day. Ja, but it is great to be alive.

In Indiana Republicans have awakened. Think – they have shaped a platform where they require "Tariff of Revenue only," election of United States Senators by direct referendum – of the appointment of an impartial tariff commission. This is something we Prohibitionists have declared we are in favor of for the last 15 years, but few had cutting words for it.

The papers would not even mention such foolishness; but now – when it comes from a political organization with its rules and regulations that have filled the country with many millionaires, society "graft," and politics with utter rottenness – well then, the plutocratic bodies promote and praise these tremendous reforms.

Thus it may indeed be a comfort to us Prohibitionists that we have done the political thinking of the past 20 years – and it is worthwhile that some of the old parties' platforms today have come from us. Now it is spring!

I had to get out here one day, lie down on the ground, salute the green blades of grass that pricked up out of the ground. Took some in my hand, greeted them, talked to them. How delightful it is to see them. They also spoke to me about the resurrection, of life, and of a primordial force that will never die – and in connection with these eternal forces, these thoughts of God, his breaths, we shall celebrate, if we are true. While I lay there on the green grass among these small blessed children of the resurrection something came into me and said:

Lo, now it is spring –
South winds so slowly move
and warm the small flowers, kissing the leaves,
and showers of rain come and give them a bath,
while little birds twitter and sing:
Lo, now it is spring.
Lo, now it is spring.

Oh, what a song –
It's the river in the valley, interpreting its need,
it is sobbing and cheering, it is crying and laughing –
and sometimes it is like thousands are praying
and everything gathers for a devotion in the field.

Oh, what a song.
Oh, what a song.[183]

During the spring, feelings on both sides of the County Option question escalated. Conversations buzzed, opinions were expressed – often with vitriol. Local newspapers kept the fires burning. Over in Pope County, just across an invisible line from Holmes City Township, the battle was literal. Iver M. Kalnes, later to figure prominently in the Lobeck story, was publisher of the *Starbuck Times*, against the saloons; Fred O. Larson, favoring the liquor interests, of the *Lowry Union*.

Larson editorially joked about preachers and Temperance believers; Kalnes retaliated. As Kalnes walked across the street on March 28, Larson and others were waiting. Verbal sparring took place, one side accusing, the other side denying, until Kalnes told Larson, "Get out of the way and let me pass." "Not until you fight," retorted the larger Larson. Larson lost his temper, grabbed Kalnes, hit him in the head, and gave him a "good drubbing." As Kalnes ran, Larson followed him, continuing to hit, finally knocking him down. Kalnes was struck again and kicked in the back several times. He rose from the ground, bleeding from nose and mouth. No arrests were made and, apparently, the townspeople had a good entertainment.[184]

Chapter 8
Running for Re-Election Again

On May 26, 2010, E.E., now a two-term incumbent, announced his candidacy as state representative on the Prohibition ticket come September's primaries. In early June, there was talk of nominating E.E. for governor since he was a "vote-getter" and had carried Senator Knute Nelson's home county in the last two elections.

At the Prohibition State Convention in Minneapolis on July 1 – a gathering at which the party's chairman, George W. Higgins, "predicted that some of the delegates of the convention 'would live long enough to see the death of the liquor traffic and to be in at the death'" – E.E. was nominated for governor but declined. If he ran for governor, he would have to give up his seat in the legislature and he, and others, were very confident he would easily retain his legislative seat. Members of the opposition were strongly pushing for his nomination, which caused suspicion. He probably could not win the governorship and would have given up his seat in the legislature; thus, they would not have to contend with E.E.[185]

In late July E.E. and Carrie Nation shared the same stage on separate nights for a week's Prohibition rally in Duluth. Nation, the famous saloon buster with the aid of her trusty axe, entitled her speech "How She Smashed, Why She Smashed, and How You Can Smash."[186]

The WCTU

E.E.'s candidacy for re-election was strongly aided by an organization – mentioned previously in this book – that his wife, Martha, devoted much effort to.

She was currently serving as district president of the Woman's Christian Temperance Union. The WCTU originated in the mid-1870s; the Minnesota chapter was among the most active and influential.

Martha spent many hours forming "unions," the organization's term for chapters. Her friend, Eva Wold, wife of the *Echo* editor, was president of the Alexandria union.

As mothers, the women of the WCTU were interested in matters of home and family. Women's suffrage also became part of their platform. They still did not have the right to vote – except in school elections. Not many women exercised this vote either, for fear of being the "only one" and perhaps intimidated. So the Alexandria WCTU members decided to go to the July school board meeting as a group and exercise their right to participate in the discussions and cast their vote. They had decided to back Rev. Tindall of the Methodist Church as their candidate.

After nominations were made, an "alarm was given downtown and in that hour they rustled up sixty-four votes of all classes of men to defeat the ladies." The men scurried in with ballots already prepared, written on brown wrapping paper, and cast their vote for the opposite candidate.

The women, though disappointed, were not discouraged. "Some of them never dreamed they could raise such a commotion and just began to realize how much more powerful they are with the privilege of the ballot than without it."[187]

The WCTU was deeply interested in anything that affected homes and families: suffrage, poverty, health of mind and body, living wages, protection of children and, obviously, Temperance.

The nearby "dry" town of Evansville was suspected of selling illegal booze. So, in June, the ladies of the WCTU hired a private detective to verify their suspicions. By August their suspicions were confirmed and reported to the county attorney, who swore out search warrants. Large quantities of beer, some whiskey and brandy, as well as Hamm's maltum (a two percent beer), another name for beer to be sold in no-license towns, were found at Joe Miller's and P. Hedeen's places of business. Miller pled guilty and paid $60 [$1,800] and costs; Hedeen's fine was $50 [$1,560] and costs.

The *Echo* encouraged sympathizers of the Temperance cause to raise a fund under the County Law and Order League to meet expenses, since "the expense of securing this evidence has been quite heavy on the ladies and their friends."[188]

The WCTU attacked another issue in this busy summer, one that E.E. also opposed – the "evils" of the moving picture shows. Movies were a new wonder in this fast-changing age, and just like iPhones and iPads in our day and age, held viewers fascinated.

A historic boxing match held in Reno, Nevada on July 1, 1910, between Jack Johnson and James Jeffries, the "Great White Hope," was filmed and quickly distributed around the country. It was scheduled to play at the Crystal Theater in Alexandria in late August.

The WCTU took action to stop it on grounds that it was "detrimental to the moral character of the children who patronize these ten-cent [$3.00] shows." The women appealed to the mayor to prevent its showing and that of any other similar movie in the future. They were successful. The movie was banned in several major cities throughout the U.S. It did have racial prejudice overtones. Johnson was (in the language of the times) Negro and Jeffries was white. Johnson's easy win over Jeffries, a previous champion, provoked widespread racial violence.[189]

The state WCTU convention heartily endorsed Lobeck because "he is women's best friend at the legislature." In the last session, as noted in the previous chapter, he had succeeded in passing two White Slave Traffic laws and an Age of Consent law, all of which were bills that directly impacted women. The law still had a way to go, however. While the Age of Consent was increased from 16 to 18, this language from 1905 was unchanged: "But no conviction shall be had for abduction or compulsory marriage upon the unsupported testimony of the female abducted or compelled."[190]

The *Minneapolis Tribune* on Feb 23, 1910, under the headline "Minnesota State Federation of Women's Clubs Holds Annual Midwinter Luncheon in St. Paul," reports a speech by the acting chairman, Mrs. A. T. Hall.

> We believe that crime and immorality cannot flourish in the light of investigation, and we would agitate a crusade in behalf of that vast army of young women who leave their homes unfitted mentally and physically to cope with unusual conditions in large cities. Knowledge of conditions and prevention go hand in hand. We ask your help in disseminating such information.

We also ask that you know the men who become candidates to our next and every legislature; that you know personally your county attorney, your city attorney and judges; that you follow such cases through the courts, as directly concern women; that you persuade your county and city officials to appoint women matrons in places frequented by women.

One phase of the work to which the committee has devoted much time investigating is the white slave traffic. Federal investigation shows 15,000 foreign girls brought to this country, practically as white slaves, and that 56,000 American girls are annually led to destruction.

We deny the newspaper report of a month ago that "No White Slave Traffic Exists in Minnesota." This purported to be a report of a federal inspector. Authorities in Washington state that no such representative has been in the employ of the government, and no investigation of Minnesota was ordered. Thousands of pamphlets containing Attorney General Lewis' report of the "White Slave Traffic," and three laws passed in our legislature pertaining to this matter have been mailed extensively throughout the state. The time is at hand when the state will take a decided step in moral questions, and dictate to parents the observance of those natural laws essential to the full development of life, and at the same time more directly purify that vast field outside the home where human activities must take place.[191]

E.E. (right) on the campaign trail

Meanwhile, E.E.'s campaign was coming along nicely. Newspapers around the state, including the *Minneapolis Journal*, stated that a Lobeck win would be "easy sledding." By early October, though, the politics began to get more difficult. Billy Hamm of Hamm's Brewing Company came to town and strongly urged liquor dealers and saloon owners that Lobeck must be beaten because they couldn't "use" him. Lobeck refused to be bought off and swayed by money.[192]

Dirty tricks

Unsubstantiated rumors were circulated. E.E. was accused of "graft" while raising funds for construction of a county hospital. He was chosen by local businessmen to canvass the field and secure subscriptions. He raised $3,500 [$110,000] in subscriptions. He was accused of pocketing $5.65 [$175]. His report showed expenses of "repairing cutter, $1 [$31]; shoeing horse, $2 [$62], deducted from Thanksgiving collections of $8.65 [$270]." The balance was reported but the money was still in his possession when he had to leave town for a speaking engagement before turning it over.[193]

Knute Nelson came to town and gave a "ho-hum" speech, according to the editor of the *Echo*, that lasted two hours, about the achievements of the Republican Party.[194]

Lobeck was endorsed by the powerful Anti-Saloon League and the Temperance Law and Order League. "If there is one man in the legislature whom the brewers want to defeat, it is E.E. Lobeck. Are you going to let them do it?" The election was seen as a struggle between the people and special interests.[195]

More rumors against Lobeck continued right up to the election. It does not appear that E.E. retaliated in kind or engaged in underhandedness as the opposing side did. He did not sway from his principles. Admirable but, perhaps, naive.

Lobeck lost the election to John Anderson by 54 votes.

Election returns from Holmes City and Leaf Valley were slow in coming in and telephone connections were shut off. Prodger was sent out to both places during the night to get the returns. About 5 o'clock Rev. Tindal who took an active interest in Lobeck's candidacy received a telephone message. He was informed that Lobeck was beaten so badly that Wold had lost all his whiskers. In the morning he found the front steps of the church covered with John Anderson campaign cards. Again on Thursday morning a goodly supply of cards and tobacco juice was covering the Methodist church steps.[196]

Newspapers around the state reported surprise and disappointment at Lobeck's loss. E.E. gallantly issued a public statement to his friends and supporters. attempting to assuage the disappointment. There would be a next time.

> A great struggle it was and we lost after a severe fight against fearful odds. We had to buck a strong party organization, a well-equipped political machine, four out of the five papers in the county were against us, lies, falsehoods and dirty stories were circulated all over; but there is only one thing under the heavens we as self-respecting reformers can do – fight to the last ditch.[197]

A couple of weeks later E.E. was feeling despondent, bitter, and betrayed when he wrote to the editor of *The Reform*.

From E.E. Løbeck
Alexandria, Minn., 6 Dec 1910

Dear Editor,

Now that the dust cloud has settled and the smoke of battle is blown away, I can stand out of the way to see the battlefield and make observations. I was knocked out of the field by 54 votes – and so there is nothing to say. The battle was horrible! It is said that at the last, $17,000 [$530,000] was sent into the county to beat me in the election – and the catchphrase was that it was four times more necessary to prevent my election than it was to select the governor. Automobiles crisscrossed the county in all directions – some days up to 20 of them – and were paid from 10 to 25 dollars [$300-$780] for each machine that was in use since they must be paid. My rival candidate could not pay this. Knute Nelson took the time to peddle Anderson's cards, and saloon owners in the city did the same. Among Germans in Millersville and Leaf Valley Joe Myers, one saloon friend, Andrew Peterson, a saloon owner, and Lew Kent, the saloon party's sheriff candidate, told the Germans that if they voted for me, they would not have a glass of beer. In Alexandria the brewer Birkhoffer, bartender Billy Jones – and a few Methodists, G. G. McCaw and Mr. Strang, represented the liquor interests. In other parts of the county the lie spread that my rival candidate was just as much in favor of the County Option as I was. There was an abundance of lies and stories – and then came election day. Twenty automobiles were out for Anderson. They took sick people out of their beds, carried them out to the automobiles, and carried them into the polling places. They did their duty. When the election results came in, I found out that over 150 of my friends were sitting at home on election day. It was not worthwhile to waste some time to go and vote, as I was the sure choice. They could not believe that anyone would vote for my rival candidate. So it came to happen that I was defeated. – There is nothing to say about it if you are defeated in open combat with the enemy, but that one's friends must cause that you lose is a little difficult. Brewer interests got its will though. They had said that they would pay more money for my scalp than anyone else in the entire state. The battle is not yet over. God lives and not all Vikings are dead.

Yours,
E.E. Løbeck[198]

He seemed to draw strength from being "out in the field" where he felt important, appreciated by crowds of people, where his mission was clear and the responses of his audience validated his work. It must have been difficult for Martha to remain in Alexandria during his defeats, while he was able to leave.

Reflecting on the loss

E.E. wrote in the local newspaper.

Some Traveling Experiences of Hon. E.E. Lobeck

Some of the Peculiar Results of the Late Elections in this Country. Discussions

On a dark murky day, I started for North Dakota. A thin sheet of snow covered the ground, the wind was howling and the flowers and hopes of summer had gone. We, as individuals, have our seasons. A springtime with the blossoms of hope, a summer with realizations and disappointments, a fall with glimmering sun and aspirations faded, a winter with gray hairs and tottering feet on the verge of the grave.

The train sped along, stopped at the stations, let people off and took people on – and those who came and left were discussing the political conditions in the country. Roosevelt got it in the head – in the eastern states – in that almost all whom he recommended had the pins knocked away from under them. The Democrats, it is said, will have control of the next Congress, and "then," said one man, "it is time for me to leave this country." "Good-bye" said another, "it will not make very much difference whether you leave or stay – such a small cog in the big wheel of government will not amount to very much."

In the midst of joking of this kind there is a serious undercurrent to be noticed. The people are restless, a feeling of dissatisfaction is prevalent all over and when this undercurrent breaks through and commences to flow on the surface something will drop. Every revolution that has shaken this earth from pole to pole has originated in one man's brain. The last election was one of the most peculiar ones in the history of the country. Dishonesty and fraud, falsehoods and wonderful propositions were dished out and the people are getting tired.

Some day the common people will work out their political salvation in spite of party machines and bosses.

Came to Galesburg, N.D. One, Mr. Kyllo, took me out to his home by Elm River. Well, all that was left of the river was the place where it once flowed. It has dried out completely – that's the way with many things and many people, nothing left except the place where they have been. Had a very good meeting out in a church close to Kyllo's place in the afternoon, and in the evening a grand meeting was held in Galesburg. The people in North Dakota are somewhat dissatisfied with the election in many sections. The old parties have put up law-breakers in some sections in order to catch the vote of the bad element, and so they put up good men in some places in order to keep the good people in line. Now after the election is over and the people see these things, they are getting mad.

Came to Roseville. There they started a Temperance society in 1885 and they have held their regular meetings ever since. The result is that the people are well-to-do and every father and mother in that community have given their children a college education. The old veterans in the battle against the Devil Rum felt good at the meeting. Drove into Portland, N.D., in the evening and met the largest audience the people have seen for many years.

In one of the North Dakota counties, a man was elected sheriff – a man who once was a saloonkeeper in Breckenridge and conducted his place so badly that even the authorities of such a place kicked him out. He went to N.D. and began his operations and succeeded in being elected sheriff. In the section of the county where good people lived he came with a smile and talked about churches and religion, in other sections he came with beer and cigars and talked about something else. But he got what he wanted – the office – and the people got fooled.

Something similar to that we had in Douglas County, this fall in the works for County Option – Joe Myers, an insurance man, and Andrew Peterson, the saloonkeeper, and Kent, the aspirant for sheriff, were up in Millerville, told beautiful stories and worked for County Option. In Alexandria we had Billy Jones, the bartender in Foslien's saloon, Birkhoffer, the brewer, and E. E. McCrea, the Sunday School man, united as brothers in the same great work. And P. J. Christopher in Kensington, also a church man, linked hands with this beautiful combination and worked for County Option. I know that P. J. C. did not like the idea of being hitched to Billy Jones and pulling his way (he said so himself that he wished Billy Jones would stay at home), but Peter stuck to it to the last. Those who believe that they shall be able to build up a good government through such combination will be badly mistaken. McCrea and P. J. Christopher with their Bibles, Birkhoffer and Billy Jones with their bottles going hand in hand, working for the same party, the same principles and the same men shall never bring about "Thy Kingdom come."

In Hatton, Northwood, Buxton, Harwood, Finley, Binford, and the country districts the meetings were large. When I sent word that I would speak once in a place, the people had arranged sometimes for three meetings. Good cheer and glad hands were extended, and the talks on the drink traffic and white slave trade certainly create a sensation in the meetings.

It is nearing up to Christmas – the wandering ones are turning their eyes homeward – soon the Christmas bells are ringing and among those we love we will forget strife and struggles and be children again.[199]

And simultaneously in *The Reform* he published a poem, "Julen 1910" (Christmas 1910).

> *My dreams carry me away from sorrow and troubles.*
> *Christmas is drawing close and I'm homewards bound,*
> *Along with swarms of others, who are yearning for home.*
> *There, in the living room, you just ought to see*
> *How the children are decorating their Christmas Tree -*
> *There it's sheer pleasure for me to be.*

Every window, every door is standing slightly ajar.
Inside them are my dear ones, and soon I'll be there,
Singing with them the beautiful Carols
That so deeply touched my heart in my childhood.
So calming and mild, like waves that gently break
On distant beaches in the sunset.[200]

Chapter 9

To the West Coast

Early in the new year, 1911, E.E. was on the go again, first to Michigan.
On the way he saw evidence of success long ago – and admitted to a
lapse of his principles. The train dropped him off

> in the cold at four in the morning in the deformed little town of Pembine
> [Wisconsin]. Ole Broder Olson and I were there one time 17 years ago
> and found to our edification five houses, three of which were saloons. It's a
> little better now, but the only hotel is connected to a saloon – and my
> innards would scream, before I should go in and eat at such a place. Still, I
> did once.

On returning home from the stint in Michigan, E.E. quickly prepared to
go the other direction, "a long trip to the west coast" that was sponsored
by the Pacific Coast Total Abstinence Association.

He was mesmerized by the scenery – mountains, valleys, forests, snow on
stumps and rocks looking like "a colony of giants, angular, with humps
weighing many tons." And the outward view turned inward.

> There runs a valley just against a wall of rock, bends slightly to the side
> and finds its path further ahead – a creek at the bottom is singing out the
> longings of this obscure world – every object has its own melody, the
> mountains their great song in their loneliness. The grass stems are putting
> their minuscule melodies in the wind, and life sings through thousands
> upon thousands of yearnings, and the soul has its own song, because it has
> its own land. In a blink my thoughts were turned from the outer world to
> the inner.

> What a landscape, what a view – scarred, wrinkled hills and peaks, deep,
> dark valleys, where I still have not seen the bottom, rapid rivers, which

from time to time are grinding life to foam – but then there is light from other suns than the one that shines upon Earth, and so my whole inner being is rocked in eternal arms, and the soul is bathed in a light that is purified in its own clarity.

But "being rocked in eternal arms" soon gave way to more somber reflection.

This is a dangerous point in the Cascades. A year ago an avalanche[201] started up in the mountain side, brought along big rocks, snow and ice, took two trains that happened to be there, and threw everything to the bottom of the valley, ground and kneaded everything together, death and destruction. A thunder went through the valley, and the echo rebounded from the mountains, snow dust filled the valley, cries of woe rose to the heavens, and then everything was silent. Ninety lives, they say, were taken in a moment.

Some 52 hours after embarking, E.E. was met by friends at the Everett, Washington train station. "Now I was at the west coast, safe and sound. For a safe journey and safekeeping of life and limbs we thank thee, O God!"[202]

Remembering wooing

In Washington state E.E. was in the territory of Ole Svendsen Sneve,[203] an immensely popular Norwegian-American poet, who at the time was 65, and would die a couple of years later. "Oh no, I had better stay away from making verses out here in the poetry country of Sneve. I started thinking that if I should start sprinkling my verses over the poetic fields of Sneve, it would seem like tares among the wheat."

Then, in a classic instance of what is known in rhetoric as apophasis – the raising of an issue by claiming not to – E.E. waxes poetic, about memory in general, and specifically the memory of his wooing Martha.

We'll see when the sun comes out and the fog lifts, if the mind will soar. But how the memories are alive; they are all but devouring me – makes the day long, and at night they come in thousands upon thousands, until my complete existence looks like sunset on an unfinished mission. Therefore I have been tempted to sing:

Come, veil of forgetfulness, and descend upon my mind –
lock the door of Memory, so nothing can come in;

Through the day and through the night
my heart is the playground of an army of memories.
Like stars in Heaven they all lit up,
as if all and every one of them have been awakened.
Here come the memories of memories, day and night,
diving into my anguished soul.

But what is it I am writing? Are not memories the only ones that come visiting when I am lonely? Are they not the faithful companions that bring the reliving of past times to my mind? Without memories life would have been night. Even the things that made me cry are vastly softened when memories of them come to me in later years. They show me the same things over and over again, until they become one with my inner soul. The memories make me live twice – live my life both ways, and the longings follow, to support the hope of the soul, and the loss fills the emptiness and mends my shortcomings. And when the songbirds of life as wages for their song take my hopes one by one, and the hopes break in front of me, the memories grow behind.

There is no use in speculating about this mystery of existence – this which lives inside one – deep inside – like behind a veil – seems never to come forward into the full light of understanding. Some of it seems to be explained in the light of memory; but it does not understand. Still, I love my memories. Should they be extinguished there would be night in my heart.

I clearly remember my childhood time.
Smiling like the sun of May;
When autumn winds surround me now
I live my life in the glow of memory.

And then there is all the mercy of God; what if one wasn't allowed to remember them – I had better tune my harp strings again:

Yes, come ye memories, come in thousands
and make my inner me a meeting hall.
I settle down in evening glow,
and you may bring me the finest wreath.

I well remember the wonderful valley
where she stole my heart one summer's night.

I remember the cabin, remember the sounds of the creek,
while everything devoutfully lay down on the meadow.

I warmly thank for every smile and every word
that she gave me on this forsaken earth.
Her gentle voice, so low and soft,
like evening breeze when it goes still.

So, memories, loss and longings may well live
within my soul, and build a bridge
between me and days gone by,
that, like a shadow, vanished into eternity.

From reverie to the practical. Right after "vanishing into eternity," E.E. gets to the regular business of recounting his Temperance meetings.

On Camano Island, in Puget Sound, his meeting was small ("because of a misunderstanding"), but he witnessed a dramatic instance of "progress."

> They had settled between tree stumps and rocks, and put dynamite under the tree stumps, lit the fuse and hid behind felled tree tops. Then there came a shake of the earth, like a gigantic sigh, a bang like an accident – earth, rocks and rubble, with splinters from the stumps flew sky high, and then descended again all around with a great noise and rolled around on the ground.

> Then the pioneers crept out again and gave another of these giant stumps the same drastic purgative. It was certainly interesting. One gets strong from such a life, battling the old and well rooted. It has to go if anything new shall shoot up and grow.

When he got to Bellingham, E.E. learned that much had happened there recently.

> The saloons were given the boot from Bellingham last year, but there was a riot in the town. Of course it had to go bankrupt. The wives of the saloon owners got anxious about the wellbeing of the town, and started an organization where they could ponder out plans to save the town from ruin. They had their meetings and forced their heads to think, probably for the first time. And yes! – an idea came to one of them. Each church was to be taxed five hundred dollars [\$15,600]. But when they made their plans known, the whole town laughed so hard at them that they had to hunker

down. And then they started moving out, went to the outer limits by the
sea. The trains at times overflowed with this furniture on the move.

On the way to Westminster, British Columbia, E.E. was sick – but was
not about to let that stop him.

I had got a bout of this infernal modern appendicitis, but it would be
strange if such a small piece of entrails should be able to lay a grown man
on his back. Off we went, northwards through the fields, and in one-two-
three the customs officer was upon us like a hawk. The bags were opened,
and he put his fat fingers into them and dug around – and then he left.
Then came another, asking questions about nationality, citizenship, etc.
That was quickly cleared up. …

I could barely get around to the meetings. It has gone up and down for
weeks, but I am still on my feet, and get to experience the word: "As your
days are, so will your strength be."[204]

The recall law

Seattle provided E.E. an example of what he called "a superb weapon
that people in a free country should always have" – "a 'recall' law."

The city's mayor Mr. Gill got it into his round skull that the city would be
what is called "wide open." And open it was. Saloons were filled with
cheating, filth, and deception. The immoral houses play first violin and the
white slave trade operated its abominable work entirely unchallenged.

So, finally, the "better element" circulated a petition for a special election,
if possible, to kick Mayor Gill out the door and get a better man. It was
this that kept the city in excitement the day I got there. Oh, what a
commotion! Big-bellied saloon owners, and businessmen, looking like
emaciated salted herring, talked big about Mr. Gill's virtues. The better
element laid their plans. Ja, there was movement in Seattle. It was certainly
not many in town who noticed the sublime nature around them. Those
who worship the almighty dollar were probably not aware of those peaks
pointing on high.

A beast of a man, a devil in human form stood on his two legs and in a
loud voice recommended that immorality should be made into a shop, a
"business proposition."

The women have got the right to vote in Washington. Now they should be
tested. The "better element" were reluctant to register, but then discovered

that the women from the immoral trade came in the mayor's automobile singing praises in his favor, and when that became clear, the good women had to get their act together. There were registrations, mass meetings, and debate. Election day came. Other traffic also came through town and it seemed like everything rolled on wheels. People were snyste [muzzled], threatened, hit and kicked – when they went on a pilgrimage to the polling stations. Eighty-year-old women and women of twenty-one, old gray-haired men and boys in their best years – a part of the evil, other for the good – a duel between the better and the worst part. We were excited for the result, you spoke with your votes. One faction lit up in the face, the other darkened – and when all the votes were added up, it turned out that Mayor Gill was defeated by thousands of votes and the women were blamed for it, of course.[205]

"The rich man does what he likes"

There were many more stops in the Pacific Northwest – Puyallup, Ellensburg, Spokane (a "battle city"), and into Idaho – Sandpoint, Potlach, Bell, Moscow. Then, back to Seattle, where E.E. revealed political concerns that would escalate enormously six years later.

During E.E.'s years in the Minnesota Senate (1915-18), the issue of the U.S. engagement in World War I would come to loom large in the political views and fortunes of the Prohibition Party, and there will be much to say about that when chronology takes us there.

But on this stay in Seattle in 1911, E.E. saw something that triggered ponderings about the role of the U.S. on the world stage – ponderings that foreshadow his take on President Wilson's decision to enter the World War, and that reflect his persistent suspicion that money explains most things that happen and don't happen.

Pastor Iversen in Seattle had a special meeting scheduled for me in Bremerton in the evening. Bremerton is our country's naval base on the west coast, and there lay a great deal of Uncle Sam's big killer barges. I'm pondering on this until I got dizzy. What right has a nation to kill another nation's population? If I were to pummel a man in the skull, so the spirit left him forever, then I should be hanged. What right has a nation rather than the individual to murder? My questions and musings came to a sharp halt. A telegram came that the fleet should mobilize and head to Mexico. A monster black beast of a battleship was in the port of Seattle and ate the western coal to see if they would stand the test. Now this monster spewed this lousy junk of the West into the water and took on board eastern coal, polished guns – oh, yes this was really going to be something! Bremerton was busy as never before. What should the fleet do in Mexico? …

It was the Japanese that should be beaten because they would not keep their hands out of the pie down there, some said. It did not take long for some before they had beaten the Japanese, completely blue. Still others had already given the Japanese the Hawaiian Islands and would be creepy enough when Japanese cannonballs began to come in through the windows of Seattle and other cities on the west coast. Then there came a quick halt to all these speculations, and the main question reappeared: Why on earth is the fleet going to Mexico? Well, it never got underway, and then we were told that this whole commotion was to test the army and fleet personnel, whether they were on the alert.

Then ventured a man who knew himself to write [almost certainly E.E. himself] that it was the American rich men who were the cause of the war in Mexico and that was why the fleet should be ready to respond to help these children of destruction in their robberies, and God alone knows whether or not this was true. The rich man does what he likes and woe to us in the future.[206]

E.E. kept up a strenuous lecture schedule southward through Oregon and California. By the end of March he was finished, and stopped in Salt Lake City to visit an old friend and relax a day or two.

Homeward bound, he was aboard a Rio Grande passenger train when it derailed near Price, Utah, overturning the coach where he was seated, spilling everyone into a jumble. Though quite shaken up, no one was seriously hurt, as the train was moving at a speed of only 15 mph.[207]

He arrived home in mid-April, a few days before Easter. His children always remembered this trip because of his long absence and the frightening episode. E.E. wrote many letters home while traveling – to Martha and, individually, to his children. Some of the letters to the children have survived.

Left to right: E.E., Kari, Ola, Inger, John; Ingerinus in middle

Chapter 10

Run for Governor

E.E. headed to the Østerdalslaget in Minneapolis in mid-June 1911. Lefse, spekekjød, rømmegrøt, and gammelost in abundance, much visiting, songs, and speeches paying tribute to Østerdalen. The attendees visited the lakes and parks of Minneapolis – Minnehaha Falls was a favorite destination – before departing for home. E.E., probably accompanied by his brother John, continued on to Willmar for the Annual Convention of the Lutheran Free Church.

E.E. spent the summer in speaking engagements closer to home – around the state and occasionally over into the Dakotas. Meanwhile there was some talk of having Lobeck as a candidate for governor in 1912. In his favor was the White Slave Traffic bill he was successful in getting passed while he was in the legislature.

On June 12, 1911, the U.S. Senate passed a resolution amending the Constitution to elect senators by direct popular vote instead of having state legislators select them – making moot the sort of controversy E.E. had been embroiled in when, during his first term in the Minnesota legislature in 1907, he proposed a Prohibitionist to challenge Knute Nelson. The 17th Amendment, passed by Congress on May 13, 1912, was ratified on April 8, 1913.

In early September E.E. began three months of three lectures a day throughout Minnesota for the state Prohibition Committee. This would let him test the waters about a run for governor the next year.

WCTU weighs in

Meanwhile, Martha spent considerable time and effort in her WCTU work. It enhanced her husband's Temperance efforts, of course, but, as a mother, a woman, and a homemaker she believed in the cause as well. Serving as district president required hours of organization, traveling throughout the district, recruiting members, and lending a presence in affairs previously decided only by males.

The *Park Region Echo* carried detailed reports of WCTU activities. Meetings were held every two weeks in a member's home. Martha, as district president, gave a talk at each meeting.

"Mrs. E.E. Lobeck read an article on dancing in the public schools, supplementing the reading with some very convincing remarks. The discussion which followed brought out some facts not known by most of us."[208] No surprise, she was against dancing.

Two weeks later, Martha hosted the meeting at the Lobeck home. The topic for discussion for the evening was "Purity" "Mrs. Haskins read an article on teaching sex hygiene in the schools. Quite a discussion followed when the meeting was adjourned."[209]

At the next meeting, at the Carlos Hotel, "Mrs. Lobeck in her talk showed how doing little things often developed far beyond any expectations." She told of a young man in her Trysil neighborhood by the Sheyenne who organized a Temperance society there when she was growing up. It was necessary, she said, because nearly everyone drank. The Temperance organization wasn't very popular, but the young man persisted. Eventually he got nearly all the young people in the neighborhood to join and sign pledges and then succeeded in getting many of the parents to join. Now that the young had grown up, they carried this influence with them.[210] In a nutshell, this illustrated the reason for and plan of the Temperance movement.

A committee of the WCTU met with the city council concerning the granting of another saloon license in the Unumb building on Main Street. The women didn't feel they could change the outcome, but wanted to protest the presumed decision. Alderman Kraemer stated if they needed any help from the women they would ask for it, but Mrs. Wold countered that they had a right to present their views since the men received a large amount of time to present theirs. Mr. Kraemer replied that it "had been trouble, trouble the whole year over the saloon question and he was tired of it."[211] The saloon license was granted, but the women had the satisfaction of making their protest. The women weren't done yet though. They were successful in getting the saloons officially closed for Christmas Day.[212]

Should E.E. run for governor or not? That was the topic at the February 1912 meeting of the Douglas County Law and Order League. Mrs. Wold said the state WCTU favored Lobeck for representative because he would more likely be elected and he could do more good in the legislature.

"Is it God's will?"

Constant Larson stated that now was the time for Lobeck to throw in his hat for the governorship. He, Larson, had thought so for the last two years and almost urged the state Prohibition Committee to nominate him then, adding that Lobeck had nothing to gain by running for representative. In the next breath, unwittingly, it seems, he remarked that if the Republicans put up a County Option man, he wouldn't be able to support Lobeck.

Lobeck said that he was not afraid of defeat. "The main question is 'Is it God's will?' It makes no difference how many times I am slaughtered in this way, I am willing to go into the fight if it serves the cause any good purpose."

Larson moved that Lobeck be endorsed by the Law and Order League as candidate for governor. Someone moved that the motion be amended to endorse Lobeck for representative. In the end, the vote was 19 -3 in favor of E.E.'s candidacy for governor.

Larson would then be running for representative. But, "What if Larson is defeated at the primaries?" someone asked. Though it would be a good idea to have a backup plan and have a Prohibitionist run in the primaries, it would be the responsibility of all to work for Larson's nomination and, if successful, then the Prohibition candidate would quietly drop out and all support would go toward Larson.

Just then, someone recalled Larson's earlier remark that he would support the Republican candidate for governor, even though Larson had pushed the hardest for Lobeck to be the candidate.

The meeting heated up at this point. Larson had exposed his true intentions. Lobeck had stepped aside to promote Larson for representative and now Larson would not support Lobeck, even though Larson came to the meeting to get the League's endorsement for himself. He had maintained quite vigorously that Lobeck's chances for election as governor were very probable but, obviously, that wasn't true. Larson apparently felt that neither of them would win and the seat would be lost to the liquor interests.

Other members were angry and told Larson, in no uncertain terms, that as a member of the League he was expected to go along with whomever they endorsed. Now Larson was angry and emphatically stated he wouldn't accept advice from anyone.

The meeting ended on unpleasant terms. No decisions were made.[213]

Off again on a lecture trip, E.E. returned for the spring elections and to assist in carrying the city in voting for no-license. Temperance work was having results. Alexandria voted "dry" after 16 years of "wet." Throughout Minnesota, 90 towns voted "wet"; 91 voted "dry." A dissatisfied businessman sold out and went to Canada because Alexandria was "going to the bow-wows."[214]

In May, a special meeting of the Law and Order League was held in the *Park Region Echo* office. E.E. had called for the meeting between the League and the state Prohibition Committee, hoping that they could get together and come to an agreement about whether he should run for representative or governor.

A calmer Constant Larson spoke first. He stated he was and had always been "squarely against the saloon," that he had stood by Lobeck even when it personally hurt himself politically. As county attorney, he felt he had done what he could in that capacity for the Temperance cause and now wanted to serve in the legislature.

E.E. spoke next "from a spirit of self-defense," since his supporters and friends were pulling in different directions.

At Easter time when he came home from a lecture trip he was surprised to find there were petitions out asking him to become a candidate for representative and people asking him to consider the proposition. He told them he was not a candidate. ... As for himself personally he has no political aspirations. He does not care to be a candidate for either position ... but what would be best for the cause.[215]

Was Lobeck just being disingenuous? Self-effacing? Health issues? His heart problems began about this time.

The meeting ended with Lobeck endorsed as candidate for governor, and no endorsement for Constant Larson as candidate for representative.

On the domestic front, E.E. and Martha purchased a larger cottage on Lake Darling. It was spacious enough for the whole family to sleep under one roof instead of in tents. By now, E.E. had purchased a car, a 1910 20-hp five-passenger Ford[216] which made it easier to drive the two-three miles between home and the cottage – though there was a small stable for the family horse, "Jennie," and the wagon on the property.

1912 State Prohibition Convention

The State Prohibition Convention took place in Minneapolis July 4-5, 1912. When E.E. was unanimously selected as temporary chairman, resounding cheers exploded from the 300 delegates. The business of adopting the planks demanding better working conditions, equal taxation, equal reapportionment of legislative districts, laws about white slave traffic, conservation of natural resources and, of course, the evils of alcohol, were easily agreed upon. The strong feeling that the brewers owned the government and it must be returned to the people was evident throughout.

Next the excited crowd named Lobeck as their candidate for governor on the Prohibition ticket. A "storm of applause lasted wholly five minutes and was followed by a score of seconding speeches." The delegates really felt that this was their chance to win, because messages had been pouring in from all over the state for months urging Lobeck's candidacy.[217] E.E.

reluctantly (at least publicly) accepted the nomination of his party for governor.

For nine months I have pleaded in vain with the State Committee and others not to bring my name up before this convention in connection with the candidacy for governor. I do not believe that that is the place I ought to occupy on the ticket in this campaign. I do not believe that I should be the standard bearer. I most firmly believe that I can do more for the cause fighting in the ranks. I appreciate your good will, I am thankful to you for the honor conferred upon me, I am gratified to know that I have been deemed worthy of your confidence and that you believe in me.

Each and every one of us has seen the awful tragedy of desolation, carnage and blood, and it has bound us together with strong bonds in friendship and love. United we stand for the protection of the home against corporate greed and legalized vice. **The supreme thing for us is to be true to our principles. They are dearly bought, they cannot be given up. Principles are mighty things for a man who will strive to live his life truly amidst a struggling, suffering humanity. "The man who speaks not what he thinks deceives the people and the state."** No worse charge can be laid up against a man than this, that his opinions and language are not the same. Let us be true to those principles, that will permit us to live in that atmosphere where we refuse to permit party feelings and sectional hatred to drag us down and warp and narrow our souls. Personal gain and selfish aims will have to be set aside, and we will have to acquaint ourselves with the fact that in fighting for the uplift of humanity, we will sometimes have to go out into the wilderness alone and be fed by the ravens. But it pays to be true.

For forty years and more the Prohibition Party has been struggling against fearful odds, fighting the battles of the people against the legalized drink traffic and corporate greed. We sent our words into the wilderness and it took years before the echo came back, but now we are heard. Our planks are eagerly snatched up one by one and incorporated into the platforms of other political organizations, except the plank calling for the destruction of the liquor traffic, this the greatest curse of all the curses of humanity. They do not dare to touch that – they evidently believe that we have the first mortgage on that plank. (Applause and laughter.) But aside from this we should be glad that our principles are taken up and advocated today by the greatest men in the nation – and we ought to be proud of the fact that the

Prohibitionists have been doing the political thinking in the country for the last twenty years. (Applause.) Every advanced idea that has been brought forward by the Republicans and Democrats of late has for years been shining like a beacon light to progressive statecraft in the Prohibition platform. (Applause.) If the people will elect us into power, we will put into political deeds the trust and statesmanship of our political thought. (Applause.) **If the people in this state at the next election, will elect a Prohibitionist governor and a Prohibition legislature the doom of the saloon will be sealed, provided we can chloroform the present Senate and send it to a better world.** (Laughter.)

We have refused to fuse and shall refuse to fuse with any and all political parties that cater to the support of the demon rum and greedy corporations. A compromise where principle is involved is a victory for the devil. If our Bible, our conscience, and our intelligence tell us that we are right and we make concessions to those who we know are wrong, we will be the worst cheated people in the whole universe of God.

The Prohibition Party arose amidst the numberless plaintive cries of starved children, pale mothers, and ruined fathers who stood on the brink of destruction with the cruel grinning demon of drink behind them – just as the Republican Party of old sprang up in God's own good time when the sound of clanking chains, the crack of the slave whip, and the blood-curdling bays of bloodhounds and moans of the dying darkies filled the land. [If this sentence sounds familiar, it is almost verbatim what E.E. said in his speech nominating a Prohibitionist senator against Knute Nelson in 1907; see page 106.] The Republican Party fulfilled its mission when it killed human slavery, and the banner of Abraham Lincoln at that time planted in the blood-soaked ground is still floating on high and shall remain floating as long as we have in this country, redeemed with blood and tears, men and women who will dare to do what is right before God and man. (Applause.) Lincoln wrote upon this banner, "Down with human slavery!" and by so doing forged together again the broken family ties of the black race. We will inscribe upon the same banner, "Down with the flag of corporate greed and up with the banner of the toiling masses, the plain people." "Down in the dust with the abominable rag of the white slave traffic and up with the shining shield of the law for the protection of the homes!" Down, forever down with the anarchistic institution, the licensed saloon – this unmitigated, blood-stained iniquity, and let us humbly but bravely bring to the ballot box, that sacred shrine of patriotism, our humble tribute to the cradle.

Comrades! With ardent soul, a burning heart and an open mind let us go forward to win. (Applause.) And in the name of him who maketh the seven stars and the Orion and turneth the shadow of death into morning and maketh day dark with night; that calleth upon the waters of the sea and poureth them out upon the face of the earth, the Lord Jehovah is his name – and in the name of him who giveth power to the faint and to those who have no might he increases strength – I very unwillingly and very reluctantly and yet with thanks and gratitude accept the nomination for governor on the Prohibition ticket. (Applause and cheers.)[218]

Lobeck knew his audience and was a master at weaving religion and politics together, holding the audience spellbound. Indeed, it is evident that he wanted the governorship. Prohibition was a top political issue – on everyone's lips.

Now all for automobiles

Prohibition campaign car

E.E. now understood the value of using automobiles in his campaign. He had been very critical of them years earlier, but felt his campaign for the Minnesota House in 1910 was lost, in part, by not using automobiles. So in mid-August the Prohibitionist-owned automobile was out canvassing the state for the candidates, holding open air meetings.

Preston, in Fillmore County, declared they were planning an auto party for Lobeck "in whirlwind style about the middle of August."

They are lining up a parade of six automobiles with which they propose to tour the entire county with E.E. Lobeck ... holding big meetings on the streets and a number of picnics in the country districts. ...

The plan will include about 30 men. ... The machines will all be decked with banners and the first automobile will carry a quartet of singers, who will gather a crowd with two or three selections. Another machine with campaign speakers will address the people for a half hour, after which the third machine will bring Mr. Lobeck, who will make the closing address. ...

The county is athrob with interest in the novel and elaborate campaign plan.[219]

Gust and Ida Loo, Eva and Carl Wold, John and Emma Lobeck, Martha and E.E. Lobeck and niece, Helga Petterson, motored out to the YPB outing (Young People's Branch of the WCTU) for a picnic at Ida on a hot, dry August Sunday. No movies on Sunday, but political speeches were okay!

One hundred fifty people gathered under the thick summer foliage of the trees on the shore of Lake Chippewa and attentively listened to E.E. Lobeck's instructive talk for an hour while the gentle patter of rain on the leaves above merely gave each a feeling that the dust would not be so thick on the return home as it had been thither. The Lobeck and Loo choir sang songs as a treat to all. ...

Lobeck explained his right to talk so-called politics on Sunday by stating that government, if right, is a God-given institution as is the home. No one denies the duty of all to study on Sunday is the best way to bring the individual and the home in conformity with God's laws. Then is it not also a duty to study the way to serve God as a member of the nation? ...

After the program five gallons of lemonade and ten of ice cream were served while each attendant was given a buttonhole bouquet.[220]

The 1912 Minnesota State Fair opened on September 2 – the exciting programs complete with horse races and the famous Dan Patch; "aeroplanes" show; automobile races; five gas balloons ascending every afternoon carrying women "aeronauts" who parachuted to the ground; the newest farm machinery; menageries of animals and poultry. The Prohibition building near the fair entrance made its presence known with music, speakers, political literature, and sported a large picture of E.E. Lobeck painted on one of the building's gables.[221]

Martha Lobeck and Eva Wold attended the State WCTU Convention in St. Paul for several days in late September. An item on the program was the "Prohibition Symposium" with E.E. Lobeck. When he walked on the stage he was greeted with "cheers and cheers." The WCTU fully embraced him for governor.[222]

C. H. Larson ran for representative in the September primaries and lost. Carl Wold then stepped up to run for representative.

E.E. and a Mr. Stewart engaged the Prohibitionists' automobile for the last weekend in September to canvass Douglas County. With car troubles, the schedule was a bit upended, but they covered much of the county. Saturday morning they were slated to begin in Osakis, but the car broke down in Melrose and they were forced to take the train to Alexandria in the afternoon. They spoke in Alexandria and then backtracked to Osakis in the evening, returning to Alexandria for a good night's sleep.

Sunday they had the repaired automobile in service and covered multiple towns with good response before returning to Alexandria for the night. However, the next morning, Monday, the automobile needed more fixing. When they got to Farwell, children had been dismissed from school so they "could take advantage of the lectures."[223]

Early Friday morning, October 4, five automobiles loaded with Prohibitionist dignitaries departed the Vendome Hotel for the Union depot in St. Paul to greet Eugene W. Chafin, the Prohibitionist presidential candidate (in both 1908 and 1912; he received approximately one and one-half percent of the popular vote each time). The cars were "bedecked with banners and pictures of Lobeck and Chafin." The group breakfasted together at the YMCA. Lobeck excused himself to catch a train and speak at the county fair in Cokato while Chafin made speaking engagements around St. Paul. Lobeck, well received in Cokato, then hustled back to Minneapolis where he spoke in the evening.[224]

A few days later the campaign toured Carlton County and then on to Duluth, which was eagerly anticipating the candidate. A Prohibitionist from California accompanied Lobeck; they could split up and cover more territory because of Duluth's size.

Duluth Prohibitionists are anticipating a big day with the advent of the big touring car which is carrying their candidate for governor and his party. ... At noon and 5:30 the party divides, holding two meetings at the same time. ... The City Fife and Drum corps has been engaged to furnish music for the evening rally at the courthouse square. Other musicians accompany the auto party. ... During the day ... the autos will parade the streets, with music playing and banners displayed. ... Tomorrow the party will start for the Range.[225]

Lobeck generated great enthusiasm on the Iron Range. When speaking in the town of Virginia, he was greeted with prolonged applause and was persuaded to speak another 45 minutes. He returned to his hotel and got himself ready for bed when he got a call from the Finnish Temperance Hall asking him to come speak to them. It was after 11:00 p.m., but he hurriedly dressed and was on his way. Arriving at the hall, he was greeted by over 400 men, whom he addressed for more than an hour.[226]

The last couple of weeks before the November 5 election were a flurry of campaigning throughout the state. E.E. received endorsements from various groups, including Gustavus Adolphus College. But all to no avail. The automobiles had not been enough.

Incumbent Republican Governor Eberhardt won with 41 percent of the vote. The Democrat got 31 percent, the Progressive 11 percent, and Lobeck nine percent, trailed only by the Public Ownership candidate, with eight percent. But Lobeck did carry Douglas County by a 200 vote plurality.

WCTU in the aftermath

The WCTU served a three-course Prohibition Banquet for 100 people the evening of January 6, 1913. Inga Petterson and Evangeline Lobeck were two of the young "misses" who waited on tables. E.E. acted as toastmaster and introduced various speakers. The oldest Prohibitionist present, Mr. J. E. Southwick, sang "The Home That Used to Be" and "For Molly and the Baby."

The first verse of "The Home That Used to Be" is a short lesson in the main motivating concern of the Temperance movement:

No, our home is not what it used to be
In the cheerful and glad days of old,
When the boys and girls were so happy there

And Jamie's heart was good as gold.
But that home once so cheerful has changed for the worse
Since the whiskey jug entered the door,
And the sweet peaceful joys of those happy days
Have pass'd, I fear to come no more.

[Refrain]: No, our home is not what it used to be
For poverty stands at the door,
And the happy days we once did used to see
I fear will never come no more.

In the other song, "Molly, a 'patient little woman' and the baby, who 'ought to have a show' from his father, await the drunken husband at home. In this song, the man gives the 'whiskey up,' takes up the 'coffee cup' for 'Molly and the Baby, don't you know.'" [227]

The Alexandria WCTU held their annual "Due Tea" in January. It was an opportunity for members to socialize without taking up serious tasks. Spouses were invited. The program began with a "white ribbon tying contest." White ribbons, actually bows, were identifiers of members of the WCTU. Members were encouraged to wear them on their lapels. Some WCTU unions fined their members a meager amount if they did not wear them, especially to union meetings. "The white ribbon bows were selected to symbolize 'purity' and the WCTU's watchwords were 'Agitate – Educate – Legislate.'"[228] On this evening, the contest was to tie the bow the fastest. Those who were not wearing the bows were given one. This little exercise reminded members of the importance of broadcasting their beliefs and, of course, advertising the WCTU. The short program continued with music by Miss Evangeline Lobeck and a recitation by Miss Dagny Lobeck.[229]

E.E. boarded the train for Chicago the end of April. He would not be home until mid-June. "The nation's most prominent social reformers and half a dozen of the well-known Prohibitionists" were planning a "crusade against vice, corruption and law violations."[230]

In August, Martha, as district WCTU president, and chairwoman of the "entertainment" (housing) committee, was in a whirlwind organizing for the state convention in Alexandria. The call went out for volunteers to host attendees. Women found it more acceptable to stay in private homes. Those who volunteered to host would furnish a bed and breakfast to their guests; all other meals would be furnished by the convention committee.

This meant that the local WCTUers were busy in their kitchens preparing food for the larger group and this, too, had to be organized. The Lobecks hosted six attendees. In Martha's capable hands, all went well.

Tuesday, August 19, opening day of the convention, the weather was cool and drizzly and quite disagreeable. The Great Northern added two special coaches to accommodate the 200 women who arrived on the afternoon train. Several automobiles were volunteered to meet the women at the depot, transport them to the registration point, and then to their accommodations. E.E. helped with his horse and buggy.

Tuesday evening, "Welcome Night," nearly all the speakers were men: Rev. Secord, the mayor; E.E. Lobeck, listed as "Mrs. Lobeck's Husband"; Senator C. J. Gunderson, who was not a Prohibitionist but was all for Women's Suffrage, he said; and Carl A. Wold, editor of the *Park Region Echo*. The last speaker, however, was a woman, Mrs. Eva Wold.

Women's Suffrage and anti-liquor efforts were the main emphases during the convention – especially Women's Suffrage. Women were beginning to feel that suffrage should be accomplished first so that they would have the vote when the Prohibition issue would come up for a vote.

The convention was a success. The women were inspired and eager to go on with their cause.

> A large number of delegates returned on the early morning trains Saturday morning. ... The railroad company was not prepared for so many. ... Some were compelled to stand until they reached St. Cloud where another coach was secured. But during this time, the conductor and train auditor were well decorated with white ribbons and "Vote for Women" pins. They also tried to capture the brakeman but he escaped.[231]

Back L-R: Torarin, E.E. holding Genevieve, Martha, Evangeline, Constance, and Dagny in front

Chapter 11

State Senator

On the last day of 1913, E.E. threw his hat in the ring for senator in the
Minnesota legislature. He had been urged for quite some time to do so
but had refused until Senator Gunderson decided if he would run. As
soon as Lobeck heard Gunderson would not run, he immediately filed.

A first order of business in 1914 was the city election in March. The day
before, the Alexandria WCTU organized a children's parade of 400-500
schoolchildren marching for Temperance. Decked out with tags "Vote
Dry for My Sake," and flags and banners, they marched, led by members
of the White Ribbon Committee, color bearers with "Uncle Sam," and a
band. For a finale they gathered in the 6th Avenue and Main Street
intersection, singing "America" and "Alexandria is Going Dry."[232]

Alexandria voted "wet."

The three oldest Lobeck girls – Evangeline, Dagny, and Constance –
were now involved with Temperance work through the WCTU. The two
oldest were in high school, their brother Torarin in eighth grade,
Constance in sixth grade. Genevieve was in third grade and Martha was
five months pregnant. At WCTU and YPB (Young People's Branch)
meetings the girls often participated in the programs. Eva and Constance
played the piano; Dagny gave recitations. The YPB meetings sometimes
drew 40-50 attendees, especially when they finished up with ice cream
and cake and a lively game of charades. Eva was elected vice president;
cousin, Alice Daly, treasurer; Dagny, a delegate to the WCTU district
convention and the executive committee.

May 26, 1914, Martha Aagot, destined to be called Baby most of her
early childhood, was born. Mama Martha was one month short of her

fortieth birthday; E.E. was nearly fifty. The older children ranged in age from seventeen to eight.

Moving kept the whole family busy when, in mid-June, E.E. bought the old house at 527 West 7th Avenue on a hill overlooking Lake Winona. It was purchased for $3,700 [$110,000 today. E.E. took out a mortgage for $3,500 [$104,000].

This seems to pinpoint the beginning of money problems.

It was a lovely home – large bay windows in the spacious dining room overlooking the lake; library for Papa and all his books; front parlor; inviting, open front porch spanning the width of the house. The back door opened into the kitchen. Steep steps led up to four bedrooms on the second story, two quite large with creaky floors and a low door opening into E.E. and Martha's bedroom. One other very tiny bedroom served to accommodate Uncle Ola and young Torarin. Another tiny bedroom was used for company.

A white ribbon on the youngest Lobeck

The annual District WCTU convention – with all the Lobeck women in attendance, even Baby Martha – was held in Nelson at the new YPB building. Martha was re-elected district president and "a very touching service was conducted when Mrs. Scovell tied the white ribbon on the wrist of Mrs. Lobeck's two-month-old baby and dedicated it to the Prohibition cause."[233]

The issues of dancing and Sunday baseball went hand in hand with the WCTU's advocacy of banning alcohol. In their view, dancing and Sunday baseball were frivolous activities – noisy, subject to vices, and against God's commandments. The *Park Region Echo* refused to publish notices or announcements of such activities, and Wold condemned the other local papers that did.[234]

Protection of Sunday was state policy. The register of state laws for 1909 includes the following, much of which had been in place for decades:

All hunting, shooting, fishing, playing, horse racing, gaming and other public sports, exercises, and shows; all noises disturbing the peace of the day; all trades, manufactures, and mechanical employments, except works of necessity performed in an orderly manner so as not to interfere with the repose and religious liberty of the community; all public selling or offering for sale of property, and all other labor except works of necessity and charity are prohibited on the Sabbath day: Provided, that meals to be served upon the premises or elsewhere by caterers, prepared tobacco in places other than where intoxicating liquors are kept for sale, fruits, confectionery, newspapers, drugs, medicines, and surgical appliances may be sold in a quiet and orderly manner. In works of necessity or charity is included whatever is needful during the day for good order, health or comfort of the community; but keeping open a barber shop or shaving and hair cutting shall not be deemed works of necessity or charity, and nothing in this section shall be construed to permit the selling of uncooked meats, groceries, clothing, boots, or shoes.

But that was not all. The register continues, with an exception that Rep. Lobeck had vigorously opposed:

Provided, however, that the game of base ball when conducted in a quiet and orderly manner so as not to interfere with the peace, repose and comfort of the community, may be played between the hours of one p.m. and six p.m. on the Sabbath day.[235]

At the first Sunday game after the law was changed, between the St. Paul Saints and the Minneapolis Millers, there was "an outpouring of fans that swamped the facilities of the park and cut down the playing area by almost half. The grandstands and bleachers were packed literally and the overflow completely circled the field 10 rows deep."[236]

The Prohibitionists continued to rail against these activities. E.E. strongly believed doing any of them, including card playing, noisy games, picture shows, etc., was against God's word, particularly on a Sunday which was a "day of rest." Though the children didn't like it, they mostly obeyed, and when grown and married, attempted to impose some of the same rules into the next generation. The world had changed. The effort was largely unsuccessful.

Mrs. Wold sounded off her opinions in a lengthy *Park Region Echo* article concerning the WCTU. She declared that five women, one of them the wife of Mr. Kinney who was editor of a rival newspaper in Alexandria, were attempting to upend the progress of the WCTU union. The issues were mostly small matters but – as is the nature of "small" matters in such circumstances – served to cause dissension. "It is our opinion that these five would not be behaving themselves as they are if it were not for the political bosses working through them to break up the union for fear the union might make itself a force in Mr. Wold's election and we think equally as much, Mr. Lobeck's this fall."[237]

By September the newspaper, which usually carried only local and Temperance news, expanded to carry news of war in Europe. The war caused growing anxiety among immigrants who had family in Europe. One local resident, returning from a visit to Norway, had a difficult time securing passage home. Though she sailed on the Norwegian-American Line, the ship crept along a different route for fear of mines in the sea. She feared for Norway because it largely depended on imports, unable to be self-sufficient.[238]

"*Genevieve døde igår kveld,*" stated the letter to Inger Nordby, dated October 5, 1914. Eight-year-old Genevieve was taken ill with appendicitis in early September. The appendix ruptured, and she had an operation on September 10. At first there was improvement, but peritonitis set in. With no antibiotics, little Genevieve suffered a painful death. Her sister, ten-year-old Constance, talked in later years about going to the hospital to visit her little sister, her best playmate. "The smell was gagging," she said, "from the peritonitis."

Genevieve had an "exceptionally sweet disposition," a "happy smile sending a ray of sunshine." She was a very bright little girl who frequently participated in Sunday School programs with solos or playing a part. Several of her playmates were pallbearers and flower girls.

A month later, E.E. won his election for state senator by 339 votes (2,755 vs. 2,416). Carl Wold was elected state representative by 287 votes (1,514 vs. 1,287).

E.E. left for St. Paul on Monday, January 4, 1915, to take up his duties in the Senate.

The Lobeck-Anderson Bill

The year got off to a quick start. The state Prohibition Banquet in St. Paul on January 12 drew 500 strong Prohibitionists from throughout the state, all desiring the legislature to support statewide Prohibition.

Sen. Lobeck and Rep. A. V. Anderson from Goodhue County wasted no time in proposing statutory statewide Prohibition in late January: "A bill for an act to prohibit the manufacture, sale, barter, gift or transportation of alcoholic liquors for beverage purposes, within the state and providing for the enforcement of the provisions of this act."

The Lobeck-Anderson bill called for implementation by January 1, 1916.[239]

The *Minneapolis Journal* stated the bill was the "product of an enthusiast, and it exhibits the sincerity and the limitations that usually mark the work of one who is pre-possessed with arbitrary opinions." The newspaper opined that being so "radical" would do the cause more harm than good, as it would "arouse antagonism to the Temperance movement." Lobeck fired off a sarcastic retort to the *Journal*, which they didn't publish, but the *Park Region Echo* did.[240]

According to the *Echo*, members of both houses of the legislature now began receiving messages from their constituents urging them to vote for the Lobeck-Anderson bill. Petitions were circulated to urge passage. The thought was that if the Lobeck-Anderson bill was supported it might pull through. If not, it might pave the way for County Option. The prospect of statewide Prohibition before their eyes created even more enthusiasm. Even the liquor interests, fearing passage of statewide Prohibition, were now advocating County Option because it was the lesser evil for them.

On February 4 the County Option bill came up in the Senate. The Local Option law that was in effect meant that only voters within city limits had a voice in the matter. County Option would give farmers a voice as well. The debate over County Option in the Senate was lengthy and thorough. Having passed 36-31 in the Senate, the bill was sent to the House on February 24. The gallery was packed. Opponents relentlessly tried to kill it by requesting recesses, leaving because they were hungry, or when that didn't work, putting forth various amendments. In the end the bill passed in the House 66-62 on February 25.[241]

> This measure, now the law of the State, provides that when a petition, signed by twenty-five per cent of the voters of a county, based on the number of votes cast for governor at the previous election, is presented to the county auditor asking for a special election to vote on the liquor question, the Auditor is required to issue an order for the election which must take place on a Tuesday not less than forty days or more than fifty days after the filing of the petition. The question to be voted upon is "Shall the sale of liquor be prohibited?" If the majority vote "yes," then the county goes "dry." No more saloon licenses may be issued and every saloon in the county must close up within six months. If the county goes "wet," then the present local option law remains in force and each city or

village may license saloons or not according as the people wish. In either case the question may not be submitted to the county again for three years. This is the first radical measure aimed at the liquor business in Minnesota which has passed the legislature since the high license law was enacted more than a quarter of a century ago.[242]

Next came the debate on statewide Prohibition. The Lobeck bill came up in the Senate on March 11. Statutory did not seem to be the best option, since the current legislature could pass it and the next legislature could repeal it, constantly pitting the "wets" and "drys" against each other, but the advantage of the bill would be its having almost instant results. When Lobeck's bill came up for a vote, only 17 voted for it and some of those only voted because they had high regard for Lobeck. Most opponents deemed the bill too radical.

A constitutional amendment on Prohibition would mean submitting the question to a vote by the people in the next election, November 1916. It did not pass in the legislature.

County Option and Women's Suffrage

In the March Alexandria city elections, the town had just voted "wet" again.

The WCTU women were emphasizing the issue of Women's Suffrage, and the legislature took up the discussion of the proposed amendment on March 4. The anti-suffragists had been out in full force. Even a group of women <u>against</u> suffrage made the outrageous claim that most Minneapolis women, 90 percent of them, did not want the vote. (It was later found that wealthy men were the "women" against suffrage.) The anti-suffragists in the legislature, all of them, of course, men, brought forth their usual arguments that giving the vote to women would undermine the family and destroy the social unit. "If women want or need anything, let them come to us (the men)." Lobeck voted for Women's Suffrage. In the Senate the issue lost by one vote.[243]

E.E. was officially designated as the campaign speaker for Douglas County during the County Option campaign. Besides his lecture, he showed stereopticon slides, and all were encouraged to engage him at any and all occasions, no admission charge. A free-will collection at the close of the meeting helped to pay expenses. He drew large crowds "in spite of very disagreeable weather and roads almost impassable." Enthusiasm was evident when people slogged through mud to go to a Temperance lecture. Every Sunday he spoke in two or three places around the county, covering it all.[244]

The *Echo* announced in its June 3 issue that Douglas County had voted "dry."

The County Option issue settled, E.E. left for the Canadian provinces to assist in their Temperance campaign. He was gone five weeks. In letters home he tells of such great interest that the people stomped their feet while clapping and screaming. He credited the papers with saying that he delivered the most logical and objective speeches on behalf of Temperance. The rigors of travel, however, were not always so wonderful. "The travel has been demanding and tiring, especially last week. Three days in a row I was in a buggy, sitting there nearly 12 hours. In between I had meetings."[245]

He was a happy man on July 22 when he telegrammed Martha, from Calgary, that Alberta province had gone "dry" by an overwhelming majority.

The WCTU and the Douglas County Law and Temperance League planned a countywide Rally Day on October 26, right before the elections, to promote the issue of statewide Prohibition. All churches and Temperance groups throughout the county were strongly encouraged to participate. Most did.

Newspaper battle

Beginning in late September and until the elections, the *Park Region Echo* and the *Alexandria Citizen* were in battle. In the October 7 issue of the *Citizen*, editor Kinney wrote:

> Has it ever dawned upon the unsuspecting readers of the *Echo* that Mr. Lobeck and Mr. Wold are the only men that have represented the people of Douglas County in the Senate and the House who have increased their bank account?[246]

The implications were clear. Wold and Lobeck were being accused of bribery as members of the legislature. The *Citizen* was using the political trick of planting seeds of doubt in minds of the voters just before the elections. Wold and Lobeck denied such, and demanded that the *Citizen* show evidence of the accusations, but Kinney continued his attacks. Wold then described the expenditures of the County Option campaign.

Lobeck, as the appointed campaign speaker for the county, only charged $5 [$150] per evening as opposed to other speakers who charged $10-$25 [$300-$750] per lecture; Wold, as head of the *Echo*, provided much of the printing at no charge. Wold stated that the entire campaign in Douglas County cost the people $200 [$6,000], significantly less than most other counties.[247]

Wold had further words in Lobeck's defense:

> Mr. Kinney appears to continue to find fault with Lobeck for asking a fair wage for services during the recent County Option campaign. ... Lecturing for Prohibition is Mr. Lobeck's business. It is his duty to provide for his family and he is entitled to a fair wage. If the people of Douglas County did not want to pay him this they would not have invited him to lecture and campaign for the cause, and contributed for the purpose of paying towards this salary. ...Would Mr. Kinney ... put in a month's time without pay ... ?[248]

It was later determined that someone on Kinney's staff had obtained mortgage records concerning Wold, "from one of the few men who have access to the records in a professional capacity." Kinney picked and chose the facts that cast suspicion on Wold and published them. Of course, this made public knowledge of the financial affairs of every person with whom Wold had done business. Wold was furious. He met with all with whom he had had business dealings and everyone agreed that since their names had been brought into the controversy, Wold had to publish the full story in detail.[249]

The *Echo* had been running a contest for several months during the summer to get new subscribers. Wold stated the contest was being handled by an outside manager located out of state who specialized in managing contests. The prizes consisted of a new Ford automobile as grand prize, a piano or jewelry as lesser prizes. The contest realized enough success in new subscribers that the *Echo* was able to purchase a new linotype machine, the only one in Douglas County.[250]

The struggle goes on

E.E. still believed a statutory Prohibition law would be best until the constitution could be amended. He relates the struggle.

> There was to be a wrestle with Belial [the Devil] in Hennepin County.

The preparations were finished, and 12th September it all started for real. Broad shouldered and big bellied King Alcohol has rolled around in Minneapolis for many, many years; but now there was to be a battle – and so it did for real. All church societies joined the fight, with the exception of the German-Lutheran. I am sorry to say that that society, when it comes to drinking, is even behind the Catholics. All Temperance organizations joined ranks. Here now stood a united army, and speeches were held in churches, halls, and out on the street corners. The culmination point was reached in the Armory building Saturday evening the 3rd October. There you found excitement aplenty.

Long before 8 o'clock the people started gathering. Along Washington and Hennepin thousands of people stood waiting for the parade. And there it came, with ringing music and waving banners. Spite was thrown against the marching column, and songs were given in answer. The mob swore, but those participating in the parade just ignored it. So does everyone who has a great cause to fight for.

At half past eight the first banners wafted in through the doors of the Armory. The music band was playing. The assembly rose up and received the parade with high shouts and "a great din of battle." One by one the participants – from churches and organizations – a wonderful sight – came in, each carrying its banner. Ex-governor Van Sant jumped around like a boy in his joy over this glory. Then came the Augsburgers [teachers and students of Augsburg Seminary] holding their heads high under their banners. They carried the names of the "dry" counties, and came in, singing the National Hymn.

Van Sant tried to assist with good advice, but soon became hoarse, and after that he mainly used his arms, while the people slowly entered like a mighty stream.

But am I seeing ghosts – through the door comes a band of Vikings under a great banner, upon which is written: "Viking blood fighting drink." Halberds, spears, and axes are held high, and shiny helmets blinked in the light. They made their way through the crowd and up on the platform, and to the cheering of thousands they first sang "Du gamla, du fria, du fjällhöga Nord,"[251] and then "My country 'tis of Thee."

The mighty building was now filled to the brim, and the speeches began. Van Sant was president, and on the platform were some 20 people of various political importance. Van Sant let the crowd know that that night he was the happiest man in Minneapolis.

Who should not feel happy? Here was nourishment for a long time. One stood like in a great embrace – a warmth of the soul and heart that seemed to build a bridge between Heaven and Earth. A holy zeal shone from thousands of faces, so it warmed a supporter to his soul. Stafford was the first to be called, but no one heard him. This was no occasion for narrow-chested people, if they wanted to be heard. One had to fill one's lungs with air and then shout with all one's might.

Excitement shone in thousands of eyes, and the crowd raised their banners and shouted when the speakers did their things well.

The Norwegians seemed to have the best lungs and the strongest voices. …

The Norwegians were fully on level with the great American speakers, including the famous Catholic prelate Cleary.[252]

Pastor Sumstad of the Norwegian Synod worked like an electric battery. Every nerve was agitated and he made a very good speech. Senator Sageng has always something good to say, as he never brings grain unless it's well grinded.[253]

Senator Lende, too, lays a burning heart on his tongue, when he makes speeches.[254] Doctor Frank Nelson made a very beautiful, stirring speech.

Dr. Bushwell and a couple of others, whose names I have now forgotten, really took on King Bacchus.

The crowd cheered, and strong yearnings were lifted in songs.

Such a meeting will be remembered for a long, long time. To me it was like a blessing to participate.

Then election day came, and we lost terribly, but the Liqueur Demon shall know this: The war is not over – and still are not all Joms-Vikings dead.[255] What we now should aim at is State Prohibition – go the straightest way to the goal – make the legislature pass a law, prohibiting sale, production, and import of intoxicating drinks.

As the case stands now, and after the lesson we got in Hennepin, it will be a waste both of time and human lives to wait for a constitutional amendment to be passed.

We have dried up some forty counties, and the total majority is a little over 20,000. We will not be able to dry up very many more through County Option. Take a look at the position! Minneapolis and Hennepin gave a majority of 9,500 in favor of the saloons – St. Paul will roll up 15,000. Then we have Duluth, Winona, and St. Cloud. Then we have counties like Straus, Carver, Brown, Rice, Dakota, Winona, Waseca and others with a powerful majority for the saloons. How shall we be able to have an amendment passed? The salvation of Minnesota lies in electing a legislature that will pass a statutory Prohibition Law. Right now I can see no other solution. Let the legislature give us such a law first, and if it will, let it also pass a proposal for a constitutional change and present that to the people, then we have this to fall back upon. With united effort this will succeed.[256]

E.E. was engaged for another five-week speaking tour in Canada and arrived home the first Saturday in December. The following day was delegated Constitutional Prohibition Sunday by the WCTU, a day to call the issue to public attention all over the state. The WCTU had requested pastors of all churches throughout the state to use the theme "Constitutional Prohibition for Minnesota" for their sermons.[257]

All in all, 1915 had been a good year for the Temperance cause. They gained more ground than they had done in years. The ball was rolling, but big struggles lay yet ahead.

Chapter 12

War and Congress

Every day brought the war in Europe increasingly into the consciousness of every citizen. The *Echo* had been dedicating one full page in nearly every issue all year to "Notes from the Fatherland" – and articles printed in German Gothic script. The Lusitania was torpedoed and sank on May 7, 1915.

Christmas 1915

Will we this Christmas be free to sing: "Peace on Earth"?
Will we feel free to preach, "pleasure" to one and each?
Now that thousands are killed with bayonet and dagger,
And the spear drinks heart-blood all the way up to its case,
Whilst millions are torn up under the thunder of bombs.
All over Europe the field gun's rumble roars –
What a scene of horror is displayed to you this Christmas, O Son of God!

The fire and sparkling of grenades spread death and pain,
Indescribable agony and bitter loss:
On battlefields strewn with corpses wolves howl and ravens cry.
In the turmoil of battle, Oh Christ, your name is forgotten by all.
Men's hatred blossoms like fire in everyone's heart.
To this hard and blinded mankind
Oh God, in your mercy let thine Angels of Peace descend!

On every hill, every mound cannons are positioned.
Like wide open devil's mouths they spew fire and death.
With the blood of young lads they paint the field crimson red:
Pain, madness, and sorrow is spread, heartsickness and hardships,
Where the filthy, inhuman drama of war is played.

Can you now, White Christ, let your peace
To this bloody and pain-ridden earth descend?[258]

Thursday, December 29, E.E. and I. M. Kalnes boarded the train to Chicago to attend a conference of Prohibitionists. "Leaders from all parts of the country were in attendance and preparations for a national campaign begun."[259]

In early January 1916 E.E. returned from Chicago, quite enthused about the conference. Prohibitionists were pulling together from all over the country. A scant four days at home with the family and he was off again, planning to be away for quite some time, speaking throughout northern Minnesota.

Martha received word that her brother, Torgal Nordby, long suffering from tuberculosis, was now failing quickly. Ten days later, Torgal died, and Martha summoned E.E. home for the funeral. E.E. was not feeling well himself. With severe pain in his leg, he consulted a doctor who diagnosed varicose veins and sent him home to rest and, presumably, elevate his legs. The pain was so severe, he canceled all of his lecture tour. He was advised to "securely bandage the limb the remainder of his life." He was unable to walk for a couple of weeks.[260]

E.E. had advocated strongly for statewide Prohibition, since he did not believe County Option would suffice, especially after the defeat of County Option in Hennepin County, home of the state's largest city, Minneapolis.

> There has long been a feeling that the Minneapolis, St. Paul, and Duluth brewers controlled the County Option situation from its inception, with the idea of promoting their personal interests and securing a practical monopoly of the liquor business of the state. The big victory in Hennepin County is still further evidence of the power of the big brewers in the state.[261]

Proponents of statewide Prohibition argued that County Option may have chased saloons out of the "dry" counties, but the saloon owners then moved to the larger cities in "wet" counties. "The twin cities have become a Mecca for the undesirables from all over the state, and a wave of crime is resulting."[262]

There was some truth in this argument. Years earlier, the Scandinavians and Germans in Grand Forks County, North Dakota had voted "dry."

This was not because they themselves objected to drinking, but they didn't want their hired hands to imbibe. Immediately the saloon owners and bartenders moved across the river to East Grand Forks, Minnesota, and opened up their shops. East Grand Forks became a "'boomtown" financially, but brought consequent ill fame to the town with its houses of prostitution and crime.[263] The only answer as the pro-statewide Prohibitionists saw it was to have the whole state go "dry" as a next step toward all out Prohibition.

A major flaw in the County Option issue was the opportunity to throw over the "wet" or "dry" outcome in the yearly elections. Late January, Hans Birkhoefer, a Douglas County brewer, filed for Wold's seat in the Minnesota legislature. Wold had already filed and was confident of re-election, but Birkhoefer's entry promised to make it quite a fight.[264]

"Do you want war?"

Carl Wold ran an anti-war, isolationist article by a friend of his, entitled "Do You Want War?" The article was originally published in a socialist magazine and reflected the thoughts of Wold – and, apparently, Lobeck – against the war and those – the rich men – who favored it. Wold continued to print columns about Germany, in both German and English.

"In the Fatherland," written by a Mrs. Hall of Minneapolis, who had lived in Berlin for three years, stated that life in Berlin was running along normally, the theaters and operas, ample food. Only the sight of an occasional wounded soldier reminded her there was a war going on. Mrs. Hall was impressed with the "sincerity of the Germans in their cause."[265] But negative feelings were growing, and pressure was brought to bear on "hyphenated" Americans. The Scandinavian-Americans and the German-Americans, especially, were hassled to show their allegiance and loyalty to the United States. Many churches began having worship in English.

Children at school were punished if they spoke their native tongue, even at recess. Many ethnic organizations were careful to sing "America" and pledge allegiance to the flag, assuring others that they were American. Most recent immigrants agreed with President Wilson and favored "Isolationism." Yet the newspapers carried news of frequent sinking of ships by German torpedoes, attacks on Paris, and Zeppelins raiding England.

Wold asked the question, "Why was the American press bitterly condemning German militarism? Now the same press is advocating 'Preparedness.'"[266] In a full-page ad bragging about the *Park Region Echo*, Wold stated "his policy is to edit the *Park Region Echo* in harmony with his convictions. He is independent of any combinations or influences outside of what he considers right." He advertised an opening on his staff and wished to hire a German-speaking young man as stenographer.[267] His liberal views would bring him much trouble as the country gradually moved toward war.

"The Cost of Feather Ornaments" was the title of a "splendid" article read by Mrs. E.E. Lobeck at the WCTU meeting in early February. Adorning women's hats with feathers required nearly five million birds a year to fill the demand. The death of so many birds was a big cost to agriculture and caused difficulty in raising fruit and other crops. "What a price for an ornament."[268] If war were to come, agriculture was needed for the war effort. This was probably an unstated reason for the WCTU's interest in discouraging feather-laden hats. Ladies were also discouraged from the use of artificial flowers on their summer hats because the poor women and children who fashioned them toiled in "disease-infested tenement houses under very bad working conditions."[269]

E.E. was very much in demand as a speaker and had more invitations than he could fulfill. Requests arrived from Michigan, Milwaukee, Chicago, Nebraska, and locally. His schedule was heavy. Winnipeg invited him to speak at a festival there in May.

Running for Congress

Senator E.E. Lobeck filed in late April as a candidate for U.S. Congress for the Seventh Congressional District. (Back in 1898, E.E. had made a run for Congress on the Prohibitionist ticket – and received four percent of the vote. This filing, 18 years later, counts as his first serious attempt.) Since the District was in favor of Prohibition, success was possible, even probable. His "great abilities and wide popularity" were in his favor.[270] His opponent, Republican A. J. Volstead (of Norwegian ancestry), who had held the seat since 1903, initially thought it would be an easy election, but he was now worried.[271] A week later, W. G. Calderwood filed as Prohibitionist candidate for U.S. Senator representing Minnesota.[272]

Late spring and summer were full of celebrations.

E.E. went to Winnipeg to speak at May 17th (Syttende Mai) festivities, returning home in time to speak at Decoration Day ceremonies in Alexandria at the Soldier's Monument, honoring Civil War veterans. He composed a poem for the occasion; music was composed for it. The newspaper published the words and requested participants to bring their copy and sing along.

America, crown of the lands,
The country of the free;
With fertile valleys, sunlit strands,
With mountain peaks like lifted hands,
To thee, dear country, yes to thee
We sing our jubilee.

It took our fathers hundred years
To build this nation strong;
They labored, suffered, shed their tears,
They toiled and prayed, 'twixt hopes and fears.
But now we stand, a mighty throng,
And sing our freedom's song.

We never, never shall forget
How open wounds gushed blood,
How hearts were pierced, how foes were met,
How heroes shed their bloody sweat,
How firm and resolute they stood
And battled for the good.

Now all is calm, a sunny rest
Is reigning o'er the land;
In war and peace we have been blest,
By heavenly grace we stood our test;
And now we pray with lifted hand:
"God save our country grand."

On June 7 and 8 Oscar Lake Church, E.E.'s home congregation in Holmes City township, where he had sung in the choir as a boy and young man, celebrated its 50th Anniversary Jubilee. Former pastors were there. Music was provided by the choir, an orchestra, and the Farwell Cornet Band. A large crowd of nearly 500 gathered – some "autoing" from 60 miles away. There was much renewing of friendships and

The Oscar Lake Church celebration; E.E. and daughters Constance and Dagny circled.

reminiscing about the old days when, as pioneers, they "ventured into the wilderness far from railroads and market places to hew a home from the primeval forests and break the sod of the prairies that had for ages been the stamping ground of the buffalo and the red men." E.E. spoke several times.[273]

There was much activity on the political front.

Wold and Birkhoefer received nominations as candidates for legislature from their own parties in the primaries. Aggressive plans were being laid out for Lobeck's congressional campaign. Anti-Prohibitionists were organizing to repeal County Option.

Excitement was running high for the Prohibition National Convention in St. Paul, July 18-22. Autos were driving overland from as far as Massachusetts and New York, taking two to three weeks for the trip and stopping along the way to hold meetings for the cause.

One of the most elaborate (auto) parades ... will be that of Goodhue County. One string of machines will start from Red Wing, emblazoned with pennants and banners, and another will come from Wanamingo, picking up re-enforcements en route, the two uniting at Hastings and forming a grand procession the rest of the way to St. Paul. They will stop at various places along the road making addresses.[274]

Railroads offered special reduced rates for the convention. Twelve hundred delegates were expected, and thousands of visitors.[275] Martha attended as an interested onlooker. Eva Wold attended the male-dominated convention as a delegate chosen by the male voters of the Seventh Congressional District, and served on the credentials committee.[276] The National Prohibition Party had the Women's Suffrage plank in its platform, and displayed its belief in women's right to vote by choosing a female delegate.

Main planks in the National Prohibition platform included Prohibition and Women's Suffrage. A third, "peace and preparedness," was defined as opposition to militarism, promotion of a world court, support of army and navy coast defenses (isolationism), and opposition both to private profits in manufacture of war equipment and to "universal military service and participation in the rivalry that has brought Europe to the shambles."[277]

E.E. and Martha autoed over to the Willmar Prohibition Committee headquarters in early August to map out the campaign. Plans included organizing strong committees in each of the Seventh Congressional District's fourteen counties; an auto tour by Lobeck to every town and village at least once, and many of them twice; picnics in each county and rural district.

Speakers at the picnics, besides Lobeck, would include I. M. Kalnes, Lobeck's campaign manager and chairman of the committee; W. G. Calderwood, Prohibition candidate for U.S. Senate; and others. Posters and announcements covered the windows, posts, and trees throughout the district. Campaign lapel buttons were available at the *Echo* and other places. The National Prohibition Committee selected this campaign as one of three nationally on which to concentrate their efforts.[278]

The *Willmar Tribute* offered a rebuttal to a *Dawson Sentinel* endorsement of Volstead.

Where the fight was the thickest during the past twenty years, there was Lobeck. In season and out of season he has stood unflinchingly on the battle line. ... He has made good in the State House of Representatives and in the state Senate. He is the apostle of clean government in western Minnesota. He is in close sympathy with the demands of the common people and has the ability and force to speak for them.[279]

Andrew Volstead

Newspapers in the district touted Lobeck as a strong candidate against Volstead, the quieter, reserved, non-Prohibitionist incumbent. Nevertheless, Volstead was described as a man who "had his ear to the ground and voted so as not to offend his district."[280] He had been in Congress for fourteen years and had never really had to campaign.

With Lobeck as his opponent, that changed. Volstead was forced to wage a campaign. At one picnic event the reporter for the Willmar newspaper commented, "The congressman [Volstead] spent nearly all his time with a select local committee of so called local leaders, seldom shaking hands with any of the hoi polloi, while the senator [Lobeck] seemed to be just as well pleased to meet a farmer or a day laborer as the president of the First National [Bank]."[281]

In late August E.E. autoed to Lac qui Parle County to speak at three picnics. People came from over a hundred miles to attend. Over the three meetings the estimated crowd totaled more than 4,000. Lobeck returned again in mid-October to the Lac qui Parle County Fair, where he shared the stage with Volstead. It was Pioneer Day at the fair. Lobeck held the audience in his hand with stories of his pioneer days.

> We knew of no such luxury as underwear in those early days, and if anyone of you would like to know how nice and cool a pair of overalls are in the winter without any underwear, just try the experiment and test the whistling breeze of a nor'wester when it is about 30 degrees below zero.[282]

On the final day the folks from Dawson pinned a badge on him and stated Lobeck would get almost a solid vote in Dawson.

At the Big Stone County Fair, again the people responded warmly. After speaking at the fairgrounds, E.E. was approached by members of a rural community about fifteen miles farther west. They asked him to come and speak there in the evening. When the campaign group arrived, they were greeted with a crowded house and everyone there declared they would vote for Lobeck.[283] With so much positive reinforcement, an election win for Lobeck seemed plausible.

The Nonpartisan League

The Nonpartisan League (NPL) began organizing in Douglas County in late summer 1916. NPL was a farmers' movement that began in North Dakota in 1915, brainchild of A.C. Townley, an avowed Socialist, brilliant organizer, and frustrated farmer who was in debt because of bad weather and middlemen at the grain elevator.

A.C. Townley

A 1901 graduate of Alexandria High School, Townley had gone to Beach, North Dakota, to farm with his brother. A few years later he had become very successful and expanded his acreage, purchased more machinery, and stood to make $100,000 [$3,000,000] on his crop in 1912. Early frost and unprecedented snowstorms changed everything. The market fell and he was left bankrupt, owing $80,000 [$2,450,000].

In 1914 he ran unsuccessfully, as candidate of the Socialist Party of North Dakota, for the state legislature. Not one to give up, Townley came up with a plan to organize farmers, whom he saw exploited by middlemen in the grain elevator, packinghouse, stockyard, and cold storage industries. In 1915 he crisscrossed the state, signing up farmers in what he called the Nonpartisan League. Though decried as socialist from its inception, the League actually rejected the third-party approach, choosing instead to endorse whichever candidates pledged to support their program.[284] Townley's plan also included NPL banks that would extend loans to farmers at cost.[285]

The League's success in North Dakota was astounding; its candidate, Lynn Frazier, would become governor in the 1916 election.

Word about the NPL spread quickly in Minnesota. The farmers in the Seventh District became interested in the League's plan and joined up. Four hundred farmers attended the meeting in Carlos. Before long, the names of Holmes City farmers – including Lobeck and Wold – appeared on the membership list. The consequences for E.E. would eventually become momentous.

Volstead beats Lobeck

E.E. headed north in late September under the auspices of the
Saskatchewan Scandinavian Total Abstinence Association.[286] The
previous year the province had gone "dry" under statutory law, but now
they were in the process of ratifying it by popular vote. He returned to
Saskatchewan again in November and campaigned for them until the
election in early December. The liquor stores there were voted out by an
overwhelming majority.[287] Several provinces had now gone dry, and E.E.
saw clearly the necessity of statewide and national Prohibition at home.

Senator Knute Nelson and Volstead toured the Seventh District together
to stir up votes. Lobeck had carried Nelson's home territory in previous
elections. The WCTU organized a Temperance Day in the Alexandria
Public Schools the day before the election. Lobeck spoke to the students
about obedience and forming good habits. Supposedly the students
would help sway their fathers' votes.

Come Election Day, the range of parties on various ballots was broad:
Republican, Democrat, Socialist, Prohibitionist, Progressive, Industrial
Labor. Wold lost re-election for the House to Birkhoefer, the brewer.
Volstead beat Lobeck by 9,339 votes, carrying all 14 counties (though
Douglas by only 85). Lobeck kept his Minnesota Senate seat (the 1914
election had been for a four-year term). Birkhoefer went to the Minnesota
House as a representative of the totally "dry" county in a "dry" district.
The *Echo* added: "A few for spite and jealousy were willing to disgrace the
whole county by sending a brewer down to represent it rather than have
Mr. Wold elected. It is the first instance in the state of a brewer
representing any county."[288]

Continuing her Prohibition work, Martha hosted the December WCTU
meeting at their home. Discussions were lively – about Women's Suffrage,
Bibles in the schools, and opposition to carnivals which were a "perfect
nuisance and carry with them all kinds of gambling devices and vice."
Constance played the piano and all the daughters served as hostesses.[289]

1916 ended with brutally cold weather between Christmas and New
Year, dipping to minus-38 degrees and a blizzard impacting church
services and travel.[290]

Passage of the Prohibition Bill

Brutal cold continued well into January 1917. The first week of February
another blizzard, "the worst of the season," slammed down on

Minnesota, swirling snow so one could barely see, stopping traffic and blocking trains, while the legislature took up a Prohibition bill.[291] Despite efforts of the Anti-Saloon League to change wording in the House Constitutional Prohibition bill, the Minnesota House passed it, 86-44, in the form favored by the WCTU.

The Anti-Saloon League asked to eliminate the word "transportation" from the bill. This amendment would permit brewers, distillers, wholesale liquor dealers, and liquor catalogue houses to supply the people of Minnesota liquor for "personal use" and open wide the doors for bootleggers and blind piggers.[292]

A week later the Senate Temperance Committee took up the bill but agreed to amend it to allow breweries and saloons some time before Prohibition would go into effect. Lobeck, still advocating for statutory Prohibition so as to have it immediately, voted against the measure as it stood. He wanted to restore the original wording as received from the House. However, the vote in the Temperance Committee carried for the amendment 5-4.

Here is C. J. Buell's account of what happened next.

> When this bill came up in the Senate Feb. 15th, on Special Order, the "wets" and "drys" had reached a compromise to extend for six months the time before Prohibition should take effect. As a result there was no contest. All the speeches that had been prepared for and against the bill remained undelivered; and the large crowd that had gathered to witness the contest was doomed to a certain degree to disappointment. But to most of them it was a joyous disappointment, for when the vote was taken, without a speech having been made, the drys won by 49 to 16. …

> And so the state wide – Bone dry – amendment to the constitution has passed the ordeal of the legislature by two to one in the House and three to one in the Senate.[293]

Now the vote for Prohibition in Minnesota would be up to the people.

War fever

War in Europe was posing profound political questions. Much discussion revolved around whether Congress should retain the power of declaring war or allow one man, the president, to do it. Wold felt Congress should have the power to declare war as the Constitution stated.

Even more fundamental was the question whether the policy of isolationism should continue, or should war be declared? Both Lobeck and Wold leaned toward peace and isolationism, but events were moving quickly toward war. The WCTU was pressing harder for an amendment to the constitution for Women's Suffrage. There was much talk about patriotism; every organization found reasons to tie their efforts to it.

The wildfire success of the growth of the Nonpartisan League, made up of 20,000 Minnesota farmers so far, marked them as targets. Grain merchants, big businessmen, and Chambers of Commerce perceived them as a huge threat to doing business as usual – which was gouging the farmers. They feared the farmers' votes at the next elections. Thus, they branded the NPL as "disloyal pacifists" and "unpatriotic," and concentrated their efforts to destroy the NPL.

One ploy was to file incorporation papers as the "Minnesota Nonpartisan League," a sham organization to confuse the potential member. They claimed to be advocates on many of the same issues. A. C. Townley quickly got out the word that it was not his organization, and the farmers would know because "the Nonpartisan League that is the farmers' organization is not incorporated in this or any other state. There is no more need to incorporate it than the Republican or Democratic Party. It is not a business institution and not a profit taking one." Townley surmised the Minneapolis Chamber of Commerce was behind the sham organization.[294]

For over a year, propaganda aimed at drumming up pro-war sentiment, much of it by England, had some success in slowly swaying people toward war. As American lives were lost in the sinking of ships by the Germans, the drumming became more intense. It was time for a decision.

The Park Region *Echo* on March 27, 1917, wrote:

> Overt Act Has Surely Come – 3 U.S. Ships Sunk by Germans May Mean Actual War – with Thirty Americans Missing. Unofficial Opinion is that State of War with Germany Exists. – President May Call Congress Immediately – Sending Warships to Clear Sea Lanes of Submarines is Regarded as the Next Move – President Has Power to Treat Attacks as Act of War.

In the April 3 *Echo* Wold announced that even though his German readers had greatly appreciated his columns in the German language, he was discontinuing them because the company who furnished the articles had discontinued them. Though most newspapers were now publishing pro-war material, Wold was not.

On April 6, 1917, President Wilson declared war on Germany.

Meanwhile the Minnesota legislature needed to finish up their business before adjournment in mid-April. The item of statutory Women's Suffrage was "blasted when the Senate, by a vote of 35-31 defeated the Putnam-Sageng bill allowing women to vote for presidential electors." The debate lasted over four hours. Lobeck spoke up in favor and voted for suffrage.[295]

The following week the Senate took up the issue of constitutional Women's Suffrage and defeated it 49-14, even though it had passed the House by a big majority. The women themselves who were ardently working for suffrage decided the amendment should not be submitted because of timing. The Prohibition amendment in the 1918 elections would be so important, and should not be cluttered with the Women's Suffrage amendment at the same time. The women planned to spend their time campaigning for the prohibition constitutional amendment. Lobeck, however, voted to submit the suffrage amendment immediately.[296]

The Minnesota Commission of Public Safety

The Minnesota Commission of Public Safety (MCPS), established by legislative statute four days after the declaration of war, ushered in a dark period in the state's history. The seven-member commission was given "almost dictatorial powers" and, unencumbered by any jurisdiction, stomped freely on civil rights.[297]

"Hyphenated Americans" who spoke in their native tongues – Gerrman-Americans especially – were suspect, as were members of unions, the International Workers of the World, and the Nonpartisan League. Norwegian-Americans, many of whom leaned toward pacifism, were among the suspects. If one was not enthusiastically pro-war, charges of treason or sedition were possible. The MCPS encouraged attendance at "Loyalty" meetings, signing "Loyalty" oaths, and patriotic displays of allegiance.

> While these sovereign powers were in their hands, the safety
> commissioners spent more time defending the existing socioeconomic
> order against a rising tide of radicalism on the prairies and a growing
> labor-union militance in the mines, forests, and working-class wards than
> they did cooperating with the federal mobilization effort. ... The
> commission's top objective – defeating trade unionism and the
> Nonpartisan League.[298]

On April 10 Wold wrote this in his *Echo* editorial, "United States
Declares War on the German Government":

> It is sad to note the bitterness, the hatred, the spite, the vengeance
> displayed on all sides. Madness seems to be in command and anyone who
> dares to express personal views in variance with these elements urging war
> is at once condemned as a traitor – or worse. The attitude of these
> elements, to a large portion of the American people appears undemocratic
> – quite autocratic. Our constitution guarantees the citizens of these
> United States freedom of speech, a free press, and the right to petition.
> But anyone who has ventured to exercise those rights during the past few
> weeks respecting the war propaganda has been vigorously condemned as
> pro-German and even a traitor to his country – the United States.

Mail between the United States and Germany and its allies was
immediately stopped, separating families for the duration of the war.

Military preparations were underway in Alexandria within four days of
the war declaration. A big rally was held on Tuesday evening, April 10, to
send off some of the boys. A parade was organized with veterans of
previous wars (including the Civil War), firemen, bands, and schoolboys.
They marched from the school, down to the depot, and then back to the
high school auditorium that was filled with a large audience to listen to
the speakers. Constant Larson strongly criticized those who do not "agree
with this war scheme and pronounced as 'traitors' all papers that claimed
the moneyed interests of this country had anything to do with bringing
on the war." After the rally, several more young men enlisted.[299]

During the week, dinners and farewell meetings were held. The partings
were sad – young men leaving home, most of them for the first time. All
tried valiantly to keep up their enthusiasm to the last, singing "Rally
Round the Flag, Boys," shouting school yells, and harboring unsaid
thoughts about when or if they would see each other again.[300] The older

Lobeck children watched their classmates leave, and, anxious to be of some help, the girls volunteered to knit socks, roll bandages, and make "comfort bags" for the boys.

Wold had been called names before for his stand on Prohibition and his independent views; Constant Larson was probably directing his "traitor" remark at him. Wold published an article about free speech and free press a couple of weeks later, defending his right to these freedoms, and quoting President Wilson: "I can imagine no greater disservice to the country than to establish a system of censorship that will deny to the people of a free republic like our own their indisputable right to criticize their own public officials."[301]

Though the Wolds and the *Echo* were the target of some disgruntled unknown individuals, the newspaper was the largest and most widely read in the county. However, besides offers of buyouts, boycotts, and criticism, they faced vandalism, threats of tar and feathering – "or even worse" – and a bomb threat.

> One night a home-made bomb was placed in the hall door of our plant and found there when we went to work in the morning. The fuse had been lighted but went out before reaching the powder in the container. Mr. Wold laughed it off, thinking it was a scare-prank, and without opening it ... slipped it under a shelf in the office and forgot about it. When it was found more than a year later, the new manager found enough powder in it to have done much damage.[302]

Blanche Wold, their daughter, and Constance Lobeck were friends. Constance remembered staying one frightful overnight at the Wolds when a mob pelted the house with stones. Friends worried about the Wolds' safety and suggested he keep a gun, to which Wold replied, "If there is going to be any shooting, it will be by the other fellow."[303] He continued to publish what he thought right, including Prohibition, NPL, and war issues. He published notices from the World Peace Association – their creed "forbids its members to participate in war in any form" – and informed his readers of an exemption clause in the War Department Draft bill to claim as a conscientious objector.[304]

Meanwhile the Lobecks kept on with their Prohibition work, as reported in the "Personals" column of the *Echo* throughout May. E.E. was lecturing and Martha was involved with her WCTU work. Both of them performed lead parts at the WCTU special cantata, "The Saving of Daddy," held at the Swedish Lutheran Church in mid-May. At the monthly Mothers meeting, Martha tied the white ribbon on eighteen little ones and made them members of the White Ribbon Recruits.

With the war in progress, the issue of Prohibition was set back. Nationally, Wartime Prohibition was adopted by the Democratic caucus, but the "wets" bolted. Rather than split the party, they adopted the motion that no legislation on the issue would be taken up in the current Congress unless it received recommendation by the president. The administration needed a united party for the war effort and could not risk taking a stand on the Prohibition issue.[305]

In response, the Prohibitionists began to frame their issue as a patriotic war duty because it would save grain needed for food for the young soldiers overseas and for the people at home. It shouldn't be wasted for breweries. Having enough food was a major priority, supported by all political parties, and the farmers were immediately pushed to raise more food as their patriotic duty – even plow up their fence corners for more available space.

The U.S. Senate approved, 38-32, an amendment forbidding the use of cereals or grain in manufacturing intoxicating liquors during the war. Senator Knute Nelson voted against the amendment.[306] The Prohibitionists were quite excited about the amendment, since it gave a big boost to eventual national Prohibition. May 15th, two days later, this clause was thrown out by a vote of 47-37. Nelson again voted against the bill. Wold expressed his disappointment with Nelson's two-facedness. A couple of weeks earlier, Nelson had responded to the local WCTU that he would vote for Prohibition issues whenever they came up, and now he had voted against it when the wets needed his vote.[307]

Wold noted further that "Sen. Nelson also voted for the press censorship clause in the espionage bill which was so drastic as to literally prohibit free speech."[308]

In mid-May Wold defiantly wrote an article in the *Echo*, "Are They Trying to Bluff the Editor?" and declared he would stand by his convictions even though some of the local businessmen had withdrawn their advertising in an effort to "shape the editorial policy of the *Echo*." Wold said his was the biggest paper in the county and the lost advertising

War and Congress

would not hurt him at all.[309] Wold would soon feel the wrath of Senator Nelson, as Lobeck had felt it ever since 1907.

Secretly, Nelson's long arms reached out to the recently established Public Safety Commission, headed by Judge John F. McGee, a Nelson supporter. In a letter to McGee, dated June 7, 1917, Nelson wrote:

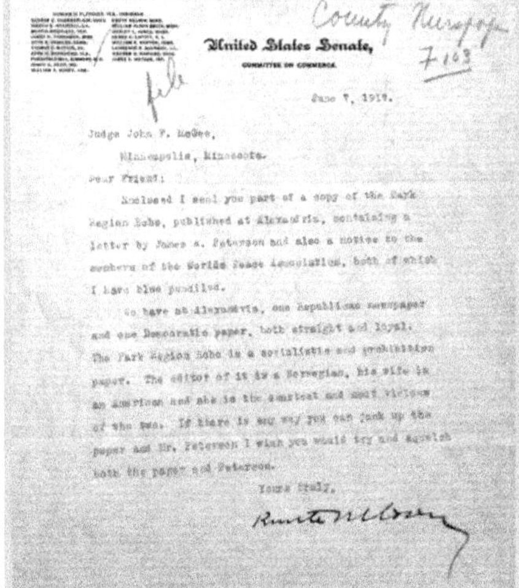

Judge John F. McGee

Minneapolis, Minnesota

Dear Friend,

Enclosed I send you part of a copy of the Park Region *Echo*, published at Alexandria, containing a letter by James A. Peterson and also a notice to the members of the World's Peace Association, both of which I have blue pencilled.

We have here at Alexandria, one Republican newspaper and one Democratic paper, both straight and loyal. The Park Region *Echo* is a socialistic and Prohibition paper. The editor of it is a Norwegian, his wife is an American and she is the smartest and most vicious of the two. If there is any way you can jack up the paper and Mr. Peterson I wish you would try and squelch both the paper and Peterson.

Yours truly,

Knute Nelson[310]

In the May 29 issue of the *Echo*, Wold published an excerpt about war from Mark Twain's "Mysterious Stranger" and an editorial entitled "Why Are We in the European War?" Of course, he had no proof of who was operating behind the scenes, but he likely would have continued publishing his convictions anyway.

During the summer E.E. attended some Nonpartisan League picnics, where he chose to be something of an observer. When asked to speak, he agreed that there were problems for the farmers, but he wanted people to know that he had not voted to create the problems and did not agree with some of the views of the pro-war people.

Throughout August Wold gave considerable space in the *Echo* to the Nonpartisan League, promoting the scheduled NPL Labor Day Rally to be held in Alexandria. A. C. Townley and N. S. Randall of the League would be the main speakers. He sent news releases to the other local papers which barely mentioned it. The editor of the *Post* insinuated that he would make no further announcement because of the *possibility* of promoting anti-draft feeling, making the meeting "undesirable."[311] Wold gave little space to the Loyalty meeting scheduled for August 26 on the courthouse grounds.

Farmers planned to turn out by the thousands on Labor Day, and all town citizens were invited to come. The farmers felt they had shown their patriotic duty and loyalty throughout the summer by raising more food, and were upset that their loyalty should be questioned as members of the NPL, which had been branded "socialistic" and "anti" by businessmen, bankers, and the Public Safety Commission.

The farmers had grown weary of the constant demand to "grow more food" and to "plow up their fence corners" when they had been working to the best of their abilities to do just that. Some of them had sons in the military, which left them short-handed, and the entire family was overworked. The farmers decided to circulate a petition to plow up the golf course and put it into cultivation. It had the desired effect. No more was said.[312]

Eva Wold and Martha Lobeck engaged the WCTU to create large numbers of comfort bags for the soldiers. As mothers they felt it was something important they could do, and it showed loyalty and support. The bags were small enough to carry in a pocket and consisted of bandages, thread, yarn, pins and needles, small scissors – and leaflets on Prohibition, antitobacco, and purity, in addition to the New Testament.[313]

Forces behind the scenes were still trying to shut down Carl Wold and his paper.

Throughout the summer, the Wolds had increasingly been threatened and abusively criticized, followed by the planted bomb that, thankfully, did not explode.

The *Echo* under threat

Another attempt was now made to close down the *Echo* by denying mailing privileges. On August 20 Wold received a notice from the Third Assistant Postmaster General in Washington to give a reason why he should not be denied these privileges. Wold was to give his answer and appear in Washington before the postal department by the 24th.

The Alexandria postmaster had been informed that the *Echo* issues of July 24 and 31 violated a paragraph in the espionage bill. No further explanation was given. Wold, in confusion, went back to the office and looked over the issues in question and could only surmise that his criticisms of Constant Larson's war speech at the Independent Order of Good Templars anniversary picnic in Holmes City in mid-July was the reason.

Larson had lauded the work of the Commission of Public Safety, and then proceeded to condemn anyone who didn't agree with the war party of the United States as "socialists, I.W.W.'s, disbelievers of Christian religion, pro-German, and traitors." Furthermore, he condemned any newspaper that claimed war propaganda is directed from Wall Street, and "the awfulness of men who have been soliciting membership among the farmers of Holmes City for an organization that is bent upon throwing a monkey wrench into our present political and economic machinery. These he declared are socialists, I.W.W.'s and usually against religion." After these direct hits on the NPL and the *Echo*, Larson justified the war with quotations from the Bible. Wold rebutted these items in his coverage of the picnic and used Bible passages as well.[314] Still, Wold was not absolutely clear about why he had been accused of violating his mailing privileges.

Wold hurried to St. Paul and, apparently, engaged someone to speak for him in Washington. In his August 28 editorial Wold reiterated his loyalty to the United States and stated his new policy. He would refrain from expressing personal opinions about the war. He repeated President Wilson's statement about the danger of censorship and thanked his supporters, if this should be his last issue.

September 4, 1917 the *Echo* informed its readers that the postal department would allow second class mailing privileges and the paper could be mailed as usual. So as not to annoy the postal department or government, the new policy was to avoid any discussions of the war and confine itself to matters of the Nonpartisan League.

The well-organized Nonpartisan League Labor Day Rally on September 3 was a huge success. It was expected to begin at 11:00 am. Naysayers looked around town at 10:00 and saw little evidence of any gathering. But between 10:30 and 11:00 Alexandria was literally invaded by farmers. Attendance was estimated at 8,000-12,000, twice as large, at least, as the Loyalty Meeting a week earlier. People arrived from several counties and townships; over a thousand automobiles drove into town.

A theme of patriotism was in the air. Nearly everyone wore a small flag. At noon the festivities began with a parade, led by the NPL banner and a large United States flag. With over 400 automobiles, and marching bands playing, the parade estimated at three miles long wound through the main streets of Alexandria, culminating at the courthouse where the program began.

The first speaker was Mayor Syverud, who welcomed all and stated he was in sympathy with the NPL movement. A specific invitation extended to the Alexandria Commercial Club was turned down. None of the members showed up.

In his speech, Townley repeated that the Nonpartisan League was not a political party and rebutted words of Sen. Nelson that insinuated differently. The lovely weather, positiveness of the day, and the feeling of strength in numbers contributed to the celebration's triumph. Many more farmers signed up for the League in the days following the rally.[315]

The full coverage of the NPL rally angered the gang that hoped to close the *Echo*. Nameless individuals devised another method.

> Thursday morning [September 13] when the editor of the Park Region *Echo* arrived at the *Echo* office he found the door had been forced open. On the floor were scattered bills, receipts, and letters from the *Echo* letter files. Upon investigation he found the filing cabinet had been cleaned out and the contents taken away. Further on he discovered the linotype had been ruined. The delicate mechanism had been wrenched and broken. ... In the other room attempts at demolishing the large press had been made. ... It would appear the intruders had left their work unfinished in this room and hastily departed, leaving one light burning.[316]

The destruction of the linotype was serious, but the situation was made even more critical by rules for mailing privileges. "If we fail to be in the mails at the proper time two issues in succession, we will be denied the second class mailing privilege."[317] The September 18 issue had to be sent to Minneapolis for typesetting because of the linotype loss, and almost was late due to a "mistake or miscarry"; it was not sent out from Minneapolis in time. But Wold used what material he had, printed, and mailed it without up-to-date news because it was imperative to get the next paper out in time.

Wold took the afternoon train to St. Paul to seek out an expert to examine the broken linotype and determine the next step. He also engaged a business to have his typesetting done in Minneapolis until decisions were made about what to do.

The Lobecks and other friends and supporters of the Wolds immediately came to offer support and words of encouragement as well as cash. When a group of supporters, E.E. among them, met at the *Echo* office on Saturday, the decision was made to buy a new linotype. Lobeck and a dozen others donated money that day amounting to $100 [$2,300].

Most likely, the Wolds wondered whether to continue against the constant barrage from opposition. It was obviously dangerous. Moreover, Wold's health was beginning to fail because of cancer. But, overwhelmed by the backing, he wrote: "This is no private matter for the editor. By the action of these men who on Saturday put up the first $100 it has become a public undertaking." And using a phrase from the NPL, he ended, "We'll stick, we shall win."

Re-energized, Wold continued,

> The battle is on. It is a fight to the finish. The *Echo* will be published as usual and continue the same policy as in the past. It shall devote much space to these farmer movements and we hope that the paper may continue to do its bit to secure justice for the masses and help to establish a truer democracy in our country.[318]

The opposition forces had failed again.

The linotype was funded by encouraging his readers to pay up in advance for a four-year subscription, though any donations and subscriptions of any length were welcomed.

Over the next couple of weeks the *Echo* reported the new linotype had been ordered, bigger and better than the destroyed one, the fund was well on its way for the linotype – the $1,000 [$23,000] needed for down payment was in place almost a week before the first payment was due – and the subscriber list had grown by 150.[319]

The October 16 issue happily informed its readers that the new linotype had arrived.

On October 23 the new linotype was installed and the current issue set on it. With freight, other expenses, and the cost of the machine itself, the bill came to $2,100 [$48,000]. Over $1,700 [$39,000] had already been raised, and the last $500 [$11,500] was not due until November 1. There were now over 200 new subscribers. The money (and a little extra) was raised by October 30, in time to make the final payment on November 1.

Quite ill, E.E. arrived home in early December from a lecture tour in the southern part of the state. The cause was not clear, but he had severe, painful attacks which seemed to be in his abdomen. Barely able to eat, he remained bedridden throughout December and was only able to be up a few hours during Christmas.

The Saturday after Christmas, Eva and Carl Wold had put in a busy morning of work at the *Echo* office and donned their warm winter coats for a stroll home to eat dinner at noon. A friend approached as they stepped out the door and joined them in conversation as they walked together up the street. After a short distance a man, Charley Watters, called to Carl to stop and talk to him. The women continued ahead. Watters began talking and then punched Wold in the face. As Wold tried to retreat into a store, Watters jerked Wold back, threw him to the ground, and started pummeling him over the head. Luckily, Wold was dressed in a heavy cap, heavy dogskin coat with collar turned up, and heavy buckskin mittens, and wasn't seriously hurt. The *Alexandria Post News* added this detail to the *Echo* account: "Mr. Watters' action was due to an article in the *Echo* criticizing Frank W. Murphy, president of the 'America First' association and by whom Mr. Watters had been employed as farm foreman for many years."[320]

Fearful of the idea of mob rule taking over, a committee largely comprised of farmers, NPL members, and officers of the Farmers Society of Equity met on December 31 and formed a resolution to support Wold and the paper financially and legally if there were more unfettered violence.[321] They called for law enforcement and decency. Wold gathered the names and addresses of eyewitnesses in preparation for a meeting with the county attorney.

As 1918 began, on January 4 Wold and Joseph Gilbert, the Manager of the National Nonpartisan League, met with County Attorney H. E. Leach. Wold intended to file charges, and have Watters arrested and tried.

Leach, seemingly wanting to downplay the entire incident, responded that conviction was very doubtful, given "existing personal feelings," and he feared the revival of old resentments because of the "peculiar mental temper of people in time of war." Leach's suggestion was that "personal controversies be discontinued." "Again, he added, in respect to punishment of Watters it may be considered he has already suffered enough since he was the worse injured of the two, having badly bruised his hands and broken a finger so he is now wearing a splint and carrying his arm in a sling."[322]

Gilbert agreed to let the matter rest as the NPL was not eager to get into local controversies; the object overall was to prevent and discourage the growth of mob rule.

The *Alexandria Citizen* on January 4, 1918, in an article headlined "Wold is Thrashed," viewed the controversy differently from the *Echo*.

Saturday noon Charles Watters met Carl Wold, editor of the *Echo*, on the street in front of Unumb's store, and gave him a thrashing. The trouble arose over the publication in the *Echo* of an article reflecting on F. W. Murphy, a personal friend of Mr. Watters. [The *Alexandria Post News*, in a similar story on January 3 headlined "The C. A. Wold Affair," noted that Watters had been employed by Murphy for some years as farm foreman.] Mr. Murphy is a well known citizen of Wheaton and is president of the State America First Association.

With his usual cunning and deceit, Wold is now attempting to make capital and create sympathy for himself because he has been chastised. In his issue of January 1 he asks: "The question confronting the people of Douglas County, shall they permit this tendency to mob rule to develop?" We fail to see where the "mob" comes in. Does one man constitute a mob? The fact that Watters alone met Wold and gave him a beating with his bare fists in broad day light, upon the main street of the town, should convince any reasonable man that there was no "mob rule." Any attempt by Wold to create such an impression is rank falsehood. It was simply a personal matter between Watters and Wold and was not any attack on anyone else or any organization or society.

Wold agreed to let matters rest, with the understanding that other local newspapers "cease their personal attacks on Wold, the NPL and League leader, Townley." He, in turn, would not respond with personal replies. It was also to be understood that both sides should be free to discuss the principles involved. If the other papers agreed also to these points, and Leach could guarantee the terms, the matter would rest. If not, the NPL would take up the fight.[323]

Chapter 13:

Nonpartisan League under Siege

The good news in January 1918 was that just a month before, the 18th Amendment, mandating Prohibition, had passed Congress. Success was imminent – the states needed to ratify it, which would happen a year later, on January 16, 1919.

The bad news was that all-out war appeared to be declared on the Nonpartisan League and, apparently, Douglas and Todd counties were identified as the hotbeds of NPL activities by the Minnesota Commission of Public Safety (MCPS).

The same issue of the *Echo* that carried the article describing the meeting results between Wold, Gilbert, and County Attorney Hugh Leach, also carried a lengthy article about the NPL opening their state campaign for Minnesota. The top NPL organizers were in town, among them the aforementioned Gilbert, N .S. Randal, state organizer, and organizers from North Dakota and Wisconsin. The meeting opened with the singing of "America," Evangeline Lobeck at the piano.

Gilbert, mentioning the Wold situation, informed the crowd that he had met with Leach and found him to be a reasonable man. Gilbert had taken Leach at his word that there would be no recurrences. The rest of his speech was devoted to the plight of the farmer at the hands of middlemen and big business.[324]

A week later, in the *Echo* of January 15, a plot to destroy the League was revealed.

A tall tale

League organizer W. E. Quigley from Lincoln, Nebraska, had been approached a couple of months earlier by members of a group of businessmen who desired to see the NPL destroyed. The group wanted Quigley, for pay, to act as a spy and furnish them with "secrets." They hoped to tie the League to pro-German activities and money, which would certainly kill the NPL. Additionally, a member confessed to Quigley that it was in the interests of the Republican Party to discredit the League in order to preserve itself. Quigley reported this overture to the NPL national office in St. Paul and was encouraged to play along. He did.

Quigley, a writer, was asked to compose anti-NPL pamphlets. They were published by a member of the group who was publisher of the Grand Forks, North Dakota newspaper. The plan was to make the pamphlet publishing appear self-sustaining in order to conceal the source of the $200 [$3,400] per month which was coming from the Republican Party to pay Quigley. Finally, Quigley saw that his lies to the group were about to expose him, so he concocted a wild tale for them, reported to the NPL in St. Paul, and went back to Lincoln, Nebraska.[325] The *Echo* stated that documents and contracts existed to back up the incident.

Quigley's tall tale went like this.

He said he met a special agent of Townley's, in Lincoln. Since the businessman group was so anxious to tie the NPL to German money, the fictional agent supposedly gave Quigley the fictional story that Townley would receive $20,000 [$340,000] in German money. Quigley called this imaginary agent Ryan.

Helping the invented story along, the supposed Ryan was on his way to New York, got drunk, was arrested in Lincoln, called for Quigley, and gave him an envelope to be posted to a German spy named Burnstein. Quigley continued with the farce, stating he had steamed the envelope open and found an unsecured note by Townley on which the money was to be advanced.

Quigley then suggested that the Secret Service in New York should know these alleged facts. One of the businessmen, Carpenter, deciding it was so important that he would go himself, took off for New York to meet the imaginary Burnstein. Quigley was to go another route and impersonate the imaginary Ryan and catch the imaginary German spy in the act.

Instead, when Carpenter left for New York, Quigley went to St. Paul, told the incident to the national NPL with his documentation and papers, then headed back home to Lincoln.[326]

The MCPS, in an effort to stop the League, was spreading a wide net and using its powers of arrest quite liberally. Joseph Gilbert, national NPL manager, and N. S. Randal were both arrested on the same day with "warrants charging them with discouraging enlistments." The remarks, supposedly made six months earlier, were denied by Gilbert and Randal. Their lawyer, who had recently been arrested himself by the MCPS on rioting charges, which were dismissed in district court, intended to bring charges of perjury against the accuser, a member of the legislature.[327]

The MCPS met all day on February 5 in their chambers in St. Paul, concluding their work at 11:00 p.m. They resolved to have county directors investigate disloyalty charges and report activities of NPL officers in Minnesota. Douglas and Todd counties, especially, were singled out.

Hugh Leach and other Alexandria businessmen, along with Constant Larson, Secretary of the Douglas County MCPS, were also there consulting with the commission. The results of the meeting were not long in showing.

The following morning, February 6, a petition was signed by several Alexandria townspeople to stop a scheduled NPL meeting in Osakis. Leach and some deputy sheriffs left for Osakis to order it stopped. The farmers had their meeting anyway. They got back in their sleighs, crossed the county line into Todd County, and 400 of them had their meeting, standing in the cold in a sympathetic farmer's yard.

It seemed the spectacle would repeat itself the following day in Alexandria. The businessmen had signed another petition to stop the NPL meeting, but Leach declared it could go on as advertised. Rumors had been deliberately spread around town on Wednesday evening and Thursday morning that the NPL meetings scheduled for that afternoon would be stopped, but, despite loud shouting on both sides, the farmers crowded into the Howard Theater until it was filled to capacity. There were no incidents.

With rumors circulating that Leach was ordered by the Public Safety Commission to close the *Echo* office, Wold called up Leach to ask for verification. Leach said it was only a personal matter about Mr. Wold. Probably quite frustrated without any real information, the Wolds met Leach on Friday afternoon and saw a copy of the complaint.

The complaint concerned an editorial, dating back to May 8, 1917. No one had expressed anything publicly about it at the time. This was the very article Knute Nelson had referred to when asking McGee to "squelch" the *Echo*.

Saturday afternoon, February 9, at 5 :00 p.m., Leach phoned the Wolds and told them to come to the office of Joe Prodger, Justice of the Peace. They went immediately and waited for a half hour for the sheriff to show up. Papers were served on the Wolds, they were arrested, and bonds furnished. The complaint was signed by Henry Sherman of LaGrand township, who later served as one of the grand jurors.[328]

Patriotism and the Constitution

Leach, Constant Larson, and other members of the Douglas County MCPS met on February 13 and decided it was their patriotic duty and in the best interest of all to ban Nonpartisan meetings, so as to keep peace, and the people could use all their thoughts and energies to support and win the war. This would effectively shut down the NPL cause, they thought.

Wold and NPL supporters saw it differently. By this act, they were "preventing the local citizens their Constitutional rights of peaceful and free assemblage." The farmers and citizens framed a resolution to demand from the county attorney, the sheriff, and other county officials that their right to free speech and peaceful orderly assemblage be not interfered with or denied.

The sheriff was invited by the NPL to the next meetings, in Nelson and Carlos, so he could report back to the MCPS that nothing libelous, seditious, or treasonable was said. The turnout of farmers continued to swell, seldom fewer than 300-400 each meeting.

The Wold case was tried in early March, drawing reporters from the *Minneapolis Tribune*. The courtroom was packed to the limit with farmers who traveled a long distance, reporters, and interested locals. After a day and night of choosing jurors, the trial was set to begin with attorney Thomas V. Sullivan, legal counsel for the NPL, defending the Wolds. The three attorneys for the state included Hugh Leach.

From the beginning, it seems, the outcome was already decided, but they went through the motions. Nearly all evidence for Wold was thrown out on some technicality. The prosecution focused on the one article from May 8, 1917. Articles in the *Echo*, showing Wold's encouragement for various aspects of the war effort, support for the Red Cross, Liberty Bonds, his loyalty to the U.S. – all these were not admitted as evidence. However, the prosecution used the occasion to grandstand their patriotism, and told stories unrelated to the matter at hand. The state attorney read articles from the *Echo* and put his own interpretation on them.

The trial began on Wednesday morning, March 6. Wold admitted to writing the contested article. Questioned about the *Park Region Echo*, Wold stated it was incorporated and that E.E. Lobeck was nominally the president. However, there had not been a stockholders meeting for the last eight years, and Lobeck had turned his stock over to Wold a year prior, in 1917. Wold declared he, alone, had acted as editor, business manager, and publisher since 1910.

Forcing Lobeck's name into the trial was undoubtedly an effort at "guilt by association." E.E. was a good friend of Wold's and a staunch supporter of the NPL, so Lobeck would be suspect by association with a "criminal" and the NPL. This suggests Knute Nelson's directing the MCPS, since Nelson's feelings against the NPL were well known and, as Lobeck had stated years earlier, he, E.E., was in "Nelson's crosshairs."

The indictment charged the Wolds with "interfering with and discouraging the enlistment of men in the military and naval forces of the United States." It goes on to quote the lengthy passage in the *Echo* that was "wrongfully, unlawfully and feloniously" printed and published. Wold felt the war was really for the moneyed interests and to "overthrow the growing power of labor and farming classes," and "the prejudiced press call these classes socialists when they begin to control politically and instantly issue calls to down the socialistic doctrines same as the Kaiser of Germany." The end results would not be good for the "common people."

Therefore, the indictment continues, the article "advocated and attempted to advocate that men should not enlist in the military or naval forces of the U.S. or Minnesota; and which article and printed matter, then and there did teach and advocate that the citizens of this state should not aid and should not assist the United States in prosecuting and carrying on war with the enemies of the United States."[329]

It seems the MCPS painted with a broad brush and a thin "veneer of legality." Any rhetoric or behavior that did not agree with their pro-war propaganda was subject to the charge of sedition. Many others were arrested during the same period, most with the charge of "discouraging enlistment."

The lawyers made their pleas to the jury that evening. At 10:00 on Thursday morning the case was given to the jury. By 6:00 p.m. the verdict was in. Carl Wold was found guilty. The sentence was a $200 fine [$3,400] and three months in jail. A sick man, Wold was taken to the county jail where he spent two nights until his lawyer went to Fergus Falls and appeared before the judge with a motion for a stay, pending motions for a new trial and appeal to the State Supreme Court.

A sixty-day stay was granted. Wold was released from jail on Saturday with a $1,000 [$17,000] bail furnished by Chas. J. Lindstrom and Robert Peacock.[330] As for Eva, her trial was scheduled for September.[331]

Carl Wold went on editing the paper for a few more months, though barely able to stay up a whole day because of his stomach cancer.[332] The *Post News* and the *Alexandria Citizen* editors continued berating Wold and the NPL with name calling, sarcasm, and undocumented, so-called "fact." "Yellow journalism" widened the wedge of bitterness between people. The newspapers had a heyday calling Wold "disloyal," "criminal," "supporter of the NPL." These newspapers show that Wold attacked issues more than he attacked people, and his writing seems more thoughtful when he lays his conclusions before the people.

Nelson in the background

Knute Nelson looms in the background of this story. He did pull strings, usually secretly. In their book *Norwegian Yankee*, Millard Gieske and Steven Keillor say that "Nelson did not condone vigilante harassment of Wold, but he did nothing to stop it. His harsh attacks on the NPL, Wold, disloyalty, and Copperheads [Democrats] encouraged the 'rough element' to settle local scores violently."[333]

The overt acts against Wold and the *Echo* on a regular basis began after the letter written by Nelson to McGee on June 7, 1917 – the attempted bombing, the attempted denial of mailing privileges (Constant Larson had asked Nelson to intercede with the postmaster in Washington to deny the privileges), attacking Wold physically on the street, breaking into the *Echo* office and destroying files and presses, arresting Wold and putting him on trial. Yes, it is clear that Nelson set things in motion behind the scenes and did nothing to discourage the violent behavior, which is the same as condoning it.

A letter written to Sen. Nelson by one of the disgruntled anti-Wold townspeople in 1918 is revealing. "We still believe we can get him legally, and get him we must for he is a menace to any respectable community. ... The rough element are in for beating them [Wold and his associates] up, decorating them with tar and feathers and chasing them out."[334]

Another letter to Nelson, December 28, 1917, from the America First Association by its secretary, R.W. Hargadine, on letterhead of Northwest Loyalty Meetings with headquarters in St. Paul, demonstrates the quasi-religious, mythical status the senator enjoyed. Hargadine quotes a speech recently given at an America First loyalty drive meeting in Alexandria by prominent economist Henry Jewett Furber Jr., Ph.D.

> In coming to your splendid County Seat, I do so as a pilgrim, visiting a shrine. The foot prints of the great are on your soil; and as from a chalice, I would drink the inspiration of a lofty soul. For I am at the hearthstone of Knute Nelson. I am not a resident of Minnesota, but as one foreign to your noble state, I may perhaps thereby become the humble vicar of the Nation in laying tribute at his feet.[335]

Judge McGee, as head of the MCPS, was determined in his war against the NPL. With the power given to him, his views continued to escalate. The *Echo* described an encounter between McGee and state legislator Magnus Johnson of Litchfield in Gov. Burnquist's office. Antagonism toward McGee and his activities had risen to such a level that a petition was presented to the governor on February 27 to have him removed from his position. Burnquist, McGee, Johnson, and an NPL representative were in the room. Speaking to Johnson, McGee said, "You little scamp, you. You ought to get your head beaten off. If I had known what you were doing that day you read that petition to the governor and if I had had a club I would have beaten your brains out."

The NPL representative responded that it was unbecoming for a public official to use such language, to which McGee responded, "I don't want to hear any lectures from you," adding that the NPL man should be thrown out of the room. Following the incident, the *Echo* reported that three witnesses filed affidavits relating the event with the U.S. District Attorney.[336]

When McGee spoke before the U.S. Senate Military Affairs Committee on April 19, 1918, his rhetoric was over the top.

> [McGee] asserted that Minnesota was rife with disloyalty and sedition, assailed the "traitorous organization worse than the I.W.W." and asserted that "firing squads should get busy in Minnesota and work overtime." Judge McGee declared that the "civil courts are absolutely incompetent," and predicted lynch law and anarchy in this state unless army officers were empowered to try and execute all suspected disloyalists at drum-head court martials. "You can fool a jury, but you can't fool any army officer," declared Judge McGee in his plea to overthrow the constitutional right of trial by jury.[337]

> "A Nonpartisan League lecturer is a traitor every time," said McGee. "In other words, no matter what he says or does, a League worker is a traitor. Where we made a mistake was in not establishing a firing squad in the first days of the war. We should now get busy and have that firing squad working overtime. ... The disloyal element in Minnesota is largely among the German-Swedish people. The nation blundered at the start of the war in not dealing severely with these vipers."[338]

President Wilson chastised McGee's proposal as unconstitutional and "inconsistent with the spirit and practice of America."[339]

The *Nonpartisan Leader* gleefully reported in its issue of April 1, 1918, under the headline "Fake 'Patriots' Are Nailed," that Joseph Chapman, president of the Northwestern National Bank in Minneapolis, and a member of the America First Association, had acknowledged in a recent speech

> that the association was organized to combat the organized farmers, but that the United States government would not lend its aid to the America First association. This is an official statement from a member of the America First association and must be taken as true. The organized farmers are to be congratulated on having a government that will not lend its aid to political moves against the farmers, under the guise of "loyalty." ...

That the federal government appreciates the loyal support of the Nonpartisan league and has not the slightest doubt about the patriotism of its leaders, has just been inadvertently admitted by a bitter opponent of the League, who let the cat out of the bag when he told how the administration refused to lend itself to an attack on the farmers' organization planned and directed by certain big business agents and politicians in Minnesota.

The *Leader* recounts the details. Organizers of an America First loyalty meeting the previous November, designed explicitly to counter the growing Nonpartisan influence, had asked that a member of the president's cabinet come "to lend his presence to the good cause." The response: Yes, if you also allow the Nonpartisan League's founder, A. C. Townley, to speak. Chapman said, "Promoters of the meeting, of course, refused to agree to this arrangement."

Chapter 14

Another Run for Congress

Still not fully recovered but feeling well enough to travel, on March 5, 1918, E.E. was in Chicago to be temporary chairman of the Prohibition Convention. Hence, he was unable to be in Alexandria during Carl Wold's trial.

The Prohibition Party was considering a merger with the newly organized National Party, comprised of Progressives, Prohibitionists, and Socialists "who have bolted the Socialist Party on account of its opposition to the war and extreme socialism."[340]

The Prohibitionists and the National Party met as separate conventions.

E.E. was the featured orator for the Prohibitionists.

> Senator Lobeck's speech was inspiring, delivered in his rich Norwegian accent, in a clear voice. His witty sallies evoked repeated laughter. ... His declaration of patriotism and pledges of loyalty to the nation in time of war was thrilling and brought storms of applause which gave no doubt as to the position of the delegates on this question.

He spoke for thirty-five minutes, encouraging the audience to join the merger for a new, larger party. While Lobeck was selected as one of the advisers for the National Party, the merger vote failed, though a majority voted for it; two-thirds was required.[341]

Meanwhile, efforts to stop the NPL meetings continued. Townley was arrested in late February on false charges of discouraging enlistments. A week prior to his arrest, farmers in Springfield, Minnesota, were forbidden to hold a meeting, and authorities locked the meeting place. The farmers got the keys, unlocked the door, and called for Townley to come and speak. Five hundred farmers attended. A group of antagonists had gathered at the railroad station to prevent Townley from disembarking, but he arrived by automobile, fooling the would-be detainers and holding a very successful meeting.[342]

NPL organizer Joseph Gilbert was arrested without warrant, kidnapped by the sheriff of Martin County, and held in jail in Fairmont for thirty-six hours without his family knowing his whereabouts.

In nearby Glenwood a meeting was stopped. A young dentist in town hired a hall for the meeting. The young man was Henrik Shipstead, who later served as U.S. Senator for twenty-four years (Minnesota Farmer-Labor 1923-41, Republican 1941-47).

Sympathizers of the NPL were called unpatriotic, disloyalists, Socialists, pro-German, affiliated with IWW. They sometimes found their meeting-places or their homes painted yellow in their absence.[343] The double standard applied by the law drove the wedge deep between townspeople and the farmers.

At its March 1918 convention held in St. Paul, the NPL framed its platform, strongly backing President Wilson and the war efforts. Labor and Farmer joined hands at this convention. Gov. Burnquist refused the invitation to attend. The *Minneapolis Tribune* commended him, noting that "he could not lend himself, he says, to anything that might be construed as an indorsement by him of propagandists who ally themselves with the I.W.W. and the Red Socialists; who attract to themselves the pro-German element of the state; who resort to base camouflage to present a show of loyalty; who stir up class feeling and foment industrial bitterness to serve demagogical political ends."[344] But there were other prominent people, some from the national government, who spoke and thanked them for their loyalty to the country.

With the mercurial rise of the NPL, the crafty, secretive Knute Nelson decided to run one more time. In late 1917, he had told friends he was getting old and thought he would retire. But when his friend, Judge McGee, head of the MCPS, heard this, he was determined Nelson should take another term.

Most likely it was McGee who leaked a fake letter supposedly written by President Wilson that declared Nelson's service invaluable to a nation at war. Other friends warned him that the NPL was gaining so much strength that his vacancy could very well be replaced by a member of the

NPL. That did it. Nelson, always secretive, sent instructions to his friend Nicolay Grevstad, editor of a Norwegian-American newspaper, that when a political supporter asked about Nelson's plans, Grevstad was to tell them that "while you don't know as to what my plans ... are ... it looks to you as though public opinion would force me into the field."[345]

Nelson announced his candidacy on April 15, claiming that he realized his services were needed – the people had insisted and it would be unpatriotic not to do so.

His one Republican opponent was James A. Peterson, the one referred to in his letter to McGee of June 7, 1917 – the same James A. Peterson he asked McGee to squelch. Peterson, a lawyer from Minneapolis, had written at least two articles published by Wold in the *Echo*. One article expressed Peterson's conviction that the war was being fought for the Allies to claim territory; the other article supported Wold and the NPL.

Not coincidentally, two days before Nelson announced his candidacy, Peterson was convicted of violating the Espionage Act – found guilty of "discouraging recruiting and enlistments." Nelson's friend, Judge Page Morris, sentenced Peterson to four years in prison, and Nelson's gang sought to have Peterson removed from the ballot.[346] The absolute proof of Nelson's fingerprints on this incident doesn't exist, but he certainly knew what was going on and gave his approval. It most certainly was a result of his June 7, 1917 letter to McGee.

Peterson remained on the ticket and never went to prison, but his chances for election were ruined.

With words most likely directed at Peterson and Wold and Townley, in the editorial in the April 4 issue of the *Alexandria Citizen* J. A. Kinney declares strong support of twenty years in prison and a $10,000 fine [$196,000] on "anybody who by word or act supports or favors the cause of the German empire or its allies or opposes the cause of the U.S. and the same penalty for opposing government war bond issues or attempting to obstruct recruiting or the draft. With such a law as this, the miserable culprits who have been convicted of crimes of this nature would not be let off with 'three months of jail.'"

Was it about this time that E.E. had words with Nelson when they met on the street in downtown Alexandria? E.E.'s daughter, Constance, my mother, was strolling with her father when the two politicians met up.

Though she didn't remember the substance of the conversation, she told me she vividly remembered Nelson spitting on her father as they parted.

E.E.'s health was greatly improved by April, yet he still lacked stamina and was unable to continue with a lecture tour. Martha was called to Minneapolis for a couple of weeks to tend to John's wife, Emma, who was quite ill with the "grippe." The Spanish flu was beginning its catastrophic spread.

E.E. advertised for sale the Lobeck family residence and the family cottage in the Mapleton addition on Lake Darling.[347] Why? The reason must have been financial. He had been very ill since early December and unable to fulfill any lecture tour. Though he would be paid for his service in the legislature, that was not enough. His main income was through lecture tours. However, neither property was sold at this time.

Running on the National Party ticket

In the midst of this maelstrom of events – abuse of constitutional rights, enforced loyalties, exaggerated patriotism, vilification and physical abuse of NPL sympathizers, the real tragedies of war, the dictatorial power of the Minnesota Commission of Public Safety, class hatred between farmer/labor and big business – E.E. on May 7 decided to file for another run at election as representative in the U.S. Congress on the National Party ticket, with the goals of securing national Prohibition and Women's Suffrage. Ten days earlier, the Minnesota Prohibition Party had voted to merge with the National Party.

The MCPS had managed with their abusive, misguided powers to have Townley arrested and convicted, Peterson arrested and convicted, and Wold arrested and convicted. Now they were referred to as "criminals" in unceasing articles and editorials written by the vitriolic editor, J. A. Kinney, of the *Alexandria Citizen*. Abuses continued to be heaped on the NPL leaders and all supporters by way of editorials, behind-the scene shenanigans, blatant physical force, and hate.

The NPL leaders, led by Townley and Charles A. Lindbergh, father of the as yet unknown famous pilot, appealed to Governor Burnquist for protection for the League meetings.

They told Gov. Burnquist that he was not fulfilling his duty as governor because he was not allowing them to meet and speak freely.

The current situation of Minnesota provides that all persons may freely speak, write or publish their sentiments on all subjects. You, as governor have failed in the enjoyment of these rights. You permitted their speakers and the candidates for public office whom they support to be unlawfully vilified, assaulted, arrested, kidnapped and mobbed. We cite here as one of the many outrages the unlawful arrest of Mayor Brandvig, candidate for the state Senate from the eighth legislative district while making a loyal speech, reading from Pres. Wilson's book "The New Freedom" and advocating the tonnage tax in a political meeting.

Burnquist said he would consider any evidence produced, but no law violations had been brought officially to his attention.[348]

Brandvig of Martin County was speaking to a small group of people during his campaign for the state Senate when the county attorney, accompanied by a group of men, burst into the meeting and placed him under arrest. Brandvig asked if they had a warrant. The attorney answered that he didn't need a warrant since he had prohibited NPL speeches in Martin County and that Brandvig was a Socialist and therefore should be jailed. Though Brandvig denied being a Socialist and proclaimed his right to make a campaign speech in his own district, the attorney ordered the crowd to leave the premises and took Brandvig to jail in Fairmont without allowing him to escort his two little boys home first.[349]

Another incident in Martin County, about the same time, involved prohibiting a speaker from the national government who was engaged for an NPL meeting. Invited to speak under the auspices of the League, he was denied permission by the Public Safety Commission, but the Commission would welcome him to speak under their auspices. Rather than cause more discord, the man refused and returned to Chicago.

Prohibition work hummed along. The Dry Federation organized to hold open air meetings in 2,000 towns and cities throughout the state to educate the populace about difficulties in amending the Minnesota constitution to achieve Prohibition.[350]

In the first week of June a huge NPL rally was held in Glenwood. "1,854 cars and over 200 horse rigs counted on the grounds. A moderate estimate of over 10,000 people attended."[351] The number of supporters was important, since the primary elections were coming up on June 17th.

Lobeck was campaigning but his name was not on the ballot, since he had no competition for the National Party ticket.

The Alexandria "Nelson-Burnquist-Volstead Club" made a strong campaign for "loyal" candidates before the primary election, though the electorate had other ideas.

Douglas County has its say

The county primary results were an unwelcome blow to Knute Nelson. He lost by 427 votes to James Peterson. Douglas County also made it clear they did not like Gov. Burnquist, voting overwhelmingly for Charles A. Lindbergh, who won by 1,400 votes. Henrik Shipstead of Glenwood beat out Volstead by 900 votes. T. J. Vickerman beat Kent, the incumbent sheriff, by 1,169 votes. Statewide, Nelson, Burnquist, and Volstead did quite well, but Douglas County had its say, despite all the political maneuverings by Constant Larson, Knute Nelson, and the MCPS.

The *Park Region Echo* was very pleased with the results. The *Alexandria Citizen* was especially bitter, claiming Douglas County was not loyal. Indignation: Knute Nelson lost big in his own home county! Humiliating! The *Pioneer Press* in St. Paul said this: "One explanation offered for the big Nonpartisan vote is the strong pro-German sentiment that has been manifested repeatedly in Douglas County." Kinney, with his ire, presented this to his readers:

> Think of it! A candidate for the sheriff's office, put forth by the Nonpartisan League with the evident purpose of securing an officer who would interfere with no kind of disloyal propaganda, receives more than twice as many votes as a tried sheriff of proved capacity, integrity and loyalty. …

> Think of it! A visionary Socialist, camouflaged for many years as a Republican but shown forth in his true colors by becoming the henchman of the unspeakable Bolshevik, Townley, gets more than twice as many votes … as the true blue governor. …

> Think of it! A convicted criminal was given 1,956 votes as against 1,517 for a man who served his country honorably in the Civil War, a man who is running again for the U.S. Senate when ready for honored retirement only because of the earnest request of the nation and its chief executive in the hour of their need for men of his capacity. … And that too in his own home county! …

Douglas County has proved that it is not loyal to the nation at the time of its greatest need.[352]

Carl Wold, in the Park Region *Echo*, countered that the county voted for James A. Peterson, as opposed to Knute Nelson, to show their dislike of the guilty verdict for disloyalty.[353]

In late June E.E.'s campaigning found him near Thief River Falls at a Red Cross picnic, where 150 people gathered on a rainy afternoon to hear him. Old Trysil friends and Scandinavians in general peopled the friendly audience. He took the opportunity to impart his thoughts about the world's conditions before he talked about his agenda – Prohibition. With the war raging in Europe, he struck a hopeful view.

> My reflection of the world situation causes me to believe that a revolutionary spirit, such as never before, is pressing itself upon the governments, the nations and the individuals. … The world has had the most wonderful time in its history, a time of inventions, of improvements, and of a civilization whose pinnacle has never been attained before, and still what has taken years to build up, and what has been the pride of nations, the benefit of individuals and the pride of civilization, is being destroyed, demolished, and with bullets of lead and steel shot to pieces in a war so horrible, and with dimensions so large that the world has never witnessed its peer. An idea prevailing with some is that this war will end in a world monarchy and with the Kaiser as a second Napoleon. … In this world we have several times noticed the attempt of one man to monopolize the world and become its chief regent, but every attempt has failed and resulted in utter destruction of the attempter, and so it shall end today. Justice shall not be set back, but shall, although not without trials, come forward triumphant.[354]

Alexandria had big celebrations for the Fourth of July with a grand parade, showcasing machine guns and war equipment, tractor demonstrations, and speakers. The Odin Chautauqua entertained at the fairgrounds for a few days. Rev. Peer Strømme was there to give talks about his travels and Professor Reimstad from Augsburg Seminary gave concert recitals. The Lobeck family spent the holiday at the festival by Pocket Lake in Holmes City township with an "immense" crowd, picnicking, licking ice cream, and listening to a speech by Charles Lindbergh.

Farmers buy the *Echo*

The July 2 issue of the Park Region *Echo* carried the note that Carl Wold was very ill and asked for understanding if the newspaper wasn't up to its usual standards. In the successive weeks, Wold was taken to Mounds Park Sanatorium near St. Paul, where he had an operation to no avail. By mid-July it was clear that he would not survive his cancer and was sent home to spend his last days. It was necessary for him to give up editing and running the business of the *Echo*.

Upon hearing this, about thirty farmers in the county met and decided to organize. They then voted to incorporate with a capital of $20,000 [$390,000] and begin selling stock as soon as possible. Staff of the NPL helped them in the organizing. The July 23 issue of the *Echo* stated that "The *Park Region Echo* with this issue becomes the property of the organized farmers of Douglas County. The noble work of Carl Wold and his fighting paper is to go on."

The organization would be known as Park Region Publishing Company; they were bonded and selling *Echo* stock at $20/share [$390] with $15,000 [$295,000] worth of stock to be sold. Carl Wold and family would receive $7,000 [$138,000] for the printing plant, and the remainder would go back into the business.

> The prospects for the paper are exceedingly bright. With the farmers of the county actually owners of the paper, the foolish and unjust boycott against the *Echo* by certain anti-farmer business interests, will undoubtedly cease. With the county in the hands of the farmers after the fall election, the paper will have ample business to more than take care of all its expenses.[355]

The masthead of the July 30 *Echo* listed I. M. Kalnes as editor and manager. The editorial column was Carl Wold's farewell.

Within a week the new Park Region Publishing Company bought a lot on 6th Avenue to put up a new building and expand the printing plant. Much money had already been raised from selling stock. Kalnes reported that he had called on several businesses in town and was welcomed with friendly feelings. The building still stands, with a plaque honoring Carl Wold affixed to the outside wall.

Tarring and feathering

An ugly incident of gang violence toward supporters or *suspected* supporters of the NPL occurred in Rock County on August 19 when John Meints, a retired wealthy German-American farmer of Luverne, was tarred and feathered. A month earlier, "just after the state primaries, when a gang in Rock County announced that it would run every man who voted for the league out of the state unless he repented. Mr. Meints was forcibly deported over the Iowa line."

Meints stayed in Iowa with relatives; then, thinking things had calmed down, he went home. Talking to a minister, who was a leader of the gang, Meints suggested they arrest him so he could have a trial. A friend of Meints warned him that the mob spirit was rising again.

Seeking justice, Meints took a train to St. Paul, hoping to see Gov. Burnquist. Burnquist was unavailable, and Meints was rejected by others. Finally, a stenographer took down his statement and telephoned the mob leaders. They stated Meints could return home if "he would go down on his knees and pray to be allowed to go back, it could be arranged." Meints refused. But he returned home.

On August 19 the mob burst into his home, promising to take him to Luverne for trial. Meints agreed. Instead, they took him to a basement of the hotel and interrogated him for hours, before they took him to the South Dakota line, threatening him with hanging. The gang handed him over to six men who tied his arms behind him, led him into the woods, stripped him, beat him with a rope, and tarred and feathered him.

At dawn he found a stream where he scrubbed his face raw with sand and water. He caught a train to St. Paul, to the U.S. District Attorney's office, where they took down his statements and photographed him.[356]

Meints sued the thirty-two men of the gang, asking $100,000 damages [$2 million]. The trial was held in Mankato. The outcome? The U.S. District Court jury (it was a federal case because Meints had been taken across state lines), instructed by the judge that "the evidence was overwhelming in support of the contention that Meints was disloyal and that there was a strong feeling against him in the community," deliberated an hour and a half and ruled against Meints. The exonerated men of the gang were welcomed home with a large delegation and a band. After an appeal in 1922, Meints settled out of court for $6,000 [$106,000].[357]

The pandemic comes

On a lovely Saturday afternoon, the last day of August, friends of the Wolds from throughout the county came to visit Carl, Eva, and their daughter Blanche, to show their appreciation for all they had done and present them with some token of that appreciation – $350 [$6,000]. E.E. was one of those who gave a short speech, thanking them for all their efforts. Carl got up from his bed, and with help managed to go out on his front porch to give his thanks to the people assembled there.[358]

As September approached, the trial of Eva Wold on the charge of sedition loomed. It had been postponed since the previous March 5. County Attorney Hugh Leach had asked at that time to have it continued. Eva's attorney, Walter H. Jacke, asked to have the case dismissed, given her circumstances and that no crime was committed. If the judge would deny the motion, he pleaded that she was entitled, by law, to a trial at once and not to continue it again. Leach, however, asked for a continuance since the case for Carl Wold was yet before the Supreme Court. He anticipated a long drawn-out trial for Carl, so he would like to have Eva's trial at the next term of court in March 1919. The court agreed with Leach. On motion by Jacke, the court agreed to release Mrs. Wold from bonds placed on her six months earlier.[359]

As the *Park Region Echo* pointed out on the editorial page, Mrs. Wold's situation was almost too much to bear – a dying husband whom she was caring for day and night, and the threat of trial still to come. Leach had failed to "measure up to his opportunity. …We are sorely disappointed in the peculiar conduct of County Attorney Leach."[360]

As campaigning progressed, some good news for Lobeck was endorsement by the Democrats. His campaign ad stated he was a "Farmer-Labor candidate for representative in Congress from the 7th district, endorsed by the Farmers' convention, running on the National Party ticket." And he attached his name along with others to a poster advocating the purchasing of Liberty Loans to help win the war by sending food overseas.

Americans were also being asked to help the Allies overcome food shortages by rationing themselves. With the slogan "Food Will Win the War," Americans were called to ration sugar, wheat, dairy, and to cut back on food consumption. "Clean your plate," "Waste Nothing," "Save wheat, meat, fats, and sugar." A notice in the newspaper in mid-September stated that sugar was now rationed to two pounds per person per month.

In late September, Martha was actively involved in a house-to-house canvass, gathering signatures on a petition for ratification of the Women's Suffrage amendment to present to the legislature.

The last couple of weeks before the election much was happening – the Spanish influenza, campaigning, and the death of Carl Wold.

By mid-October, the Spanish flu had already claimed some lives in the community, causing schools and meetings to be canceled until further notice. Obituaries of soldiers dying from influenza made the front page of the papers. It has been estimated in some sources that more than half the casualties in WWI were from influenza.

"The little blue bottle that saved America," Vick's Vaporub, a topical containing camphor, eucalyptus oil, and menthol, was an aid in opening up the air passages to enable better breathing and gave relief to the sufferers. The local newspapers advertised it. The demand was so heavy that in a couple of weeks the ads told the readers that supplies of Vaporub had run out.

On October 18, schools, churches, and public gatherings were ordered canceled because of the flu. Campaigning was reduced to the newspapers.

Tuesday evening, October 29, the phone rang in the *Echo* offices just after the paper had gone to press. Mrs. Wold telephoned with the long-expected news that Carl Wold had died. The presses were stopped long enough to insert a black rimmed box on the front page. He died just one week before the election for which he had worked so hard.

Because of the restrictions against public gatherings, the funeral was held on the front lawn of the Wold home on Saturday afternoon, November 2. E.E. had the opportunity to speak words about his good friend, reminding the gathered mourners of Wold's sacrifices, both financial and physical, to stand up for his convictions and principles.

Reasons (insufficient) for optimism

The outcome of the upcoming election, three days later, on November 5, looked favorable for Lobeck. In the last couple of weeks he received endorsements from farmers, some townspeople, and the progressives. He also received the backing of the National Democratic Congressional Committee.[361] The farmers backed Lobeck after Shipstead was narrowly eliminated, because they liked the honorable way Lobeck handled the result.

> When the League convention in his district selected ... Doctor Shipstead, Lobeck openly supported him.

> He sent a letter to the *Minnesota Leader* boosting Shipstead. ... However, Volstead beat Shipstead for the Republican nomination by a few votes, and Volstead is the Republican candidate against Lobeck. ... In supporting Shipstead for the Republican nomination, Lobeck ... said that in the event Shipstead was nominated he and Shipstead would get together and decide which would withdraw as both stood for the same things.[362]

The NPL also noted that Lobeck was a member of the League and was entitled to their support. The Progressives liked Lobeck because "of his attitude of fairness to farmer and labor organizations."[363]

His old friend, Waldemar Ager of *The Reform* newspaper in Eau Claire, Wisconsin, backed Lobeck, recounting his last 25 years of good work, and stating:

> He can't be twisted around anyone's finger – he is too big for that. Nor can he be brought down by flattery – he is too foolish for that. Neither can he be misled – he is too wise for that. He is both too poor and too rich to fall for bribery. He is too old to run away and too young to be balky.[364]

Election day. Though the race was lost statewide, throughout Douglas County every candidate backed by the NPL farmer's ticket won, from township offices to the national Congress: Vickerman for sheriff; Calderwood, Nelson's opponent, beat out Nelson in his home district; County Attorney Hugh Leach lost his position to Walter Jacke, the new county attorney, who promptly dismissed the pending case against Eva Wold.

E.E. came much closer than he had two years before, losing by 4,819 votes, and this time winning two of the fourteen counties, Douglas and Kandiyohi.

The *Alexandria Citizen* licked its wounds with some belittling words for the Douglas County winners, while announcing that Senator Nelson and Governor Burnquist and Congressman Volstead had been re-elected.

I. M. Kalnes, editor of the *Echo*, was arrested on election day for driving around in his Ford, circulating signs for Calderwood, in violation of election laws. The complaint was drawn up by County Attorney Leach – who would soon no longer be the county attorney, having just been elected mayor of Alexandria. A bond of $100 [$1,800] was given by Lobeck and the county auditor-elect to keep Kalnes from jail.

The influenza ban on public gatherings was lifted at the end of the week. Church services were held on Sunday, November 10, with school scheduled to resume the following day – but the next day, school was not on anyone's mind.

On Monday, November 11, World War I ended when Germany surrendered.

Before dawn, the good news was filtering in. The people of Alexandria began milling in the streets and creating as much joyous noise as possible. The Lobeck family joined the crowd downtown. E.E. took a stand on a corner, hoisted little Martha on his shoulders, and they shouted and applauded with the crowd.

> Tubs, horns, cow bells, tin cans, joints of furnace pipe, tin cans tied to ropes and hung to the back of cars, automobile horns and … the always flashing and flaming red fire truck, appearing and vanishing in every alley and street, a voice in the darkness bidding everyone to be up to celebrate so glorious an occasion. … Men and women appeared on the street with street clothes hastily thrown on over night clothes. …

> A semblance of order was established in the middle of the morning and an immense parade formed to escort the boys who were to leave on the noon train for training camps. The parade … led by the fire truck, in a gorgeous panoply of flags, chrysanthemums, asters, roses, carnations and ferns … and carrying its usual squad of firemen, was made of horses with bells tied to their necks and tails, decorated automobiles, hundreds of school children, the Red Cross, countless citizens and various mirth and noise producing vehicles. … The crowd then sang the "Star Spangled Banner" and the march proceeded to the Great Northern depot.[365]

The joy was even greater when the young men who left for training camp on the noon train were stopped at Sauk Centre and sent back to Alexandria on the westbound train, arriving home three hours after they left.

The Douglas WCTU met at the Lobeck home the last week of November. The topic for the evening was Women's Suffrage. Because the goals of the organization – Women's Suffrage and Prohibition – were now accomplished nationally, the women moved to reorganize as the Douglas Union and to devote "its efforts to any local worthy cause."[366]

The Union met again, the night before Christmas Eve, for a social evening. With a feeling of festivity in the air after years of war, campaigning for elections, the hard work of gaining Prohibition and the right to vote, supporting a French war orphan, making comfort kits for the soldiers, knitting socks for the Red Cross efforts, enduring the Spanish flu effects – all this in addition to their regular roles as housewives and mothers – the evening brought out a big attendance to celebrate.[367]

Chapter 15

Storm Clouds

The year 1919 started well. The war was over. Prohibition had won. On January 16, thirteen months after it passed Congress, the 18th Amendment achieved the requisite number of state ratifications; the day before, the Alexandria WCTU held a celebratory meeting, with E.E. as speaker. The Volstead Act, specifying how the 18th Amendment was to be implemented, passed Congress on October 28, with January 17, 1920 as the day it was to go into effect. In June, Congress passed the 19th Amendment, granting women the vote – an occasion for celebration at that month's WCTU meeting. The 19th Amendment would be ratified fourteen months later.

Closer to home, Martha and E.E. were re-elected to offices in the church, he as trustee, she as Sunday School superintendent. The case against Eva Wold had finally been dropped.

On January 27 the WCTU hosted a well-attended Prohibition Ratification Jubilee at the Methodist Church. E.E. spoke about his experiences in more than three decades of Prohibition work. He told many stories, and closed by expressing hope that the future would bring better economic conditions for working people.[368]

In March E.E. met with Worldwide Prohibition; they wanted to recruit him for work in foreign lands (six months, or a year, or three years, in Scandinavia). "He is yet undecided whether to go or not."[369] The *Minneapolis Tribune* in July wrote that "in most states the [Prohibition] party will pass away. Its work is done. Sweden and Norway have asked for help. Norway votes on the question this fall, and it has asked Mr. Lobeck to go there and work for the cause."[370]

The general good feeling was momentarily clouded by trouble at the *Echo*.

There were internal problems. In January the staff walked out on strike without notice. I. M. Kalnes claimed he didn't know why, since he was paying wages agreed upon. He promised to inform readers about reasons, but didn't. Kalnes struggled for a couple of months to get the paper out, engaging Eva Wold, who "did the work of three men."[371]

In March he hired more help and, after training them in, got the paper running smoothly again. But this would turn out to be a temporary reprieve; the paper's stance, so often in harmony with Lobeck, would eventually sound sharply discordant notes.

A new bank

In the aftermath of the pro-NPL Douglas County election results, talk of starting a farmer-owned bank was abuzz. On the last Saturday of 1918 four committees of five men each, representing all parts of the county, met at the *Park Region Echo* offices and hammered out plans for the venture. They agreed that stockholders would have only one vote regardless of how much stock they owned, to avert any person's gaining control, and limits would be set on how many shares could be held by any one individual. These motions were carried unanimously.

In meetings over the successive January Saturdays, other alternatives were explored. The Douglas County State Bank refused to sell a controlling interest to the farmers, asking the farmers to buy minority stock. This was promptly turned down by the committee. The Farmers National Bank offered no proposition. Therefore, at the January 18 meeting the farmers decided on a new bank – a state bank – with a capitalization of $50,000 [$900,000], all money to be paid in cash by February 15. No more stock would be sold because it was already oversubscribed at $58,000 [$1,040,000], and those who had subscribed for more than five shares were reducing their subscriptions to lower the capitalized stock to $50,000. Until the new charter was granted, the First National Bank of Alexandria would hold the monies in deposit.[372]

The subscribers met in February 1919 to select the board of directors of the new bank: E.E. Lobeck, president; L. G. Hermanson, first vice president; Sheriff T. J. Vickerman, second vice president; County Attorney W. H. Jacke, secretary.[373] On May 14 the Minnesota Securities Commission granted the charter for the farmer-owned bank.

Park Region State Bank, July 1920; L-R: Fred Proehl, August Quitmeyer, E.E. Lobeck

Labor Day 1919 was the grand opening of the Park Region State Bank. There were new deposits of $12,187.74 [$220,000]. "F. C. Proehl is the cashier of the new bank and will be in complete charge. When the Board of Directors chose Mr. Proehl as cashier, they surely chose wisely."[374] Proehl had recently been cashier of the Lincoln State Bank in Wadena.

Lobeck would before long conclude that the choice was anything but wise, but for the time being all was well. Within four months the deposits had risen to $174,657 [$3,140,000], prompting Kalnes to write that it "was splendid work done by officials of the bank."[375]

Armenian Relief

On April 24, 2021, Armenian Genocide Remembrance Day, President Joseph R. Biden Jr. issued a press statement that concluded with these words: "The American people honor all those Armenians who perished in the genocide that began 106 years ago today." It took a century for the U.S. to acknowledge what really happened – to call it by its right name – but contemporaries of E.E. Lobeck knew about the consequences of what happened. And the efforts of him and his colleagues to do something about it generated unnecessary controversy.

A July 16 editorial in the *Echo* was headlined "Negligent Stewardship."

Early last winter, six months ago now, there was a great drive in this county for the relief of suffering Armenians. We were told that babies were starving and mothers dying in Armenia for the lack of food. We were told that haste was necessary in order to keep a whole people from dying of starvation. Senator E.E. Lobeck used his eloquence to good advantage in raising many hundreds of dollars for this worthy purpose in Douglas County. With Lobeck on the committee were D. C. Dvoracek and Rev. Stauffacher and an urgent appeal for funds was published in the papers over the signatures of these men. Mr. Hugh Leach, now mayor of Alexandria, is the treasurer of this committee and Mr. Dvoracek acted as chairman of this committee.

Last Monday Mr. N. Martinson, state campaign director of the American Committee Armenian-Relief … was in Alexandria trying to find out what had become of the money which had been raised in Douglas County last winter. None of this money had as yet reached state headquarters, Mr Martinsen explained. And it is now six months since the drive was made and we were told that the drive was very, very urgent. And no doubt it was. But the Douglas County committee had not turned over one red cent of this money on Monday, July 7th according to Martinson. The chairman of the Douglas County committee had even quit. This necessitated his coming up here to locate the fund, some $2,746.40 [$49,000] which, instead of relieving the suffering of starving Armenians has simply added that much working capital to an Alexandria bank.

To say the least, this is a case of gross negligence on the part of the Douglas County committee.[376]

Kalnes had too hastily jumped to a conclusion without vetting his source. "A Retraction" was published on July 23.

> Mayor Hugh E. Leach called on the editor of the *Echo* last Wednesday morning and informed us that our leading editorial of last week, "Negligent Stewardship," was not based on fact. Mr. Leach showed us his canceled checks from the First National Bank proving that he as treasurer of the Armenian Relief committee for the Douglas County had turned over the money collected to the treasurer of the state committee, Mr. Chapman. There was no more than $10 [$180] left in the hands of the local committee. As was plainly stated in our editorial of last week, the statement was made by Mr. Martinson that the funds have not been received at State headquarters.
>
> Mr. Martinson made the statement to some of our courthouse officials, and the editor of the *Echo* was called in by them and jotted down the facts in the presence of at least three of our courthouse officials. It appears now that Mr. Martinson did not have the facts in the case as the money was properly turned over to Mr. Chapman, the treasurer of the state committee.
>
> On the basis of the statement made by Mr. Martinson to our courthouse officials, the editor of the *Echo* said last week: "To say the least, this is a case of gross negligence on the part of the Douglas County committee." As our conclusion was based on Mr. Martinson's statement and as Martinson's statement does not tally with the facts in the case, we retract our editorial comment of an adverse nature against the Douglas County committee as the facts seem to be the Douglas County committee handled the funds properly and with dispatch. We are very sorry that we should've been led to make a statement which is not true and gladly take this opportunity to correct it.[377]

It is clear that Mayor Leach, on reading the initial editorial, went immediately to the *Echo* office with his canceled check, for the next day, July 17, at a Nonpartisan League picnic, the first speaker of the afternoon was Kalnes, who "took the occasion to explain the Armenian Relief matter and showed how the *Echo* came to make a mistaken report on the matter, suggesting that possibly the thing was a 'frame up' to get the *Echo* in bad."

"Mr. Lobeck" replied that perhaps "Mr. Kalnes" thought he saw a chance to dig at him in the write-up on the Armenians, but that he would settle with him as he was the bigger of the two.[378] This riposte, lighthearted as it was, hints at a tension that would soon escalate.

The American Legion and the NPL, and what it means to be "American"

In February 1919, three months after the Armistice was signed, General Pershing, at the urging of Lt. Col. Theodore Roosevelt Jr., son of the former president, assembled some reserve and regular officers in Paris to form an organization for veterans of the war. The American Legion was born.

In May another meeting was held in St. Louis, at which a constitutional preamble was adopted:

> For God and Country we associate ourselves together for the following purposes:
> To uphold and defend the Constitution of the United States of America; to maintain law and order; to foster and perpetuate a 100 Percent Americanism; to preserve the memories and incidents of our association in the Great War; to inculcate a sense of individual obligation to the community, state, and nation; to combat the autocracy of both the classes and the masses; to make right the master of might; to promote peace and good will on earth; to safeguard and transmit to prosperity the principles of justice, freedom, and democracy; to consecrate and sanctify our comradeship by devotion to mutual helpfulness.

At the national organizing convention in Minneapolis, November 10-12 (scheduled to coincide with the first anniversary of the Armistice), 15,000 veterans marched in the parade in the snow.

Although at this convention the Legion declared itself non-political –

> this organization shall be absolutely non-political and shall not be used for the dissemination of partisan principles or for the promotion of the candidacy of any person seeking public office or preferment; and no candidate for or incumbent of a salaried elective public office shall hold any office in The American Legion or in any branch or post thereof –

there were enough contentious political issues roiling the nation to make "non-partisanship" impractical – indeed, the meeting in St. Louis had called on Congress to "pass a bill for immediately deporting every one of those Bolsheviks or Industrial Workers of the World."[379] Not just Republican vs. Democrat, but town vs. country; big business vs labor; the Russian Revolution, pitting the poor against the rich and with the goal of public ownership run by government instead of private ownership. The words "Bolshevik" and Bolshevikism" were frequently directed at members of the Nonpartisan League, whose support of farmer-owned banks and elevators could hurt big business.

How did this affect Alexandria?

The *Echo* editorial on October 29 stated:

> We note that a political program is to be pulled off at Alexandria on Armistice Day, November 11, under the auspices of the America First Association, the American Legion and the local Red Cross Chapter with Dowling, a reactionary banker from Olivia, who is a candidate for governor to succeed Burnquist, as the main speaker. In our opinion the local Red Cross is traveling in mighty poor company and it will surely discredit the Red Cross in this county.

The Legion was outraged. On November 5 a meeting was held, with Ole Langhaug as moderator.

> Ralph Thornton first spoke of how quietly the American Legion had been organized in Alexandria. There had been no advertising of the fact that a Legion post was to be organized he said. They had gone at it so quietly because they did not want to stir up any feelings with anybody. Now that they were organized with a very large membership they came before the board of the directors of the *Echo* to DEMAND that in next week's *Echo* a retraction of last week's editorial be made on the front page of the *Echo*, the retraction to be okayed by a committee of the American Legion before publishing and that an apology be also made on the front page of the *Echo* to the Alexandria post of the American Legion. Mr. Thornton explained that the editor of the *Echo* had point blank refused to retract a single word of his editorial when called on by the 15 Legionnaires last Thursday night, as related previously. Mr. Thornton termed the editorial of the *Echo* a "dirty insult." He said the committee did not want to argue or debate, but that they simply stated their "demands" and that it was up to the Board of Directors to take action on their "demands."

Henry F. Proehl [Fred's brother] asked Mr. Thornton to state the purpose or platform of the American Legion. Thornton read a part of the bylaws stating the organization was non-political. Thornton added he did not come here to debate. Mr. Proehl then said that if the American Legion was a democratic organization as they claim to be they ought to be willing to discuss their platform and principles and further that he couldn't see anything about the *Echo* editorial that should make anyone feel as insulted as they pretended to be.

Kalnes spoke, referring to his editorial. "I said what I did because a political program is being put on for Armistice Day under the guise of patriotism. I feel that the Red Cross is an organization which should keep strictly out of politics. I feel and I think the American Legion is strongly suspected of being very much like the America First. Mr. Dowling is exactly the same kind of a man as Governor Burnquist. What gets my goat is that this kind of a program is put on under the camouflage of patriotism."

C. J. Lindstrom made a motion to support the editor and editorial. Proehl seconded. John Urness said, "I don't know whether I am ready to vote to support the editorial or not." Mr. Urness then asked Thornton if the America First Association had anything to do with the Armistice Day program. Thornton didn't answer. A copy of the *Alexandria Citizen* was brought out and Langhaug read from it that the program was "under the auspices of the American Legion post, Red Cross and America First." Urness replied, "Well, if the America First is mixed up in it then I too will vote to support the editor."

Several visitors were at the meeting, including E.E. Lobeck who asked some difficult questions of Thornton.

Kalnes opined in a subsequent editorial that there might be trouble in town on Armistice Day because of strong opinions on both sides, but "Sheriff Vickerman has promised to keep order in Alexandria if it is necessary to swear in 500 farmers as deputy sheriffs."[380]

A headline in the *Minneapolis Tribune* on November 13, the day after the national convention, signaled the brewing conflict: "Legion to Fight All Things Un-American."

The conflict over what it means to be American played out in the Alexandria newspapers.

"Certain charges and vague insinuations of immoral conduct on the part of the Manager and Editor of the *Echo* have been made in a most sensational manner by certain other papers in the county," the Board of Directors of the *Echo* published in the December 3 issue. The Board formed a committee to investigate and promised to inform readers of results. In the meantime, readers were asked to withhold judgment.

In the same *Echo* issue, a recap of the paper's stockholder meeting of November 29 reported a large crowd attendance from around the county, mostly farmers. The vote was to construct a new building, increase capitalization, and "endorse the present editorial policy," along with talk of suing an individual for "damages of alleged slander of the *Park Region Echo* unless slander is retracted by individual or by Alexandria post of the American Legion within ten days."

Kalnes began the year 1920 stating his New Year resolutions. He was still trying to abide by what he had said when, earlier, Eva Wold had admonished him about so much sarcasm in his editorials: with "Mrs. Wold's calm and deliberate judgment, we have often listened to her counsel to tone down with good results." He promised to refrain from insulting personalities as much as he could. He claimed that he would not be personal unless the situation warranted it, since there were always people to deal with, not just principles. In the very next sentence he referred to the editors of the other two papers in town as "Demo-Publican Mensheviks." But he didn't want to hurt anyone's feelings, he said.

Attorney H. Zander welcomed this.

> Wonders will not cease. The unbelievable has happened. The thing long wished for and prayed for, that there be a change in the editor of the Park Region *Echo*, has happened, judging from his New Year's resolution, he has changed from a devouring lion into a humble, peaceful little lamb, harmless and docile.

> Let us all hope that all whose nerves were formerly grated by the writings of the editor, will reach out the glad hand of brotherhood so that the people of Douglas County may hereafter live in peace and harmony, the former lion feeding with the lambs, all factions, frictions and breaches having been healed. No doubt, hereafter, there will be but one flock and one shepherd in Douglas County.

Let us all be thankful for that.[381]

The *Minneapolis Sunday Tribune* ran an extensive article written by a journalist for the New York Times, labeled "Nonpartisans Greater Menace to Nation than the I. W. W.," continuing with "Terrorism and Fraud of Nonpartisans," referring to them as "Plunderers," which prompted Kalnes's January 21 editorial.

Whither are we drifting?

The nation is passing through a period of hysteria. There are interests at work trying to throw a scare into the people and the result is that the country is full of shadow fighting.

The Metropolitan press, controlled, as most of it is, by special interests, and that portion of the country press that represents the "me too" element of the rural editors, are busy these days making the nation "see red."

Some terrible thing, called by a name that nobody understands, is supposed to be threatening this country. Americanism, as interpreted by "vested rights," is held up as the one sacred thing.

It is not the Americanism of Washington and Jefferson. It is not the Americanism of Patrick Henry. It is not the Americanism of the founders of the nation. It is an Americanism that has little in common with our national tradition and still less of the nature of the principles promulgated by the "Spirit of '76" that these flag-waving patriots, of the profiteer stripe, are so lustily proclaiming.

As the 1920 election year rolled in, the Minnesota NPL hoped to mirror North Dakota's accomplishments by gaining legislative control, wider farmer support, and establishing state banks and pro-NPL hometown newspapers.

Alexandria's Frazier Club, named after the NPL-endorsed Republican governor of North Dakota, met for its regular monthly meeting in mid-January with an enthusiastic attendance of over ninety NPLers. E.E. had been head of the club previously, and now served as just an active member of the planning committee and lunch committee. A Frazier-for-president movement was being proposed, since Frazier had been so successful for the NPL movement in North Dakota. He was first elected in 1916 and again in 1918, and was instrumental in the establishment of the North Dakota State Bank and the North Dakota Mill and Elevator.

At the Frazier Club meeting in November E.E. had spoken.

Mr. Chairman and ladies and gentlemen:

In 1776 a nation was born, born to liberty and baptized in blood and fire. This nation gave to the world the principle that all men are created equal as a foundation for our political equality and self-government. Recently this same nation was fighting to establish the principle that all nations are created equal, the basis on which must be built the "Federation of Man," the "Republic of the World." This nation is the United States of America, your country and mine.

(Here the audience, upon request of the speaker, rose and sang "America.")

Seeking and accepting the guidance of Almighty God, we ought to stand ready to give our best and our all for our country, for the cause of humanity, right living and good government. Such a task can be performed only by law abiding citizens.

Lincoln said: "Let reverence for the law be breathed by every American mother to the lisping babe that prattles on her lap; let it be taught in schools and seminaries, let it be written in primaries, spelling books and almanacs; let it be preached from the pulpits, proclaimed in legislative halls and enforced in courts of justice and, in short, let it become the political religion of the nation, and let the old and the young, the rich and the poor, the grave and the gay, of all sexes and tongues and colors and conditions sacrifice unceasingly upon its altar."

Those who wrote our state Constitution had this plainly in view and they put it in this way – "Government is instituted for the security, benefit and protection of the people in whom all political power is inherent, together with the right, to alter, modify or reform such government whenever the public good may require it." Here we see that the Constitution of the state of Minnesota guarantees to the people their security, benefit and protection in article 1, section 1 of the Constitution and it most emphatically denies the right of anyone to affect the security, benefit and protection of the people in an injurious way. Our Constitution, then, is set aside, our government is trembling, our institutions are shaking as long as we have "Tar and Feather" parties and "yellow paint" brigades running at large in the commonwealth, and it behooves every loyal Citizen to be ever ready to face this vile serpent spirit and make it impossible for sentiments of this kind to exist for one single moment in the United States of America.

Section 3 of our constitution reads as follows: "The liberty of the press shall forever remain inviolate and all persons may freely speak, write and publish their sentiments on all subjects – except in Alexandria – being responsible for the abuse of such rights." This section of the movement is to uphold the law and the Constitution, to determine and specifically set forth the rugged, fundamental principles of democracy and democratic ideals, strengthen and maintain the lofty aims of our institutions in order that we may be able to deal in a supremely just manner with the political, social and economic facts and problems which affect the lives and liberties of Americans today. To adopt definite methods of political actions so as to give these principles immediate force in the government of our country where the masses today are surging to and fro, seeking for light.

To elect to office men who have courage to stand for these principles, ready to live and die for the truth as they see it, men who do not cringe for a plutocrat or creep before a sack of gold. Jesus was the founder of democracy. He came to serve and democracy rests on service.

Without unselfish service democracy will perish from the earth. The money power is a menace to the liberty in this country as well as in other countries.

Senator Borah of Idaho called for information as to food profiteering, and the Treasury in response to this resolution stated that food dealers made as high as 2.183%. It is difficult to imagine a more satisfactory result financially. It is still more difficult to imagine that stockholders in organizations and firms of that kind can take blood-soaked dividends of 2.183% during war times, when the world is bleeding and humanity quivers in agony and want, without sacrificing their claim to membership in the human family. It is up to us to help to warn our commercial and political masters that they better call a halt in their mad rush, lest the masses suddenly wake up to a sense of its age-long, monstrous wrong, losing patience in its righteous fury and destroy capitalist civilization in a welter of raging storm of a bloody revolution.

We do not desire this. God forbid it. From the depths of our souls we cry: "God save our country from a bloody revolution." We desire peaceful, educational, gradual, rapid progress by sane legislation. It can be accomplished this way, if the profiteers and capitalists will start to let the better feeling rule their conduct in the future. But if they continue to dam the River of Life with their purchased courts, their servile priests, politicians, generals and armed force and greedy profiteering then nothing can save them nor the country from the red fury of the coming storm.

History of other countries will teach us that God's righteous wrath rides not upon the resistless hurricane of social revolution.

Governor Frazier has taken his stand among the common people. He has taken scorn, abuse and vilification. He, in common with other reformers had to go out into the wilderness and be fed by the ravens. His actions and words have been misconstrued. His every move has been watched, but like a rock in the midst of a raving torrent he has stood and plowed through four great purgatorial years and come out victorious. He is worthy of our support and most earnest efforts.[382]

Half a year after Lobeck's speech, in late June 1920, a note of warning about pride going before a fall, about the temptations of success, was sounded by Eva Wold in an afternoon speech, following the dedication in the morning of the new *Park Region Echo* building, during which the memorial bas-relief tablet to her late husband had been unveiled. In the audience for her talk was North Dakota Governor Frazier. After thanking those who had given moral support and financial support through the years, she concluded with a warning for the NPL.

It is not when a movement is small and weak that there is danger. The men and women who work in the movement while it is still small and struggling are those who are in the work because they believe in principle. But when movement gets strong, then is the time to be on guard. Then is the time when outsiders will come in for their own personal benefits, when people who have been on the inside may be tempted to use the organization for their own benefit. Traitors to the movement should be watched for.[383]

As noted in chapter 3, as early as 1893 in his career as a Temperance lecturer, when he was only 23 years old, E.E. had made the same point about inside treachery: "I dare to believe that no association has been stifled by opposition from without, but it is the members themselves who destroy it."

Chapter 16

"You Must Take the Days as They Come –
They are Not All Alike"

The years 1919 and 1920 had been for E.E. a time of up and down, back and forth, light and shadow. 1921 and 1922 will be in some ways even gloomier, but there were two moments early on that were purely and simply gratifying.

Members of the First Norwegian Lutheran Church gathered at the church on the first Saturday in June 1921 and marched as a body to E.E. and Martha's home to surprise them on their 25th wedding anniversary. They brought ample food and refreshments, and the evening was spent in speaking and singing. Pastor Tjornhom gave a little speech praising both of them for their work in the church and for Prohibition work.

E.E. was speaker later that month at the dedication of a monument at the old Oscar Lake Church cemetery – where his older brother Per was buried after his accidental death. Attendees came from near and far to the location on the Nels Fahlin family land, where the original church had been built in 1864. E.E.'s parents were buried about a mile away, in a cemetery next to the new church building erected in 1884.

A Fahlin descendant told of the first funeral in the first cemetery. Twins born to the Olaf Fahlins in January 1867 lived only a few days. It was too cold and the snow too deep to bury them, so they lay frozen in their casket until spring.

E.E. talked of the old pioneers and their hardships; Norunga choir furnished music; former pastors and Nels Fahlin spoke. The inscription on the monument reads: "IN LOVING MEMORY OF THE ABOUT

TWO HUNDRED SETTLERS THAT ARE LAID TO REST
HERE. This monument was erected by relatives and friends May 30,
1921."

"Working hard to learn the banking business"

On January 10, 1921, stockholders of the Park Region State Bank met in
the *Echo* assembly room with president E.E. Lobeck presiding. Lobeck
told the group that he had been working hard to learn the banking
business. Cashier Fred C. Proehl gave the financial report and stated they
were in good shape, but … they needed more deposits in order to make
loans.

This was a problem for all NPL-endorsed banks at the time, since
farmers were living on the economic edge and had no extra savings to
make deposits. Moreover, after the war ended and soldiers returned, they
did not necessarily come back to farming. Census statistics for 1920
showed that, for the first time, over 50 percent of the U.S. population was
defined as urban.[384]

Stockholders asked about salaries. Lobeck was paid $2,000 [$31,000] a
year as president; Fred C Proehl, cashier and manager, got $2,100
[$33,000]; Quitmeyer as assistant cashier was paid $125/monthly, or
$1,500 annually [$23,000]. One disgruntled attendee objected to
Lobeck's high salary because if Lobeck was "just learning the banking
process" as stated, he, as a stockholder, did not want to pay for Lobeck's
education.[385]

The next meeting, on January 22, determined the president and board of
directors for the coming year. Kalnes was sure that L. E. Olson would be
the new president and that F. C. Proehl would continue his "fine job" as
cashier. However, Lobeck was again chosen as president. At that point
Proehl and August Quitmeyer immediately resigned. Hermanson was
elected first vice president and T. J. Vickerman was elected 2nd vice
president. William Narum became cashier. Lobeck's yearly salary was
lowered to $1,800 [$28,000].

The Proehl Case

"Lobeck Causes Proehl's Arrest" – under this headline on January 18,
1922, the *Echo* let its readers know that on December 31 E.E. had gone
before Justice of the Peace E. P. Wright with "cause to have F. C. Proehl
arrested and dealt with according to law,"[386] for "knowingly, wrongfully,

falsely and feloniously altering an endorsement with intent to defraud" a sum of $500 [$7,700] on January 20, 1920, and for appropriating $400 [$6,000] on March 9, 1920, for his own use.

Kalnes blamed Lobeck for Proehl's wrongdoing, and sarcastically carped that Sheriff T. J. Vickerman would get to go on a joy ride at the county's expense to pick up Proehl in Freeborn County.[387] Proehl was charged with forgery and bound over for continuance, with bond of $2,500 [$38,000] paid by his relatives. He presented himself at the Justice Court in Alexandria on January 12, 1922.

Kalnes's article continues: "All the witnesses had a straight story and stuck to it, except Lobeck, who contradicted himself in his testimony." Lobeck first answered "late last fall" when asked when he knew of the trouble, but later said he knew about it a day or so after the deal was made by Proehl in early January 1920.

If E.E. knew of this problem that early – and initially even said he learned of it only "late last fall" – one can wonder: Why did he wait so long to file the complaint? There is no direct evidence to answer this question, but it is plausible to suggest that he did not want the public to know, especially since the charter for the bank had been issued only half a year earlier than Proehl's first offense, and undermining confidence in the new bank would destroy it before it got a start. Subsequent developments made clear that such a concern would have been entirely warranted. When Proehl's trial took place, an *Echo* front-page story subhead read: "Prosecution Charged With Attempt to Break Nonpartisan League in Douglas County And to Break Park Region State Bank For Forced Sale."[388]

January 21, 1922, the bank board chose officers for the coming year: L. G. Hermanson, president; Lobeck, 1st vice president; T. J. Vickerman, 2nd vice president.

E.E. wrote a letter to daughter Constance at Moorhead State Teacher's College on February 11.

Dear Constance,

Sending herewith $25 [$440].

I am still in the bank. The directors did not want me to leave yet. I gave them a talking to so that two of them had to use their handkerchief to dry their eyes. I don't think they will soon forget the day I had a meeting with them.

As I understand, there will soon be further trouble in the bank, but there will be others who will have to take part of the responsibility with me.

I understand that there was a disturbance in church, but you will have to see to it that you control yourself when something unusual happens. I stood one day and spoke in a church when a drunk man came down the aisle with a revolver to kill me. I spoke just as well both before and after. A couple of men took him and set him down in a pew and bound him and he beat in the pew in front of him so that the walls rang. To have self-control is one of life's great abilities.

Can tell you that Kalnes got a petition together for himself to be mayor of Alexandria, but when the count of the signatures on such a petition was taken and he didn't get a single one, he naturally gave up on his big plan to become mayor here in town. [Kalnes had started a "straw vote" in the *Echo* naming names for different offices in the area. Readers were invited to vote. It didn't have the outcomes he wanted.]

Greet Evangeline so much. Both of you think of your Creator in your youth. You don't know how much I think of you at night and pray that all will go well with you and that you may be protected from the evil world.

From your father,

E.E. Lobeck

A bank examiner met with the bank board on January 25 and ordered Proehl to pay back to the bank $450 [$8,000] that he had "wrongfully taken out of commissions on mortgage purchases." Proehl apparently ordered the interim cashier to write a cashier's check for $450 to the bank, but Proehl never paid for the check.

On the same day Lobeck was ordered to pay back $800 [$14,000] which the examiner claimed he was not entitled to under the law. Lobeck immediately paid the sum. It was stated that "Lobeck received $2/day [$35] for attending bank meetings of board of directors and drew expense money from time to time for traveling and expenses in addition to his salary." Sheriff Vickerman, by this time 2nd vice president of the bank, testified that part of Lobeck's salary was to "pay 'back salary' for his work to promote the new bank and solicit stockbuyers from January 1 to September 1 prior to the bank opening."

At the end of February, Proehl's trial was bound over to the District Court. On March 12, 1923, the state of Minnesota indicted F. C Proehl on nine charges totaling $7,350 [$130,000] – two of grand larceny in the first degree, one of forgery in the first degree, and six of forgery in the second degree, committed between September 1919 and January 1921.[389]

Sarcasm threads through Kalnes's assessment of the bank trial (although in his long article he acknowledges that he himself wasn't present, had not gotten access to a transcript, and had been dependent mostly on conversations with Proehl's attorney, Thomas Sullivan – who, it will be remembered, was the NPL attorney defending the Wolds). He accused Lobeck of not testifying at times because he was supposedly sick. "Lobeck was sick after he testified the first time, so the county attorney couldn't get him again. The defense will probably want him too if he is not too sick to testify. Lobeck was also sick the day the board elected a new president … The embarrassing part about testifying is that Tom Sullivan insists on going into Lobeck's affairs with the bank," asking for money for traveling expenses in addition to his salary. "It seems that Lobeck could never get enough."[390]

The jury was out for fifteen hours. Bold print headlines in the March 29, 1922 *Echo* reported the verdict: JURY FINDS F. C. PROEHL "NOT GUILTY" VERDICT REBUKE TO PROSECUTION. The story credited Sullivan with a "Masterful Speech." Prosecutor R. G. Anderson, the county attorney, stated in his speech to the jury that Proehl had embezzled thousands of dollars – and then, surprisingly, added that "Mr. Lobeck had no more business being president of that bank than I have to be president of the United States and Mr. Lobeck didn't know and doesn't know now what happened in that bank."

Kalnes wrote an editorial headlined "The *Echo* Vindicated."

> The Park Region *Echo* has been quite severely criticized even by some of
> our best friends because of things that we have said during the past two
> years or so about E.E. Lobeck. The evidence of the Proehl case brought
> out facts that we have known all along but which we dared not publish
> because the hero worship is so strong with some people that they would
> not have believed us. Now the facts are in evidence, brought out publicly in

district court. And if anyone has anything to apologize for, it is not the *Echo*.[391]

A week later, Kalnes wrote regarding the bank, "if the stockholders and directors now act wisely, the attempt by certain politicians to wreck the people's bank will not succeed. …We need the bank and control should be gotten out of the hand of selfish individuals."[392]

The bank was closed April 5, 1922.

> Commissioner Smith declared that Lobeck is no doubt honest but that he certainly is no banker and had no business to be in charge of a bank and that if the bank is reopened that some man would have to be found to take Lobeck's place, that in fact the department would never allow the bank to reopen with Lobeck in charge.[393]

The brickbats flew in many directions. Some blamed Kalnes for the bank's closing because of "excessive" loans taken by the *Echo* to subsidize its new building. Kalnes countered that the *Echo* made good on payments to the bank, and "the *Echo* loans would not be excessive if it had been on farm land instead of city property as banking law allows larger loans on farm land. The loan to the *Echo* being excessive is therefore a mere technicality of the law."[394]

Kalnes submitted his resignation to the *Echo* board on March 18 and announced it to readers on April 18. It would take effect at the end of May 1922.

Paul Kinney, editor of the *Alexandria Citizen*, referring to "the red and yellow Kalnes,"

> congratulates the *Echo* upon their success on finally getting the skids under him. Since coming to Douglas County this immoral, vindictive, Socialist dictator has been responsible for creating a condition of ill feeling and distrust among former friends and neighbors that will take years to eradicate. … Possessed with an abusive style and vulgar vocabulary, Kalnes is a voluminous writer and has a knack of twisting the truth that appeals to many people. … Abuse, untruths or half truths and innuendoes come as natural to him as water to a duck. … Kalnes may now look back upon his work and view the havoc he has wrought in a business, social and political way as a result of his selfish efforts to control League policies in Douglas County and his insane desire to brand all opponents of Nonpartisan propaganda as dishonest emissaries of Big Biz.[395]

A letter of May 15, 1922, from E.E. to his daughter Connie, includes this: "There have not been many happy days for me this past year and now I don't know what I shall do in the future – and all the lies and slander that I have had to take – but it will probably be good for something."

In her later years, E.E.'s daughter Martha reminisced about those days.

> The most vivid memories I had of "enemies" was the pain and helplessness and disappointment he suffered when the Park Region State Bank of which he was president failed because the treasurer absconded with or somehow mishandled its funds. There was talk at home of having to mortgage the house, or go into bankruptcy, a sure sign of failure with (in those days) a taint of wrongdoing, unthinkable for a Christian man. There was no backing of money; he had no insurance as he did not believe in it. The editor of the local newspaper defamed him unmercifully and there was an inimical group of townspeople who joined him.

The World's Purity Federation

E.E. collected money for the Lutheran Church and served as assistant financial secretary for the Alexandria area, always eager and willing to serve the church whenever he could.

He enjoyed the annual Østerdølslaget, held in Alexandria July 1-3, 1922 – speakers, activities, storytelling, lots of music, and a sightseeing automobile tour of the lovely park region. The auto tour was a fiasco when a crowd of Shriners from St. Paul staged a parade at the same time and caused such an upset that the Østerlanders had to give up. It is not implausible that these Shriners had another identity as well. In the aftermath of the 1915 film, "The Birth of a Nation," the Ku Klux Klan mounted an auto parade on the final day of the 1917 St. Paul Winter Carnival as a promotion for the Minneapolis Auto Show. "In the decade after The Birth of a Nation's release, the Klan expanded throughout the nation. Its leaders hired recruiters, who used the film to draw new members. Klan membership spread quickly through other fraternal orders, such as the Masons and the Shriners."[396]

But a feast of food was next on the agenda, and they filled up with rømmegrøt, meatballs, potatoes, stacks of lefse, flatbrød, fåttigmand, and the enticing aroma of coffee. E.E. was elected vice president for the coming year.

In 1906 E.E. had written, in anticipation of "what we shall do once drinking has been defeated," that "there is no danger that there will be so much sense in the world that reformers will be without work." [See pages 58-59.] By midsummer 1922 he decided to engage with the World's Purity Federation, and met with B.S. Steadwell, its president, at the organization's headquarters in La Crosse, Wisconsin.

This organization – which had as one of its watchwords, "Paul's advice to Timothy, 'Keep thyself pure,' would, if generally followed, free the world of ninety percent of its poverty, disease, warfare, suffering and unhappiness, and make unnecessary most of our charity and philanthropy"[397] – worried about white slavery, prostitution, and morals of children, both boys and girls, and their moral upbringing, thus appealing to women homemakers, members of the WCTU, women physicians, reformers, and Temperance workers. It also allied itself with eugenics and white supremacy. The call for a "Purity Sunday" in July 1915, to coincide with the Ninth International Purity Congress in San Francisco, was "For the consideration of the White Slave Traffic, Suppression of Vice, Sex Hygiene, Race Betterment; Social, Civic and Moral Welfare."[398]

Central to the Purity movement's strategy was the "White Cross Pledge." One was for young men:

I promise by the help of God:

1. To treat all women with respect, and endeavor to protect them from wrong and degradation.
2. To endeavor to put down all indecent language and coarse jests.
3. To maintain the law of purity as equally binding upon men and women.
4. To endeavor to spread these principles among my companions, and to try and help my younger brothers.
5. To use every possible means to fulfill the command, "Keep thyself pure."

Another was for young women:

I promise by the help of God:

1. To uphold the law of purity as equally binding on men and women.
2. To be modest in language, behavior, and dress.
3. To avoid all conversation, reading, pictures, and amusement which may put impure thoughts into my mind.

4. To guard the purity of others, especially of the young.

5. To strive after the special blessing promised to the pure in heart.[399]

It is easy to see how readily such a movement would appeal to E.E. He told Steadwell that he would first have to confer with Martha. Unsurprisingly, Martha wholeheartedly agreed – indeed, E.E. had told Steadwell that they had subscribed for years to *The Light*, the Purity Federation's magazine, and often, when an issue arrived, had spoken of a desire to "sometime enter this field of service."

E.E. was hired as a field secretary. This gave him opportunities to be among the people and speak in schools, churches, and various other institutions – a job he loved doing and that gave him purpose. Throughout September and October, as he traveled around in his car to engagements – never far from home and seldom away overnight – Martha often accompanied him, and "as she listened to his stirring messages felt that God was speaking through him."[400]

October 11, 1922 (his birthday), he wrote to daughter Constance on stationery of the World's Purity Federation, datelined Benson, Minnesota. The fourth paragraph reflects one of the concerns that attracted him to the Federation's work.

Dear Constance,

Was home a short while yesterday and heard that you had been sick! Mama thought it was mostly because you were nervous because some of your instructors criticized you a little too much. You must take these things calmly and only do your best. You must practice to depend more on yourself so all will go well. It is not so long ago since you wrote to say that things were going well so you must take the days as they come – they are not all alike. Some are good and some are less good – all will benefit us when we only take them in the best way. Take hold of yourself and do your best.

Today I am 58 years old. It would have been fun if I could have been home this evening, but it can't be. So I can congratulate you on a father who is 58 – and it is no great man you have for a father either but he wants to do what is right both for God and mankind.

I am having good meetings and lectures. People can seldom sleep at night afterwards.

Be careful. Young girls are being snatched up all over and think what if I should lose one of mine. God forbid it.

Don't forget to pray.

Loving greetings from your father, E.E. Lobeck

Later the same day he writes:

My dear Constance,

Wrote a little too early to you today. When I came to church this evening, I found your letter and two packages, one from Evangeline – a nice box of candy, and a pair, much too pretty, gloves from Torarin. So there was a letter from you. Took all to my room and opened these things after I had removed my wraps.

Now I cannot go to bed before I have written and thanked you for your letter. It did me so much good that I sat down and cried with joy. You had no gift, but your letter was better than all the money in the world. A thousand, thousand thanks for what you wrote. Now I have congratulated myself because I have such a splendid daughter as you. Again I will say thanks. This little letter will make me stronger both in body and soul for a long time. Thanks, a thousand thanks!

Spoke this evening to 400 people. If I had read your letter before I spoke I would have spoken much better than I did, although people said I spoke magnificently.

God bless you and good night!

Your happy father, E.E. L.

Proehl Case closed – without E.E.'s knowledge

The court system was not yet done with Proehl. Proehl's case was appealed, and indictments were continued to the District Court. A date was set for September 13, 1922. On that date, Proehl filed an affidavit of prejudice against the presiding judge and another judge was appointed to begin on September 18.

September 15, Thomas Sullivan, Proehl's lawyer, called the county attorney and asked the trial be delayed as Proehl was sick, maybe with the flu, and desired a continuance.

The next day Dr. May, a "reputable physician" in St. Paul, contacted

Sullivan with news that Proehl was diagnosed with appendicitis and needed an operation, but should recover enough to stand trial on September 25. May advised Proehl to stay in bed, stated that in his physical condition it would be too dangerous to attempt to travel to Alexandria and undergo the strain of a criminal trial, and asked for a continuance. Proehl stated he was not making this affidavit for the purpose of delay, and that he was ready and willing to go to trial anytime he was able.

Sunday, September 24, at 11 a.m., Dr. David Caldwell of St. Paul and Douglas County Attorney R. G. Anderson called at the home of Fred Proehl and his wife in Minneapolis. Mrs. Proehl said that Dr. May "had left the state a few days before on account of his wife's illness and that another doctor whose name she did not know had attended Mr. Proehl Friday and was now the attending physician."

Four hours later, Thomas Sullivan and Dr. M. Lyons arrived, and in the presence of attorneys Anderson and Sullivan examined Proehl. The conclusion was that he was in moderately good health, everything normal except bad breath and a complaint of tenderness in his right abdomen. It was the doctor's opinion that the stated tenderness was doubtful, and that there was no way to confirm unless there was an exploratory operation.

Thus, a continuance to October 23, 1922 was scheduled.

On October 16 Proehl went to Mayo Clinic under referral from Dr. May to be examined for ulcer or appendicitis. He asked for continuance for his trial.

October 25, 1922, Mayo Clinic responded to Dr. May their findings. Repeated X-rays of stomach showed no ulcers. His condition might be due to appendix. Proehl also showed chronic tonsillitis and infected teeth and a history of migraines. Mayo advised that Proehl have his appendix removed, along with his tonsils and infected teeth.

The continuance was granted, and trial date set for November 20, 1922.

Judgment finally came in a plea agreement on March 18, 1923. Proehl, his attorneys, and the county attorney representing the state, came before District Court Judge Nye in Alexandria. Proehl was permitted to withdraw his plea of not guilty to the charge of forgery in the first degree and enter a plea of guilty to the charge of grand larceny in the second degree. "It is the judgment and sentence of the Court that you Fred Proehl as punishment for the offence of grand larceny in the second degree to which you have duly entered a plea of guilty, be punished by being required to pay a fine of $250.00 [$4,400] and upon the payment of that sum to the Court, the motion of the county attorney for leave to Nole Pross the Indictments now pending will be granted." "Fine paid to Clerk in open Court."[401] Case closed.

But E.E. did not know this.

He went to downtown Alexandria on Monday morning, October 30, 1922, to help plan a reception for Norwegian-American historian Hjalmer Ruud Holand the following day. At noon E.E. wasn't feeling well. He returned home. Martha and his brother Ola and sister-in-law were there.

During the afternoon the attending doctor gave injections, relieving some pain. To Martha E.E. said, "If I die now, I shall go to glory." Then he asked for forgiveness for any harm or hurt he had done them. They assured him they had nothing to forgive.

He died about 6:30 pm.

The *Echo* said this on November 2:

> To the casual observer about town he appeared to be a rugged, and exceptionally well developed example of the old Viking type. He had, however, been subject to stomach trouble and its accompanying gas attacks, and it was one of these which caused his illness Monday. At first it was regarded as just the ordinary attack from which he would recover in a short time, but his heart became affected, and finally heart failure caused his untimely end in spite of the most diligent efforts of physicians.

In family lore, to the physical cause of death was added the burden of recent developments, what daughter Martha remembered as the work of "enemies" resulting in the bank failure recounted earlier. She concluded, "It was this incident, in particular, which my mother felt strongly about his death."

Friday, November 3, his open casket was placed in the library of his home. His niece commented that he looked so handsome and as if he would awake at any moment. "How brave Martha is," observed niece Ellen Berg. "We all admire her so much, but prayer gives her strength, she says. She is busy and looks after everybody and everything as before."

The funeral service began at 1:30 in the home, followed by the church service. The church could not hold all who came. Rev. Tjornholm spoke of E.E.'s church work; Prof. Nordberg of Augsburg spoke of E.E.'s ideas and principles and how proud they were to send out a man like him, of good strong character; Prof. Stageberg of Red Wing Seminary brought greetings from many Prohibition members. Waldemar Ager, editor of *The Reform*, described Lobeck: "A wonderful man to look at, straight as a candle, light and buoyant as if he walked on steel springs. There was power, power personified, and power radiated out from him. It was also in his voice, in his language and in the pictures he described."

R. R. Rønning spoke of seeing Lobeck at a recent meeting. "I got an eye on him in the middle of a crowd. He stood head and shoulders above all others. He loved his fellow man and he stood there and looked at people as if they were all his brothers and sisters. He beamed kindness, love, and popularity out of his whole being."

George F. Wells and Charles W. Dorsett, representing the state and national Prohibition Committees, compared Lobeck to all great martyrs who died in the fight. Rev. Bergstrom of Oscar Lake Church expressed sympathy from his congregation. Trysil Church sent condolences as well.[402]

His brother John gave a stirring and heartfelt eulogy, spiced with a touch of humor.

> He had a stirring in his soul. His speeches were realistic poems, life events, translated by his vivid imagination and performed in a language of pictures that gripped and mesmerized. When Lobeck was speaking people came, especially if they knew him, to hear that speaking. And they sat and listened, or stood, if there was no sitting room – there often were not enough sitting places when Lobeck spoke – until he was finished – and it sometimes took a long time before he was finished. But time was not long while listening to the word pictures that his mind conjured up. It was like a party around him anyway, in spite of the many grim and at times outright terrifying things he announced from the drinking world. When he spoke in the schoolhouses throughout the country, the walls would burst and the ceiling be lifted by the power of his voice.

> Lobeck had an unusually large crowd of upright friends, but also some bitter enemies – which all really important men have – who sought to

destroy his good name and back and otherwise make life miserable for him every way possible. But whether he was praised and spoken well of – and it was he who was – or he was persecuted by the enemy and misunderstood by some of his friends – so through it all he preserved his Christian faith and the humble Christian way to the last. He was one who could pray for his bitterest enemies.

Lobeck was a striking figure. Over six feet in height and broad in proportion, full bodied, with his long, curly black hair, with an eagle nose of the manly expression, with eyes, which in the game of whimsical play, often random, could express deep compassion and with the powerful grip of a master almost cause dread for the listener, so strong was it.[403]

E.E. is buried in Kinkead Cemetery, Alexandria, Minnesota.

U.S. Rep. Andrew Volstead was an honorary pallbearer.

Epilogue

"All the Good He Did Lives after Him"

Other players in this story, including two who had been E.E.'s adversaries, lived longer.

I. M. Kalnes left the *Echo* and Alexandria in May 1922. His plans to head some other small-town papers did not materialize. After a couple of years he took a journalism program in Chicago, and eventually ended his career writing a column for the *Capital Times* in Madison, Wisconsin. He died in March 1959. His obituary made no mention of his life in Alexandria or as editor of the *Echo*.[404]

Fred Proehl operated a grocery store for some years in Minneapolis. In 1936 he was appointed a deputy bank examiner. The 1940 census notes his occupation as a lecturer, giving talks about dealing with money. In 1942 he moved to Seattle, where he worked for Boeing, and also got back into the grocery business. In 1952 and 1956, he was nominated as the Greenback Party's candidate for president, and ran his campaigns from the back room of his grocery store; in 1956 he received three votes. (There is no continuity between this party in Seattle and the historical national Greenback Party, which existed 1874-1884.) Proehl died in 1970 at age 90.[405]

Niece Ellen Berg said of E.E.'s funeral that it "was beautiful – more like a victory festival. His enemies had been so cruel to him, and the speakers maintained that Uncle had not lost his fight. All the good he did lives after him."

Some accounting

A century after his death, and ninety years after the 21st Amendment to the U.S. Constitution repealed the 18th, "all the good he did" requires some accounting – especially as I enjoy a glass of wine while writing about my grandfather.

It would be hard – let's say impossible – to make the case that Prohibition was a successful policy. Yes, abuse of alcohol was a serious problem (and remains so), but the belief that the problem could be legislated away ran head-on into psychological and social and economic reality.

For E.E., the issue could be reduced to two institutions – as he wrote in 1905 about Alexandria, "The spiritual need can be satisfied in thirteen churches, and the bestial in thirteen saloons. The thirteen saloons have most followers – the beast is worshiped there seven days a week, the spiritual need is satisfied once a week in the churches." And there may be no image in the whole history of Prohibition more astonishing than E.E.'s dream in New York "that the angel Gabriel was expelled from Heaven because of excessive drinking." (See page 85).

But, during the years ruled by the 18th Amendment, in Stearns County, right in Alexandria's back yard, "Minnesota 13" had a national reputation as the strongest moonshine you could get, and locals justified breaking the law by saying they were simply saving their family farms. Alcohol played very differently in the cultures of German-American Catholics and Norwegian-American Lutherans.

Temperance and Women's Suffrage going hand-in-hand may appear anomalous today, but my grandfather and grandmother, E.E. and Martha, believed them inextricably bound together. These indeed were intertwined. If women didn't have the vote and. consequently, some rights, they had no say in their wellbeing at all, and no rights to vote for a candidate who could be open to help them in times of need with a drunk husband who controlled them and their children and the money. Poor Houses were their only means.

There is a kind of long-distance exhilaration I feel when imagining how deeply my grandparents must have welcomed both the 18th and the 19th Amendments, ratified just a year and a half apart – January 6, 1919 and August 18, 1920. If I have misgivings about the support for Prohibition by the Woman's Christian Temperance Union, those reservations are more than overbalanced by my appreciation for the support of Women's Suffrage by the Prohibition Party. The fight for the rights of women has gone far beyond the "protection" of women that motivated many men of my grandparents' generation, but I do appreciate the initial advances that were made under such now-outdated auspices.

The vitriol spewed at the Nonpartisan League can sound like QAnon and Proud Boys. I lived through the "Red scare" of the Joseph McCarthy years. I now know that my grandparents were vilified as though they were agents of Lenin. I am especially proud of E.E. for his opposition to the "America Firsters" of his day, and for his ringing defense of American identity as articulated by Lincoln. There are speeches of his that could be given today and seem entirely current.

Finally, I am grateful to my grandparents for the way they managed to retain their Norwegian identity while becoming as American as anybody else. There were undoubtedly moments of nostalgia, but longing for the old country was more than compensated for by commitment to the flourishing of the new country. Some developments since his time would likely give E.E. heartburn – for instance, the fact that the Super Bowl – insult to injury, on *Sunday* – is about as big a national celebration as Independence Day. But Social Security, Medicare, Voting Rights – these are in line with values he held dear – along with Temperance. And Temperance, if understood as Aristotle meant it – moderation in all things – is itself worth drinking a toast to.

Indeed, E.E. had some warrant for what he said at the state Prohibition Convention in 1912, which had adopted planks demanding better working conditions, equal taxation, equal reapportionment of legislative districts, laws about white slave traffic, conservation of natural resources – in addition to, of course, the evils of alcohol.

> We should be glad that our principles are taken up and advocated today by the greatest men in the nation – and we ought to be proud of the fact that the Prohibitionists have been doing the political thinking in the country for the last twenty years. Every advanced idea that has been brought forward by the Republicans and Democrats of late has for years been shining like a beacon light to progressive statecraft in the Prohibition platform. (See page 164.)

And I am grateful to have as part of my heritage an ancestor whose eyes and words could take in and reflect the beauty of the world:

> In a blink my thoughts were turned from the outer world to the inner. … What a landscape, what a view, – scarred, wrinkled hills and peaks, deep, dark valleys, where I still have not seen the bottom, rapid rivers, which

from time to time are grinding life to foam – but then there is light from other suns than the one that shines upon Earth, and so my whole inner being is rocked in eternal arms, and the soul is bathed in a light that is purified in its own clarity. (See page 158.)

The forest stood with branches stretching toward the sky, seagulls moved in silence with a quiet roof overhead, flower and leaf served as the tangents from the gentle summer afternoon rising up in worship to God in pianissimo. (See page 76.)

My life both ways

The story I have told in this book began with me holding in my hand a silver pitcher, given to my great-grandfather, Engebret Persen Lobeck, on the occasion of his baptism in 1813 at two weeks of age. The story concludes two centuries later, with a completion of the Norway-America circle – a kind of testimony to E.E.'s musing on memories that "make me live twice – live my life both ways, and the longings follow, to support the hope of the soul, and the loss fills the emptiness and mends my shortcomings." (See page 159.)

But first, leading to the completion of the circle, is the story of the 32 years my grandmother Martha lived as a widow – during which time she never wavered in her belief that "his enemies, who had been so cruel to him," were responsible for E.E.'s early death.

She was left at age 48, with a young child still at home and absolutely no finances. It was difficult to stay in Alexandria. Though she was an extremely smart woman, there were no opportunities for women in those days. E.E. died intestate and Martha, shortly after the funeral, petitioned in court for administration of the estate. She retained a life interest in the homestead and the five surviving children had an undivided 1/5 each in the homestead subject to the life interest of Martha. She and her daughter, Martha, moved to a four-plex apartment in Minneapolis near the University of Minnesota and struggled to earn a living teaching people how to weave wicker lamps and other items, working as an aide at the University of Minnesota hospital, and working as a parish worker at a local Lutheran church that paid little more than a pittance.

She gave most of her time and energy to the work of her church, having served as Ladies Aid president and Sunday School superintendent for many years in Alexandria. In Hope Church she served as parish assistant, as organizer of the Glencar branch of the Sunday School, and director of the church's welfare program. She was a life member of the Women's Missionary Federation and held a life membership in the Minnesota WCTU, of which she had been president of the Alexandria district from 1909 to 1919.

Grandma Lobeck, as I knew her when I was a young girl, was kind, sweet, and never offered an opinion or complaint. She seemed to exist at the perimeter of family doings. Until I started research for this book, I never knew of her strength, her ability to take charge, her accomplishments, her endurance – and her suffering. She asked for nothing. With all her children raised, college educated, and now independent, except for eight-year-old little Martha, she remained strong.

Young Martha stayed with Mama until the age of 37, graduating high school and working to add to their meager income. Her siblings, married and busy with their lives, expected young Martha to stay with Mama and be the caretaker, though she was never asked. She had so wanted to go to college like her siblings, but that was unaffordable and a source of personal pain all her life.

By 1951, young Martha took control of her life and applied for a career in the U.S. State Department Foreign Service. She was accepted as a secretary in the U.S. Embassy in Vienna. There she met a young U.S. diplomat, Findley Burns, and they married in 1953. Findley grew up in Baltimore in a family with Scottish background, was Ivy League educated – and was Episcopalian! Not Lutheran, Midwestern, or Norwegian! That was a stretch for Grandma, but she rose gracefully to the fact. When Findley and Martha were married in Vienna, she stayed up that night setting her watch to Vienna time and read the marriage service in the Book of Common Prayer at the hour of the wedding. (In a rather nice irony, Findley Burns would later become U.S. Ambassador to Jordan and to Ecuador, where Martha – who at two months of age in 1914 had been "dedicated to the Prohibition cause" at a WCTU convention – was hostess on occasions at which alcohol was routinely served.)

In 1953 Mama's children gathered to be with her at Christmas. It was decided that the siblings would contribute to subsidize a trip for her to

Norway the following summer. Daughter Martha and son-in-law Findley would meet her plane in Oslo and take her to Trysil – her childhood home.

On June 8, 1954, she was found dead beside her bed – two weeks before her 80th-birthday trip.

While I was researching, a letter fell out of an old book of Grandma's – a letter from a childhood friend in Trysil, written soon after Martha's emigration to America in 1885. The letter told of how she missed her, and they probably would not see each other again until they met in Heaven.

On my next trip to Trysil, I took the letter with me to find out who might be its writer. I showed it to Per Oskar Strandvold. He broke into tears. The letter was from *his* grandmother. Per Oskar took me to her grave. She and my grandmother had died two weeks apart.

Appendix

E.E. the Novelist

In March 1899, when he was 34 years old, E.E. published a novel, *Billeder fra Dodens Dal* (*Pictures from the Valley of the Dead*). It was popular enough to go into a second edition in 1907 – the year E.E. began his first term in the Minnesota House of Representatives. It is printed in Norwegian Gothic script; the entire text is available both in the original Gothic and in Roman script at https://babel.hathitrust.org/cgi/ssd?id=umn.31951001016844h;seq=1;num=.

To call it a "novel" is a stretch. The title page calls it a *fortälling*, which means "narration." In the Preface E.E. disclaims authorial originality. "Almost all the events mentioned in the book are either personally known to me, or they are cut out of various magazines – events from real life. The words that are put into the mouths of the various characters are words that I have heard with my own ears or have heard others tell. It has been my endeavor to get the contents of the story of such quality that it could kindle a burning hatred of drink and the saloon among those who read it. I have the will, but I lack the ability to portray the ravages of drunkenness as they should be portrayed." Portray them, though, he does, repeatedly.

The title is apt. The pages are littered with corpses. There are the men who die from drink, but they are outnumbered by the wives, and especially the children, who from neglect, or violence, or the poverty caused by alcoholism pass into eternity too soon. There are suicides. There is an execution.

The heart of the book, taking up at least half its length, is a narration by Georg Ravn, a young man who early on attracts the eye of Alma Jacobson, who is herself a model of the pure and abstinent. We learn that "most of the youth were against her for not joining the dance. 'Alma can't have any fun,' they thought. 'She never goes to the dance.' … She liked to sit at home with a good book. … Among the youth there was no one to whom Alma could open her heart. As long as the conversation revolved around hats and dresses, horses and riding gear, they were enough; but if she brought forward thoughts of eternity and sought to bring beautiful images before the soul, that was the end of the conversation." It's easy to imagine E.E., at the time of writing, projecting onto Alma his ideals of a danceless and thoughts-of-eternity future for his own daughters, Inge Evangeline, then two, and Dagny Miranda, just born (there would eventually be three more).

When Alma first sees Georg, she notices a sadness in him. It takes a while for there to be an opening for him to talk – then he hardly ever stops. But … his story is in two dissonant parts.

First is an account of the efforts of Georg's father, an abstinence man, often with Georg in tow, to sway his church to bash the saloons. The powers that be in the town and the church, pre-eminently the cigar-smoking, slightly buffoonish mayor (who, we learn toward the end of the novel, eventually dies of alcoholism), are determined to license saloons, on the grounds that it's good for the city – brings in revenue that builds schools and roads and other amenities. "And, after all, Jesus turned water into wine, didn't he?"

The priest, because he didn't want to split his congregation, was initially in the mayor's pocket – "Because you know" he said to Georg's father, "that the majority of my congregation is in favor of the saloon, and if I am going to agitate against their interests, you know how it will go." But he did indicate his private opinion: "I'll probably mark my ballot against the saloon; that's all I can do now."

The priest finally "sees the light" and starts preaching Temperance. A church trustee counters: the Temperance people "forbid us to enjoy intoxicating drinks which are a gift from God; and if God's word is true, then the priest has sinned, and I demand that he ask both God and the congregation for forgiveness for his behavior." The upshot: the priest is eventually voted out by the congregation but is sustained by the faithful in rural areas.

Yet another option drops into the conversation when a visiting evangelist appears. Instead of arguing for licensing saloons or outlawing them, he says the only thing necessary is to convert people to Christ – they will then simply pass by the saloon. "Let us preach Christ, convert sinners to Jesus, then there will soon be an end to drinking and saloons, glory be to God!" "The drunkard must repent to God. If everyone converted to God, the saloon would soon dry up. Praise the Lord!"

But the last word is given in a trial, when the defendant exclaims: "The saloon business in this country is responsible for almost all murders, bloodshed, riots, poverty, and grief. … You legalized the saloon, which made me a drunkard and a murderer, and you are guilty together with me before Almighty God in Heaven and the people on Earth for the murder of my wife."

Among the tales of violence and abandonment that Georg relates, the one that most perilously sits between tragedy and melodrama is of the time his father hears a cry from a barn and climbs the ladder inside to find a young boy, bruised and in pain. "What did your father beat you for?" "Father got drunk and hit me because I didn't want to steal." "Have you ever stolen?" "Yes, I was once a street thief." "And why don't you want to steal more?" "I went to the mission school and there they told me about God, about Heaven and about Jesus, and they taught me: You must not steal. I will not steal again." "My little boy, you must not stay here – you will die. I will go and get help." "Thank you, but don't you want to hear me sing a sad song before you go?"

The gist of the sad song: "Have mercy, Jesus. be with me. Let me go to you soon. Oh, I want to go to you, gentle Jesus. Don't forbid it. In your Heaven full of peace, give me a place." Georg's father returns with medicines – and finds the boy dead. Georg continues the story: "Father came home with tears in his eyes, but with a heart full of thanks to God, because, as he said, 'Let the little children come to me,' not the children of rich people, nor the children of respectable people, nor children with good education or fine clothes – no, he sends his merciful angels into the poor home of poverty and need, where we will not go, in order to bring his redeemed to the peace of Heaven, even though they are broken and abused, lying alone and singing their last song."

Alma is both anguished and enchanted by the tales of heroic efforts on behalf of abstinence – "If I could, I would open my arms for the whole world's needs and quench them with my heart's blood!" But then she is caught off-guard when Georg tells her that his own story has a much darker side – "I almost regret that I have begun my story; for now also my own life must come forward; it will push you away from me."

The titles of Chapters 9 and 10 capture the continuation of Georg's tale: "Worse and Worse"; "Sacrifice upon Sacrifice."

Georg worked in Chicago as agent for his father's Minnesota dairy business, began drinking, became addicted, started gambling. To demonstrate the depth of his depravity, Georg recounts an instance when, in a gambling den, he witnessed a man kill his mother and then himself. "But do you think we stopped with our game? No! We were not ones to leave our cards, even if Death was around us. We had to finish the game." "The shame, resentment, guilty conscience, weakened strength, lack of money and penchant for drink and gambling caused me to have suicidal thoughts. I was ruined in body and soul."

He wrote a letter to his parents saying he would kill himself, but before he could carry out the threat his father came to Chicago to look for him, persuaded him to live, and wrote to his wife, Georg's mother, explaining their son's change of heart, but enclosed also the suicide note, which is what she read first – and promptly died of a broken heart.

On hearing this, Alma exclaims, "There is one who can help you, the Man of Sorrows from Nazareth, he who has come to save that which was lost, he can loose your bonds and set you free." Georg's response makes a classic distinction between Christ and Christians:

> Perhaps he would do it; but how many of those who call themselves by his name will do it? Men will not. Women will not help a wretch to tear off his deadly, Death-binding bonds. Society won't. His Church says it will, but God help us, it won't, because the majority of Christ's church followers today, on Election Day, are walking shoulder to shoulder with the saloon

owner, and the raw mob that supports the devil's most soul-disturbing work among our people. Go and investigate, and you will find my words true. You will find the majority of our priests, professors and teachers, the majority of our parishioners so blinded that in order to preserve their loved ones, the old political party can sacrifice around 75,000 humans per year on the saloon's blood-stained altar. If they apply Jesus of Nazareth's doctrine in accordance with this matter, then he has no help for me.

As Georg's story continues, he tells of being tempted again: "I was completely condemned to love the institution which I hated most of all on earth." And after many more deaths, including those of a young brother and sister frozen in the snow, Alma urges him to "gather the people together and tell them what you have told me." "I can't," Georg responds, "until I myself am freed."

Chapter 11's title tells of the turnaround, or at least its initial stage: "Wrestles." Alma loves Georg more and more, but he knows he's not ready. "In great humiliation and shame, he came to say his last farewell." She sings a song, then wails, "I've lost you." He protests: "You still own me completely!" He wants to take her hand, but she hides it behind her with these words: "If I own you, I also own the Powers that own you. ... If I ever come to you with both hands, then you own me." Georg Ravn takes his hat and overcoat and rushes out into the night.

Around Christmas Alma sees Georg again briefly, sitting on the stone where she first glimpsed him, but it's still not both hands time. Come summer, though, at a Fourth of July celebration festooned with American and Norwegian flags, Alma is scheduled to give a declamation, and when she sees Georg in the crowd, she waxes eloquent – "Because I know how hard, how painfully you struggle, I want to bring spring and song to you at last" – and then draws analogies with human emotion and nature's glories that we are familiar with from E.E.'s meditations and poems. When she's finished, Georg, unscheduled, comes to the podium and delivers a stem-winding abstinence speech.

Chapter 12, "Both Hands," completes the reversal – from Boy and Girl meet through Boy and Girl part to Boy and Girl get married.

After the celebration, Georg tells Alma, "Now I'm free. Now I am a man again, I am changed. Your prayer has been heard." "How did you become free?" "Your words, 'If I own you, I also own the Powers that own you,' pursued me day and night. I came to ask myself what Powers it was that possessed me, and to my unspeakable horror I found that it was the evil Powers. And as long as they held me, I was lost, I knew it. There was a struggle. Heavy, long, nightly struggles, until Jesus came in a quiet hour and gave me peace. Do not be surprised that I am happy and surrendered. Jesus has set me free." And the next day: "It is good that there is something called 'grace for sin.'"

Not long after,

> They came to the gate by Alma's home. She went through first, and he came after her and turned to put the hook on, and turned again to say goodnight, but there she stood with the full moonlight in her face and both hands outstretched towards him. He needed no explanation, but went and cradled her in his arms so firmly and so warmly, as if he wanted to shut out the world with all its loss and pain. Alma's mother stood by the window and prayed: "Lord, you gentle God, bless, bless these two," and the chariot lighted down on their covenant.

Pictures from the Valley of the Dead is too didactic to count as an effective novel, though it has the virtue of giving at least a hearing – if often couched sarcastically – to the other side of the issue. There are more dead bodies than necessary to make the point. Alma and Georg are not persuasively complex characters. Perhaps E.E. thought of the book as Prohibition's analog to Abolition's *Uncle Tom's Cabin*, but if so, he is not in Harriet Beecher Stowe's league. It is difficult to know, or even guess, how widely *Billeder fra Dodens Dal* was read. E.E.'s prominence in the Norwegian-American community, especially after he became a successful politician, might well have generated sufficient publicity to make a market, though it would not have gone beyond the limits of people fluent in Norwegian. That there was a second edition suggests it got some attention.

Notes

Many references are to two newspapers:

The Reform, a weekly Norwegian language paper published in Eau Claire, Wisconsin, 1886-1941. E.E. frequently wrote for the paper, with the heading "Under Blyanten" ("Under the Pencil"). Beginning with its Vol. 11 (1896), *The Reform* has been published online in the original at https://rescarta.apps.uwec.edu/Ager-Web/jsp/ RcWebBrowseCollections.jsp. The English translations were made by Magne Teppen.

Park Region Echo, published in Alexandria, Minnesota, 1908-1969. E.E. occasionally wrote for it, and he was frequently the subject of articles.

[1] Translated from the Norwegian by Constance Lobeck Kahl. Engebret E. Löbeck, *Forglemmigei: Nogle Sange* (*Forget-me-not: Some Songs*) (Eau Claire, WI: "Reform"'s Trykkeri, 1894), is available online as a Google book, https://www.google.com/books/edition/Forglemmigei/ j_QwAQAAMAAJ?hl=en&gbpv=1&dq=.

[2] Mark Lawrence Schrad, *Smashing the Liquor Machine: A Global History of Prohibition* (Kindle Edition: Oxford University Press, 2021), 15-20.

[3] Embret P Journal, Apr 14, 1893. The Journal, covering the years 1867-1894, is quoted here and throughout in the translation by his granddaughter, Constance Lobeck Kahl.

[4] Clarence J. Carlsen, *Years of Our Church* (Minneapolis: The Lutheran Free Church Publishing Company, 1942), 12-13; excellent history of establishing of the Lutheran Free Church in America. Available at https://babel.hathitrust.org/cgi/pt id=wu.89067355065&view=1up&seq=7

[5] Ibid., 13-17.

6 On the matter of perjury, Prof. Mark Tranvik of Luther Seminary suggests this: "In nineteenth century Norway the rite of confirmation was also your admission to full citizenship. And you had to be confirmed through the state church. So the free churchers were counseling against going through state church confirmation for the sake of gaining citizenship. It was a form of lying (since you rejected the official church) done to gain admission to state privileges." Prof. Mark Granquist, also of Luther Seminary, offers another perspective: "What did these pietists have against the formal, traditional process of confirmation as practiced in the State Church of Norway in the 19th century? Well, the pietists very much believed that a person needed to have a subjective, personal, experience of faith to be a true Christian. The process of confirmation was much more of an objective educational experience, where one learned the doctrinal positions of Lutheranism and assented to them. In the State Church process, yes, being confirmed was equivalent of citizenship. But I think the issue was more that one considered themselves a true Christian simply by assent and rite. Now the pietists did not eliminate confirmation, but tried to re-invent it along the lines of a subjective, conversion process – where the pietist understanding of what made one a 'true' Christian was taught. The old pietist catechism of Bishop Pontoppidan was widely used along these lines – confirmation was to urge the students to seek such a relation with God. Could 'perjury' here mean 'lying to God,' claiming to be a Christian when in fact one had not had the requisite conversion experience?" With thanks to both of these learned scholars!

7 *Østerdalslaget Mindeskrift*, 1913.

8 Excerpts from E.E. Lobeck, "Tryslinger i Amerika" (1912); original handwritten manuscript, owned by Tulla Froyen; translated from Norwegian by Constance Lobeck Kahl. Published in Norwegian in K. G. Nilsen, compiler, *Østerdølenes Saga* (Duluth, MN: Fuhr Publishing & Printing Co., 1938), 320-69. Available at http://www.dxhansen.com/osterdolenes-saga.pdf. These excerpts at Nilsen, 323-26.

9 *The Minnesota Guide, A Handbook of Information for the Travelers, Pleasure Seekers and Immigrants, Concerning all Routes of Travel to and in the State; Sketches of the Towns and Cities on the Same, etc., etc., etc.* (St. Paul: E. H. Burritt & Co., 1869); reprint facsimile edition (Bedford, MA: Maplewood Books, 2001), 8-9, 11. Text available online at Library of Congress: chrome-extension:// efaidnbmnnnibpcajpcglclefindmkaj/https://tile.loc.gov/storage-services/service/gdc/lhbum/ 01097/01097.pdf.

10 Ibid., 15.

11 "Douglas County, Minnesota," in Martin Ulvestad, *Nordmændene i Amerika: Early Norwegian Settlements in Minnesota*, 1907, trans. Olaf Kringhaug, at http://www.rootsweb.ancestry.com/ ~mnnorman/miscellaneous/earlysettle.htm.

12 *History of Douglas and Grant Counties, Minnesota: Their People, Industries and Institutions, With Biographical Sketches of Representative Citizens and Genealogical Records of Many of the Old Families*, Vol. 1, Constant Larson, editor-in-chief (Indianapolis: B. F. Bowen & Company, 1916), 176. The material on 175-78, "Pioneer Life in Holmes City," begins, "In response to a request from the *Park Region Echo*, Hon. E.E. Lobeck, state senator from this district, recently prepared the following brief review of pioneer conditions in the neighborhood of his boyhood home in Holmes City township. 'To enumerate the struggles and hardships the first settlers had to go through,' wrote Senator Lobeck, 'would take up too much space, but suffice me to say that this lot fell upon a rugged class of people, strong in body and mind, who converted the wilderness into a garden spot.'" What Lobeck wrote for 1916's book has some overlap with 1912's "Tryslinger i Amerika," but is not identical.

13 "Tryslinger i Amerika." Nilsen, 326.

¹⁴ Ibid. Nilsen, 325-26.

¹⁵ Ibid. Nilsen, 327.

¹⁶ All these details are found in Embret P Journal – in which weather is a major player throughout.

¹⁷ *History of Douglas and Grant Counties*, Vol. 1, 176-77.

¹⁸ "Tryslinger i Amerika." Nilsen, 329.

¹⁹ Ibid. Nilsen, 331.

²⁰ Agricultural census, available on microfilm at the Minnesota History Center.

²¹ Emeroy Johnson, *A Church is Planted: The Story of the Lutheran Minnesota Conference 1851-1876* (Minneapolis: Lund Press, Inc., 1948), 286, 293. Available at https://catalog.hathitrust.org/Record/005973043.

²² Ibid., 295

²³ Elroy Stock, *Church History of Wennersborg and Oscar Lake Congregations*, date unknown, 19. *Centennial Anniversary 1871-1971, History of the Norunga Lutheran Church, Lowry, Minnesota*, 6.

²⁴ Embret P Journal, Jan 1872.

²⁵ Carlsen, *Years of Our Church*, 18-20. The Missouri Synod's dogma on predestination was rejected by these other groups.

²⁶ Embret P Journal, Apr 1874.

²⁷ Carlsen, *Years of Our Church*, 37.

²⁸ A.E. Strand, compiler, *A History of the Swedish-Americans of Minnesota* (Chicago: The Lewis Publishing Company, 1910), Vol. 1. Pastor Peter Carlson immigrated from Sweden in 1854 as a lay preacher. He was ordained in 1859. https://babel.hathitrust.org/cgi/pt/search?id=njp.32101067427748&q1=Rev+P+Carlsen&sz=25&start=1&sort=seq&hl=true, 170.

²⁹ Embret P Journal, Jan 30, Feb 13, Feb 20, Mar 5, 1876.

³⁰ Embret P Journal, Mar 7, Jun, Jun 17, Jul 9, Jul 13, Oct 3, 1876.

³¹ George Strandness, *History of St. Pauli Lutheran Congregation 1874-1949* (Pope County Historical Society Museum).

³² Embret P Journal, Dec 25, 1877 (for Christmas Day reference).

³³ Ole Steen's descendants loaned me his journal.

³⁴ *History of Douglas and Grant Counties*, Vol. 1, 178.

³⁵ *Østerdølenes Saga*, 371-72.

³⁶ "Famous Minnesota Winter Storms": https://web.archive.org/web/20090107005538/http://climate.umn.edu/doc/historical/winter_storms.htm.

³⁷ Embret P Journal, right hand flyleaf.

³⁸ Embret P Journal, Jan 20, Apr, Apr 15, Jun 1, Dec, 1873.

³⁹ Embret P Journal, 1874.

⁴⁰ *Centennial History of Norunga Lutheran Church, Lowry, Minnesota, 1871-1971* (Pope County Historical Society).

⁴¹ Embret P Journal, Apr 1875.

⁴² Embret P Journal, 1876.

⁴³ "Tryslinger i Amerika." Nilsen, 332.

[44] "Frontier Scare," *Alexandria Post*, Jul 14, 1876. The story is told also in Embret P Journal, Jul 13, 1876, where he concludes, characteristically, "But we still had grasshoppers to contend with until the 21st."

[45] *Alexandria Post*, Jul 21, 1876

[46] Embret P Journal, Aug 1, 1876.

[47] Ibid., Sep 17, 1876; Sep 13,1875.

[48] "Tryslinger i Amerika." Nilsen, 331-32.

[49] Kate Roberts, *Minnesota 150: The People, Places, and Things that Shape Our State* (St. Paul: Minnesota Historical Society Press, 2007), 63.

[50] Annette Atkins, *Harvest of Grief: Grasshopper Plagues and Public Assistance in Minnesota, 1873-1878* (St. Paul: Minnesota Historical Society Press, 1984), 68.

[51] Ibid., 84.

[52] https://www.trysilhistorielag.com/trysilingers/engemoenkrisk/, from Embret P Journal, Jun 29, 1877, and *Alexandria Post*, Jul 6, 1877.

[53] *Alexandria Post*, Feb 22, 1878.

[54] Embret P Journal, 1878-1879.

[55] In 2010 Trysil Kommune received a large collection of letters that included several from Embret P to his sister Johanne Viken (1807-1884) and brother-in-law Nils Viken (1806-1894). He wrote with blue ink on pink paper and filled four pages of dense text. Delivery from Holmes City to Trysil took a month.

[56] Trysil Ladies Aid notes, at Douglas County Historical Society; Embret P Journal, Feb 1, 1881.

[57] Steven J. Keillor, "Rural Norwegian-American Reading Societies in the Late Nineteenth Century," *Norwegian-American Studies*, 33 (1992: Norwegian American Historical Association), 139.

[58] Ibid. Charter members were Christian Saugstad, John Aasen, Chris Haugen, John Pedersen, Karen Pedersen, Jacob Johanson Mollan, Andrew Knudson, Ole E. Fagerlie, Randine Saugstad, Ida Saugstad, Mette Knudson, Maria Strandvold, E. Lobeck, Albert Engemoen, B. Tøraasen, John Mattson, Ingerinus Lobeck, Kirstine Engemoen, Peter Aas, Jonas Tallgren, Eline Haugen, Ole Støen, Ole Søberg, Ola Lobeck, H.H. Tøraasen, H. Tøraasen.

[59] Holmes City Læseforening, Records, 1877-1905, at Norwegian-American Historical Association.

[60] Alexandria Justice of the Peace Docket Book, Box 128.F.1.4.F, at Minnesota Historical Society.

[61] Olaf Morgan Norlie, *History of the Norwegian People in America* (Minneapolis: Augsburg Publishing House, 1925), 277.

[62] Embret P Journal, Apr 20, 1893.

[63] "Farwell," *Alexandria Republican*, Apr 29, 1896.

[64] "Lobeck's Father is Dead," *The Reform*, Apr 21, 1896. Obituary written by E.E. Lobeck. Re: the poem: The first stanza is apparently a Norwegian variant of a text included as No. 220 in the section "Old Prayers" of *Danske Sagn*, New Series, Vol. 2 (Religiøse Sagn), collected by Evald Tang Kristensen (Copenhagen, 1928), 216-217 (https://www.google.com/books/edition/Danske_sagn_Ellefolk_nisser_osv_religi%C3%B8/Ad01AAAAIAAJ?hl=en&gbpv=1&dq). The second stanza is from "Hjertens Jesus, i dit hjerte," a hymn popular among Lutheran Pietists, by A. C. Rutström (1721-1772) (https://hymnary.org/text/hjertens_jesus_i_dit_hjerte).

[65] E.E. Lobeck, "Holmes City, Minn.," Letter to *The Reform*, Aug 23, 1892.

[66] *The Reform*, Nov 11,1922.

[67] *The Reform*, Sep 19, 1905.

[68] "Under Blyanten," *The Reform*, Nov 25, 1902.

[69] "Under Blyanten," *The Reform*, Nov 27, 1906.

[70] "Under Blyanten," *The Reform*, Apr 12, 1904.

[71] "Under Blyanten," *The Reform*, Feb 28, 1911.

[72] Beretning om Det Ottende Aarsmøde for Wisconsin's Totalafholdsselskab (Eau Claire, WI: Reform's Trykeri, 1895).

[73] Extracts from "Under Blyanten," *The Reform*, Aug 14, Jan 9, Apr 10, Jun 12, 1894; Nov 28, 1893; Jan 9, 1894; Apr 12, 1904.

[74] Extracts from "Under Blyanten," *The Reform*: Aug 14, Jun 12, Jan 9, Apr 10, 1894; Dec 30, 1902; Nov 28, 1893; Jul 4, 1905; Mar 2, 1897; May 13, 1902; Jan 6, Apr 21, 1903; Nov 14, 1905. "Drive 20 miles": A comment by attendee at speech in Fergus Falls in March 1902, as told in family papers.

[75] "Under Blyanten," *The Reform*, Jul 28, 1908.

[76] *The Reform*, Apr 17, 1894.

[77] Extracts from "Under Blyanten," *The Reform*: Apr 12, 1904; Jun 12, 1894; Dec 12, 1905.

[78] "Under Blyanten," *The Reform*, Nov 22, 1892.

[79] "Under Blyanten," *The Reform*, Apr 11, 1905.

[80] *The Reform*, Jul 1, 1902.

[81] "Under Blyanten," *The Reform*, Dec 30, 1902; Jan 6, 1903.

[82] "Under Blyanten," *The Reform*, Oct 24, 1905.

[83] Nathan Heller, "Was the Automotive Era a Terrible Mistake?" *The New Yorker*, Jul 29, 2019, 25.

[84] "Under Blyanten," *The Reform*, Nov 25, 1902.

[85] *The Reform*, Dec 16, 1902.

[86] "Under Blyanten," *The Reform*, Dec 11, 1906.

[87] "Under Blyanten," *The Reform*, Mar 10, 1903.

[88] This is the final verse of E.E.'s song "I skoven" ("In the forest"), in *Forglemmigei*, 13.

[89] A clear allusion to Proverbs 6:6: "Go to the ant, thou sluggard; consider her ways, and be wise" (KJV).

[90] "Under Blyanten," *The Reform*, Jun 14, 1910.

[91] "Under Blyanten," *The Reform*, May 26, 1908. Early reference to lecturing in both languages: "Under Blyanten," *The Reform*, Mar 2, 1897. The "name change" was also indulged in by E.E.'s close friend, the editor of The Reform, Waldemar Ager, who frequently went by William.

[92] *The Reform*, May 17, May 8, May 22, 1900.

[93] *The Reform*, Jul 3, 1900.

[94] *The Reform*, Jul 10, 1900.

[95] *The Reform*, Aug 21, 1900.

[96] Information about the rally held at Støa, June 16-17, 1900, is compiled from several sources: "Avholdsstevne i Trysil," *Østlandske Tidende*, Jul 14, 1900; "Afholdsstevne i Trysil," *Menneskenvennen* ("People's Friend": publication of Det Norske Totalavholdsselskap = Norwegian Total Abstinence Society, which changed its name to DNT Edru Livsstil in 2015), Jun 16 and 17, 1900; notes by Olaf Teppen, "E.E. Løbeck fra Holmes City i U.S.A, besøker sin fødebygd Trysil," *Årbok for Glåmdalen*, 1970, 106-07; research done by Magne Teppen, Ole Arild Bovolden, and Hilding Sponberg.

[97] "Til Folk fra Trysil," *The Reform*, Sep 26, 1911.

[98] "Under Blyanten," *The Reform*, Jul 4, 1905. On Nansen, see https://en.wikipedia.org/wiki/Fridtjof_Nansen.

[99] "Under Blyanten," *The Reform*, Apr 10, 1894.

[100] "Under Blyanten," *The Reform*, Apr 12, 1904.

[101] chrome-extension://efaidnbmnnnibpcajpcglclefindmkaj/https://www2.census.gov/library/publications/decennial/1910/abstract/supplement-mn.pdf

[102] "Under Blyanten," *The Reform*, Jun 13, 1905. The salt and light imagery is from the Sermon on the Mount, Matthew 5:13-16.

[103] "Under Blyanten," *The Reform*, Apr 11, 1905. Oliver W. Stewart (1867-1937) was chairman of the Prohibition Party 1900-05, and briefly a member of the Illinois legislature (https://en.wikipedia.org/wiki/Oliver_W._Stewart).

[104] "Under Blyanten," *The Reform*, Apr 21, 1903.

[105] "Under Blyanten," *The Reform*, Jan 8, 1907.

[106] "Clean Out the Whole Basement," *Park Region Echo*, Feb 10, 1910.

[107] *Glenwood Gopher-Park Region Echo*, Mar 8, 1905.

[108] *Glenwood Gopher-Park Region Echo*, Apr 20, 1905.

[109] *Park Region Echo*, Mar 13, 1917.

[110] *Park Region Echo*, Mar 27, 1917.

[111] *Park Region Echo*, Jun 6, 1916.

[112] "Under Blyanten," *The Reform*, Dec 11, 1906.

[113] David Dayen, "How Teddy Roosevelt Saved Football," *Politico*, Sep 20, 2014: https://www.politico.com/magazine/story/2014/09/teddy-roosevelt-saved-football-111146_Page2.html.

[114] *Washington Post*, Oct 15, 1905, quoted in Katie Zezima, "How Teddy Roosevelt Helped Save Football," *Washington Post*, May 29, 2014, at https://www.washingtonpost.com/news/the-fix/wp/2014/05/29/teddy-roosevelt-helped-save-football-with-a-white-house-meeting-in-1905/.

[115] *The Reform*, May 5, 1903. In April and May 1903 President Theodore Roosevelt, during an eight-week, 25-state tour, covered 14,000 miles across the American West. During his tour, Roosevelt gave a total of 263 speeches, seven or eight per day on average. The balance of the time he spent camping in back country: two days at Yosemite with conservation activist John Muir (almost certainly the "face overgrown with a dazzling white beard and lined with hair pale as linen" seen by E.E.), and 16 days in Yellowstone. https://www.wyohistory.org/encyclopedia/president-theodore-roosevelts-1903-visit-wyoming.

[116] "Under the Pencil," *Park Region Echo*, Dec 9, 1909.

[117] "Dancing by School Students," *Park Region Echo*, Nov 6, 1913.

[118] "For Representative," *Alexandria Post News*, Sep 6, 1906. After 1894, the *Alexandria Post* becomes the *Post News*.

[119] "Under Blyanten," *The Reform*, Nov 25, 1902.

[120] https://collection.mndigital.org/catalog/p16022coll518:1125#?c=&m=&s=&cv=4&xywh=-122%2C923%2C2232%2C1693. The online file suggests "1911(?)" as the publication date. See also the obituary for Youngdahl, https://startribune.newspapers.com/article/the-minneapolis-star-obituary-for-p-j/128287229/.

[121] https://www.loc.gov/item/usrep137086/. Youngdahl mistakenly calls the case "Crawley versus Christianson." The case was an appeal from the San Francisco police chief to a decision of the Circuit Court of the United States for the Northern District of California that granted a writ of *habeas corpus* to a San Francisco liquor dealer who had continued doing business without a license, on the grounds that he had been denied equal protection under the law as mandated by the 14th Amendment. The Supreme Court remanded him back to the police for arrest. Field, appointed to the Court by President Lincoln in 1863 as a tenth justice, added to the nine, wrote 544 opinions in his 34 years as an Associate Justice. https://en.wikipedia.org/wiki/Stephen_Johnson_Field.

[122] John Albert Johnson (1861-1909), Minnesota's 16th governor (1905-1909) – a Democrat, and only the third non-Republican to that time. He was reform minded (e.g., allowed women to own property and sue in court), and was a contender for the Democratic nomination for president in 1908, losing to William Jennings Bryan. https://en.wikipedia.org/wiki/John_Albert_Johnson.
Halvor Steenerson (1852-1926) was U.S. Representative from Minnesota's Ninth District 1903-1923; he served in the Minnesota Senate 1883-1886. A Republican, he is included in *Progressive men of Minnesota. Biographical sketches and portraits of the leaders in business, politics and the professions; together with an historical and descriptive sketch of the state* (1897; https://www.loc.gov/resource/lhbum.19129/?sp=50). https://en.wikipedia.org/wiki/Halvor_Steenerson.
Charles August Lindbergh (1859-1924; father of the aviator), a Republican who served as U.S. Representative from Minnesota's Sixth Congressional District 1907-17. That he and E.E. were on adjoining wavelengths is confirmed by his opposing American entrance into World War I and his having run for governor in 1918 with support from the Nonpartisan League (which will figure prominently in Chapter 12 below). https://en.wikipedia.org/wiki/Charles_August_Lindbergh.
Moses E. Clapp (1851-1921) was Republican U.S. Senator from Minnesota 1901-1917. The *New York Times* obituary (Mar 7, 1929, p. 25) notes that "he was associated with the Progressive bloc headed by the late Robert La Follette." Further, prior to his election to the Senate, "he had trained with the Old Guard faction in his State, and his desertion to the 'insurgent' cause created great surprise among his old associates back home."

[123] "Under Blyanten," *The Reform*, Nov 27, 1906. Charles William Dorsett (1850-1936), a Swedenborgian, was Prohibition candidate for governor of Minnesota, 1904, 1906, 1916 (primary). https://politicalgraveyard.com/bio/dorn-dorsett.html. In a reversal of the norm for this period, he was apparently upstaged – at least in the historical record – by his wife, Martha Angle Dorsett (1851-1918), who, after passing the bar exam with high grades and challenging the state's statute limiting the legal profession to men, became the first woman to be admitted to the bar in Minnesota. https://en.wikipedia.org/wiki/Martha_Angle_Dorsett. Nearly all Internet references to Charles Dorsett say simply that he was married to her. For Stewart, see Note 103.

[124] http://en.wikipedia.org/wiki/Minnesota_State_Capitol.

[125] W. J. Dean (1843-1910) was a farm implement dealer and a long-time member of the state Prohibition Central Committee. https://mnelectionarchive.datamade.us/candidate/william-j-wj-dean/.

[126] *The Reform*, Jan 29, 1907. There is no evidence for attribution to Lincoln of the words about "the teachings of Jesus Christ, the simple Nazarene." Lincoln loomed large in Prohibitionist rhetoric. The *Minneapolis Tribune* on Feb 13, 1909, recounts many local celebrations of Lincoln's hundredth birthday the day before, including 450 attending the thirteenth annual Prohibitionist gathering at which a "Lincoln Memorial Fund" of $6,330 [$217,000] was inaugurated, to "be used in furthering the party principles in the next political campaign." Lobeck, on "Lincoln as statesman," was among the speakers.

[127] "Scenes of Disorder," *Minneapolis Journal*, Apr 24, 1907.

[128] *Alexandria Post News*, May 9, 1907.

[129] "Under Blyanten," *The Reform*, Jan 14, 1908. E.E. misattributes the quotation in the final paragraph; it's not David, but Jacob (Genesis 32:10).

[130] Benjamin Blessum (1877-1954) was a notable Norwegian American painter and graphic artist who received the Royal Norwegian Order of St. Olav, First Class, for his contributions to the nation. His works currently sell for $500 or more. https://en.wikipedia.org/wiki/Benjamin_Blessum. E.E. seems to think Blessum a better orator than artist!

[131] "Under Blyanten," *The Reform*, May 26, 1908. A recent sale notice for *Life Story of Rasmus B. Anderson* (1915; self-published; note spelling of name): "Memoirs of 'the father of Norwegian literature in America,' including his education, encounters with notables including Ole Bull, Thomas Edison, Knut Hamsun, the Czar of Russia, Sarah Bernhardt, Bismarck, Ibsen, Strindberg, many others; professional career. Anderson was a tireless promoter of Norwegian heritage and interests in the United States and professor of Scandinavian Literature at the U of Wisconsin." https://www.abebooks.com/servlet/BookDetailsPL?bi=177723054&ref_.

[132] Clinton Norman Harold (1869-1955) was subject of the Religion Section, under the heading "Little Giant," in *Time* magazine, Jan 11, 1937. The notice includes reference to the thousands of lectures he had given, and quotes his colorful language. https://content.time.com/time/subscriber/article/0,33009,757276,00.html. On Dec 5, 1925, he got national attention in the *New York Times* when he wrote to Pope Pius XI, urging the Pontiff to tell American Catholics to support enforcement of Prohibition. https://timesmachine.nytimes.com/timesmachine/1925/12/05/98843169.html.

[133] In the 1908 election George D. Haggard got 2.08% of the vote. https://uselectionatlas.org/RESULTS/state.php?fips=27&year=1908&f=0&off=5&elect=0.

[134] Temperance folk frequently attributed this remark to Bismarck, but without citing a source. It is probably apocryphal.

135 "Under Blyanten," *The Reform*, Jun 23, 1908.

136 "Under Blyanten," *The Reform*, Jul 28, 1908. "If you show yourself discouraged …": Proverbs 24:10. King Gambrinus: "While some attribute the invention of hopped malt-beer to Jan Primus (John I), a scion of the stock of Burgundy princes, who lived about the year 1251, others ascribe it to Jean Sans Peur (1371-1419), otherwise known as Ganbrivius. A corruption of either name may plausibly be shown to have resulted in the present name of the King of Beer, viz., Gambrinus, who we are accustomed to see represented in the habit of a knight of the middle-ages, with the occasional addition of a crown." George Ehret, *Twenty-Five Years of Brewing* (1891), quoted in https://www.beerhistory.com/library/holdings/gambrinus.shtml. E.E.'s closing line is likely a touch of sarcasm inspired by a poem of Josiah Gilbert Holland (1819-81) that begins, "GOD, give us men! / A time like this demands / strong minds, great hearts, true faith and ready hands; / Men whom the lust of office does not kill; / Men whom the spoils of office can not buy." https://www.theotherpages.org/poems/holland1.html.

137 *Princeton Union* (Princeton, MN), Aug 13, 1908.

138 *Park Region Echo*, Oct 1, 1908.

139 *Park Region Echo*, Oct 8, 1908.

140 Ibid.

141 *Minneapolis Tribune*, Oct 23, 1908.

142 *Alexandria Post News*, Oct 29, 1908. Transparencies were pictures on translucent material that were illuminated with oil lamps from behind (or from within when they were three-sided) and carried in parades.

143 *Willmar Tribune*, Nov 18, 1908.

144 *Park Region Echo*, Nov 19, 1908

145 *Park Region Echo*, Nov 26, 1908.

146 *Willmar Tribune*, Dec 30, 1908.

147 *Park Region Echo*, Jan 21, 1909.

148 *Minnesota Session Laws 1909*, Chapter 314, HF 495, Apr 21, 1909 (chrome-extension:// efaidnbmnnnibpcajpcglclefindmkaj/https://www.revisor.mn.gov/laws/1909/0/ General+Laws/Chapter/314/pdf/). Carley's reimbursement of $314.65 is HF 496. *Park Region Echo*, Apr 1, 1909, reported that Olson had to pay his own expenses.

149 Quoted in an article written by M. Haugen, *Menneskenvennen*, ca. 1920.

150 *Minneapolis Journal*, Jan 15 and Feb 14, 1909.

151 *Princeton Union*, Jan 21, 1909.

152 *Starbuck Times*, Oct 28, 1910. On the meaning of "Cannonistic," see Note 175 below.

153 Lynn Haines, *The Minnesota legislature of 1909: A History of the Session, with an Inside View of Men and Measures* (privately published: 720 New York Life Bldg., Minneapolis, Minn., 1910), 116. The book – an intriguing example of muckraking that applies almost verbatim to today – is available at http://www.minnesotalegalhistoryproject.org/assets/Haines-%20Minn.%20Leg. %201909.pdf.

154 Ibid., 11.

155 H.F. 82, Mar 24, 1909. https://www.revisor.mn.gov/laws/1909/0/General+Laws/ Chapter/92/pdf/. See also https://www.revisor.mn.gov/statutes/1905/cite/98/pdf.

156 *Duluth News Tribune*, Apr 23, 1909.

157 "Combined corporate lobbyists" – with thanks to the Norwegian-American Historical Association for help with translating "Kombinationernes": "an alliance of individuals, corporations, or states united to achieve a social, political, or economic end."

158 William Howard Taft, "a progressive Republican, campaigned on tariff reform and won the presidential election" in 1908. "In his inaugural address … he declared that he would veto any tariff bill that did not lower rates. … In the Senate, Nelson Aldrich of Rhode Island, head of the Finance Committee. and a dedicated protectionist, made numerous additional changes to the bill [that had originated in the House], raising hundreds of rates. The legislation passed without the support of the vast majority of Democrats or of the progressive Republicans. Taft signed the bill into law and later praised it as 'the best tariff bill the Republican Party ever passed.' It lowered rates on 650 items, raised rates on 220, and made no change on 1,150. … Because the act decreased rates only slightly, progressive Republicans broke with Taft and tried to prevent him from being nominated in the election of 1912. When they failed, they left the Republican Party and formed the Bull Moose Party, with Theodore Roosevelt as their candidate. Both parties were defeated by the Democrats, and shortly after Woodrow Wilson took office in 1913, Congress passed a bill lowering the overall tariff rate to 27 percent." https://www.britannica.com/topic/Payne-Aldrich-Tariff-Act.

159 Halvor O. Sageng, born in Norway and raised on a farm near Dalton, Minnesota, conceived the idea of a self-propelled thresher while a missionary in Madagascar for the Lutheran Free Church. When he returned to the United States he set to work on it. It was announced in *Farm Implements* magazine on Dec 19, 1908: "The Sageng Threshing Machine Company recently filed articles of incorporation under the Minnesota law … for the purpose of manufacturing and putting on the market a new type of threshing machine invented by Halvor O. Sageng, of Dalton, Minnesota. A machine has been constructed by the Minneapolis Steel & Machinery Company, from Mr. Sageng's patterns, and presents some novel features. The main distinctive point is that the engine and separator are combined in one machine. The motor is installed at the rear, and is cut off from the separator by a steel partition. The whole machine is encased in steel as a precaution against fire. Another radical difference is that the separator is equipped with two sets of shakers, so that the straw is passed over double the amount of shaker surface than it is in the ordinary separator, which should surely clean it thoroughly of loose grain." https://www.farmcollector.com/steam-engines/story-of-the-sageng-thresher.

160 This was Ole O. Sageng (1871-1963; from the same region of Norway, Østerdalen, as Lobeck), known as "the Napoleon of Women's Suffrage," who served in the Minnesota House 1901-02 and in the Minnesota Senate 1907-22 and 1951-54. https://www.lrl.mn.gov/legdb/fulldetail?id=14625. See also the memorial statement made in the Minnesota Senate, Mar 31, 1965: chrome-extension://efaidnbmnnnibpcajpcglclefindmkaj/https://www.lrl.mn.gov/docs/2009/other/090735/1965.pdf.

161 The Memorial Gift (Mindegave) was a tribute from Norwegian-Americans to the home country. On Jul 4, 1914, "America's Day" at the Norwegian Centennial Celebration in Kristiania (from 1925: Oslo), "the Mindegave, or Memorial Gift, amounting to 245,000 kroner [17,100,000 kroner, or $1,543,300, today], was formally presented by Dr. H. G. Stub and accepted on behalf of the Storting by its president, Mr. J. Lövland, to be administered for the benefit of sufferers from great national calamities, and so be forever a token of the love of emigrated Norwegians for their homeland." "The Fourth of July in Norway," written by Hanna A. Larsen, editor of the *American Scandinavian Review* and published in Sep 1914, republished in the *Newsletter* of the Norwegian-American Historical Association, 153 (Spring 2014), "Archive Highlights," 2 (chrome-extension://efaidnbmnnnibpcajpcglclefindmkaj/https://naha.stolaf.edu/wp-content/uploads/2020/08/Spring2014.pdf).

[162] "Under Blyanten," *The Reform*, Aug 3, 1909.

[163] John Albert Johnson (see Note 122) died at age 48 on Sep 21, 1909, shortly after the beginning of his third two-year term. (Minnesota amended its constitution in 1958 to a four-year term for the governor.)

[164] 2 Kings 9:20 (KJV): "the driving is like the driving of Jehu the son of Nimshi; for he driveth furiously." Jehu had recently been anointed King of Israel by the prophet Elisha, and tasked with eliminating the current king, Ahab, husband of Jezebel.

[165] It appears that Minnesota's legendary jaundiced view of its neighbor to the immediate south (which that neighbor readily reciprocates) has a long pedigree.

[166] The text of Taft's Sep 17, 1909 speech at Winona, Minnesota, on the Tariff Law of 1909, is available at https://www.presidency.ucsb.edu/documents/address-the-tariff-law-1909. Albert B. Cummins (1850-1926), a progressive Republican, was U.S. Senator for Iowa (1908-1926), and previously governor. He fought to break up monopolies and to abolish corporate campaign contributions. He also worked to lower protective tariffs. https://en.wikipedia.org/wiki/Albert_B._Cummins. Jonathan P. Dolliver (1858-1910) was U.S. Senator for Iowa (1900-1910). He was a Republican who became a progressive after supporting Cummins's rival in the 1908 election. (Lobeck appears to be referring to Dolliver's reconciliation with Cummins.) Dolliver was considered by many a contender for William McKinley's vice-presidential choice in 1900. Theodore Roosevelt got the nod instead. https://en.wikipedia.org/wiki/Jonathan_P._Dolliver.

[167] On Clapp, see Note 122. James A. Tawney (1855-1919) was a Republican U.S. Representative from Minnesota (1893-1911), an ally of the anti-Progressive Speaker of the House, Joseph G. Cannon (see Note 175 below). https://en.wikipedia.org/wiki/James_A._Tawney.

[168] "Under the Pencil," *Park Region Echo*, Oct 7, 1909. On Gambrinus, see Note 136.

[169] This doesn't turn up in a search for statements by Lincoln. *The American Advocate*, a major Prohibitionist newspaper, has the following in a story by J. P. Newell, "How to get a hearing for the Cause" (issue of week ending Feb 10, 1912, 13 [733]): "The Prohibition Party demands that the men who believe the saloon is wrong shall quit voting with those who believe it right." Perhaps Lobeck and others imagined that Lincoln would have said the same about slavery.

[170] "Under the Pencil," *Park Region Echo*, Dec 9, 1909.

[171] The penultimate of the plagues visited upon the Egyptians: "And the Lord said unto Moses, Stretch out thine hand toward heaven, that there may be darkness over the land of Egypt, even darkness which may be felt. And Moses stretched forth his hand toward heaven; and there was a thick darkness in all the land of Egypt three days." Exodus 10:21-22 (KJV).

[172] William Eugene "Pussyfoot" Johnson (1862-1945) plays a huge role in Mark Lawrence Schrad's *Smashing the Liquor Machine: A Global History of Prohibition* (Kindle Edition: Oxford University Press, 2021), the revisionist history mentioned in the "Preliminary Notes" to this book. "Pussyfoot was an American Temperance activist and writer, who'd twice circumnavigated the globe to network with Prohibitionist nationalists and revolutionaries across Asia, Africa, Europe, and North America" (14). While Johnson was known for tricking saloon owners into thinking he was on their side, he was most famous for his worldwide activities, and "is seldom even mentioned in standard Prohibition histories" (522); see also https://en.wikipedia.org/wiki/William_E._Johnson_(prohibitionist).

[173] In Cherry, Illinois, Nov 13, 1909; 259 men and boys were killed in the fire.

[174] "Mr. Lobeck Writes Again," *Park Region Echo*, Jan 6, 1910.

[175] For Aldrich, see Note 158. Joseph Gurney Cannon (1836-1926) served as Speaker of the U.S. House of Representatives from 1903 to 1911 (the Cannon House Office Building is named for him). Aldrich and Cannon were prominent members of a group of conservative Republicans who were known colloquially as "standpatters."

[176] "Clean Out the Whole Business," *Park Region Echo*, Feb 10, 1910.

[177] *Duluth News-Tribune*, Mar 14, 1910.

[178] "Representative Lobeck Closes Lecture Tour," *Duluth News-Tribune*, Mar 25, 1910.

[179] "Shall Joe Prodger Run the City?," *Park Region Echo*, Mar 3, 1910; "Objects to Cleaning up the City," *Park Region Echo*, Apr 28, 1910.

[180] Elias Rachie (1875-1950), Ph.D. and LL.B, University of Minnesota; Minnesota House of Representatives 1905-1909; subsequently law practice in Minneapolis; Nordfjordlaget in America, president 1915-1920, 1943-1950; author of several books, all of which would have elicited E.E.'s approval had he lived long enough to read them: *Thor's Gold: A Novel Depicting real life in the Northwest from pioneer days – containing a story of the gift of a million in tainted gold to buy a name and redeem a soul* (1927), dedicated to "The rank and file of our people, both in church and state – the men and women who bear the burdens and build our institutions, and who will always have to safeguard and defend them diligently, if they are to remain free and true and be perpetuated from generation to generation and be of the greatest possible good to all the people" (https://www.google.com/books/edition/Thor_s_Gold/m4Uop3YdySQC? hl=en&gbpv=1&dq). *The seven rich states – the heart of America: whose people should abundantly prosper but do not; causes and solutions* (1929); *Seventeen keys to freedom* (1930); *Building America*; *"Let us rise up and build"* (1936).

For Sageng, see Note 160.

Jacob (J. F.) Jacobson (note spelling), Republican, Minnesota House of Representatives 1889-1890, 1893-1902; candidate for governor 1908. Curt Brown, "'King Jake" reigned in Lac qui Parle," *Minneapolis Star Tribune*, Jul 9, 2017 (https://www.lrl.mn.gov/LegDB/articles/12286STbio_2017.pdf), notes Jacobson's "anti-alcohol stance [which] might have cost him the [governor's] race," and then tells this vividly remembered story: "When Lac qui Parle County formed in 1871, a village by the same name served as the county seat. But when the railroad bypassed the village, nearby Dawson and Madison tangled over where to move the county seat along the new rail line. Jacobson led a group of 150 men and 40 horse-drawn wagons, hauling the courthouse 15 miles through a November blizzard from Lac qui Parle Village to Madison. 'In Lac qui Parle County, people refer to Jacob F. Jacobson as "King Jake,"' the St. Paul Dispatch said in 1926. 'On the day that citizens dragged the old courthouse 15 miles cross country to Madison, it was "King Jake" astride the ridge pole of the kidnapped building, who had charge of the abduction.'" The article includes a photo of Jacobson atop the courthouse.

Edward T. (E. T.) Young (1858-1940), Republican; Minnesota House of Representatives 1889-1891, 1893-1895; Minnesota Senate 1895-1903; Minnesota Attorney General 1905-1909.

[181] Gustaf (G. H.) Mattson (1872-1927), Republican; Minnesota House of Representatives 1909-1912.

182 Of Seaborn Wright (1857-1933), a Prohibitionist member of the Georgia House of Representatives (1880-1883; 1900-1908; 1917-1918) and of the Georgia Senate 1927 – from which he walked out before the end of the session because "he was disgusted with the whole situation and saw no hope of accomplishing anything constructive for the state of Georgia" ("Seaborn Wright, Colorful State Leader, Dies," *Atlanta Journal*, Dec 15, 1933) – it was said, in a profile under the heading "The Georgia Cracker" in a brochure by his agent, The Mutual Lyceum Bureau in Chicago, "By the power of his eloquence he has freed his clients and driven criminals and lawbreakers from his town, has won the votes of his fellow citizens in every race he has ever made in spite of his uncompromising warfare on powerful classes, has acquired a competence by the practice of his profession, and has been a powerful factor in many great reforms in the legislation of Georgia." University of Iowa Digital Library (https:// public.uni.dgicloud.com/islandora/object/ui%3Atc_63522_63519).

183 "Under Blyanten," *The Reform*, Apr 12, 1910. E.E.'s poem in Norwegian has the rhyme scheme AABBAAA CCDDCCC.

184 *Park Region Echo*, Apr 7, 1910. The story is told, with fewer details, on the front page of the *Starbuck Times*, Apr 1, 1910: "Larson Assaults Times Publisher – Attack Took Place in Broad Daylight Lending a Fitting Climax to the Local War."

185 "Prohibitionist Seers Say New Party Dawns," *Minneapolis Tribune*, Jul 2, 1910; "The Prohibition State Convention," *Park Region Echo*, Jul 7, 1910.

186 "Temperance Folk Begin Campaign," *Duluth News-Tribune*, Jul 27, 1910.

187 "WCTU Department, The Annual School Meeting," *Park Region Echo*, Jul 21, 1910.

188 "Blind Pig Raid at Evansville," *Park Region Echo*, Aug 11, 1910.

189 A video of this movie can be seen at http://www.smithsonianmag.com/videos/the-johnsonjeffries-fight/.

190 H.F. 82, Mar 24, 1909. https://www.revisor.mn.gov/laws/1909/0/General+Laws/ Chapter/92/pdf/. See also https://www.revisor.mn.gov/statutes/1905/cite/98/pdf.

191 The problem is acute today as ever; see *Human Trafficking in Minnesota: A Report to the Minnesota legislature 2019* (89 pages). chrome-extension://efaidnbmnnnibpcajpcglclefindmkaj/https:// www.leg.mn.gov/docs/2019/mandated/191234.pdf.

192 "Why Hamm Brewing Company Don't Want Lobeck," *Park Region Echo*, Oct 6, 1910.

193 "Another Falsehood Exposed," *Park Region Echo*, Oct 13, 1910.

194 Wold's comment about Nelson's speech was passed down in Lobeck family lore.

195 *Park Region Echo*, Oct 20, 1910.

196 *Park Region Echo*, Nov 10, 1910.

197 "To My Friends and Supporters," *Park Region Echo*, Nov 17, 1910.

198 *The Reform*, Dec 13, 1910. The entire letter is printed as a single paragraph.

199 "Under the Pencil," *Park Region Echo*, Dec 29, 1910.

200 *The Reform*, Dec 20, 1910. Translation by Asbjørn Hildemyr.

201 https://guides.loc.gov/chronicling-america-wellington-washington-train-disaster.

202 Excerpts from "Under Blyanten," *The Reform*, Feb 28, 1911.

203 https://www.geni.com/people/Ole-Sneve/6000000071126066854.

204 "Under Blyanten," *The Reform*, May 16, 1911. The concluding reference is to Deuteronomy 33:25, "as thy days, so shall thy strength be," relating to the tribe of Asher. The first section of the memory poem, translated by Asbjørn Hildemyr, rhyme in Norwegian AABB BBCC; the second section is DDEE; the final section is FFGGHHIIJJKK.

205 "Under Blyanten," *The Reform*, Oct 3, 1911. E.E. is here recounting events from many months earlier in 1911.

206 Ibid.

207 "Salt Lake Man Hurt in Wreck," *Salt Lake Tribune*, Apr 8, 1911. Also, "Returned from the Coast," *Park Region Echo*, Apr 13, 1911.

208 "WCTU Department," *Park Region Echo*, Oct 5, 1911.

209 Ibid.

210 Ibid.

211 "WCTU Department," *Park Region Echo*, Nov 30, 1911.

212 *Park Region Echo*, Dec 7, 1911.

213 Carl Wold, "Law and Order Meeting," *Park Region Echo*, Feb 22, 1912.

214 *Park Region Echo*, March 21, 1912.

215 Carl Wold, "Special Meeting of the Law and Order League," *Park Region Echo*, May 9, 1912.

216 Motor Vehicle Record, Vol. 5, 1912-14, Office of Minnesota Secretary of State, #65453: Lobeck, E.E., residence – Alexandria.

217 "Prohibition State Convention," *Willmar Tribune*, Jul 24, 1912.

218 "Hon. E.E. Lobeck, Prohibition Candidate for Governor." Political tract with his acceptance speech, the Prohibition platform, and list of Lobeck's successes. Boldface in original. The quotation is from Demosthenes, *Oration on the Crown*, 51 (https://sites.google.com/site/persuasionpast/home/demosthenes-on-the-crown).

219 "Fillmore Drys are Aggressive," *Duluth News-Tribune*, Jul 31, 1912.

220 "Ida Y.P.B. Outing," *Park Region Echo*, Aug 8, 1912.

221 *Duluth News-Tribune*, Sep 2, 1912.

222 Minutes of 36th Annual Meeting of Woman's Christian Temperance Union of Minnesota, Sep 20-24, 1912, 25.

223 "Prohibition Automobile Campaign," *Park Region Echo*, Oct 3, 1912.

224 "Lobeck in the State," *Park Region Echo*, Oct 10, 1912.

225 "Prohibs Will Be Busy Today," *Duluth News-Tribune*, Oct 8, 1912.

226 "Lobeck Creates Great Enthusiasm at Virginia," *Park Region Echo*, Oct 17, 1912.

227 "Prohibition Banquet," *Park Region Echo*, Jan 9, 1913. "Our Home Is Not What It Used To Be," words by J. F. Coles, music by C. A. White, in C. A. White and J. F. Coles, *Temperance Revival Songs* (Boston: White, Smith & Company, 1876), 38-39 (https://archive.org/details/temperancereviv00unkngoog/page/n38/mode/2up). Summary of "Molly and the Baby," in Josh McMullen, *Under the Big Top: Big Tent Revivalism and American Culture, 1885-1925* (New York: Oxford University Press, 2015), no page numbers (https://www.google.com/books/edition/Under_the_Big_Top/9td4BgAAQBAJ?gbpv=1#h=).

228 "Early history of WCTU," http://www.wctu.org/earlyhistory.html.

[229] "The Due Tea," *Park Region Echo*, Jan 30, 1913.

[230] *Park Region Echo*, May 1, 1913.

[231] Full coverage of the WCTU convention in *Park Region Echo*, Aug 28, 1913.

[232] "The Children March for Temperance," *Park Region Echo*, Mar 12, 1914.

[233] *Park Region Echo*, Aug 6, 1914. The WCTU had a multi-pronged plan to encourage children to abstain from alcohol and other evils. The wrist-tying ceremony began at birth when a mother presented her child and pledged to teach the child the principles of total abstinence and purity. The LTL (Loyal Temperance League) and YPB enlisted children at various ages.

[234] "Publicity for Sunday Baseball and Dances Condemned," *Park Region Echo*, Jul 16, 1914.

[235] *Revised Laws of Minnesota, Supplement 1909*, #4981. The "Sabbath" was definitely the Christian Sabbath. Section 4981 references a 1906 Minnesota Supreme Court case, State vs. Weiss, which determined "That defendant was a Hebrew and of the Jewish Church, attended such church on Saturdays, and believed Saturday to be the Sabbath, did not affect the constitutionality of said law."

[236] *Minneapolis Tribune*, Apr 26, 1909.

[237] "Misrepresenting the WCTU," *Park Region Echo*, Aug 27, 1914.

[238] *Park Region Echo*, Sep 3, 1914.

[239] *Park Region Echo*, Jan 28, 1915.

[240] *Park Region Echo*, Feb 4, 1915.

[241] C.J. Buell, *The Minnesota legislature of 1915* (St. Paul, 1915), 49-55. https://www.leg.mn.gov/docs/nonmnpub/oclc06902248.pdf. Buell's sympathies are revealed by his reference to "this pauper-breeding, crime-producing traffic" (50).

[242] *Sacred Heart Review*, 53/16 (Boston College, Apr 3, 1915), 242.

[243] Buell, 22-23. Buell comments: "For some time the vote stood a tie, thirty-three to thirty-three. Then Senator A. S. Campbell of Austin was found and voted no. To Mr. Campbell belongs the distinction of having saved the male voters of the state the labor of taking thought and voting upon this important question."

[244] *Park Region Echo*, May 6, 1915.

[245] Letter to daughter Evangeline Lobeck, dated Calgary (Alberta, Canada), Jul 7, 1915.

[246] *Park Region Echo*, Feb 3, 1916.

[247] "Some Queer Criticisms," *Park Region Echo*, Oct 14, 1915.

[248] "Faithful Service is Entitled to Fair Pay," *Park Region Echo*, Nov 11, 1915.

[249] *Park Region Echo*, Feb 3, 1916.

[250] *Park Region Echo*, Oct 14, 1915.

[251] "Thou ancient, Thou free, Thou mountainous north," the (unofficial) Swedish national anthem.

[252] Monsignor James Cleary, of Incarnation Church in Minneapolis, a major figure in the church. In 1913, on the occasion of his 41st anniversary in the priesthood, speakers included the governor of Minnesota, the president of the University of Minnesota, and Father Cleary's close friend and fellow-Irishman, Archbishop John Ireland.

[253] On Sageng, see Note 160.

[254] Ola Lende (1873-1952), Republican, lawyer, Minnesota Senate 1911-1918.

255 The Joms-Vikings were famous for their singlemindedness and fearlessness in battle (probably due to the intake of certain mind-bending ingredients before battle). Note by Magne Teppen.

256 "Under Blyanten," *The Reform*, Oct 12, 1915.

257 "Constitutional Prohibition Sunday," *Park Region Echo*, Dec 2, 1915.

258 E.E. Lobeck, "Julen 1915," *The Reform*, Dec 21, 1915. Trans. by Asbjørn Hildemyr. These are the first three verses of a six-verse poem. The Norwegian rhyme scheme for each stanza is ABBBACC. "White Christ": *Hvide Krist*: No racial implication; part of Nordic folklore, a way of making Christ more powerful than Odin.

259 *Park Region Echo*, Jan 6, 1916.

260 *Park Region Echo*, Jan 20, 1916.

261 *Park Region Echo*, Jan 13, 1916.

262 "Argument for State Wide Prohibition," *Park Region Echo*, Jan 20, 1916.

263 Stephen G. Sylvester, "The Soiled Doves of East Grand Forks, 1887-1915," *Minnesota History* (Winter 1989), 291-300.

264 *Park Region Echo*, Jan 27, 1916.

265 *Park Region Echo*, Jan 13, 1916.

266 *Park Region Echo*, Feb 10, 1916.

267 Ibid.

268 Ibid.

269 *Park Region Echo*, May 30, 1916.

270 *Park Region Echo*, Apr 27, 1916.

271 *Park Region Echo*, May 16, 1916.

272 *Park Region Echo*, May 4, 1916.

273 *Park Region Echo*, June 13, 1916.

274 Ibid.

275 *Park Region Echo*, Jul 4, 1916.

276 Eva Emerson Wold, "A Short Biography of the Honorable Carl A. Wold" and "Autobiography of Mrs. Emerson Wold" (typewritten pages, 1953), 27; Biographies in the Minnesota Historical Society's Manuscripts Collection, #P939.

277 *Park Region Echo*, Aug 22, 1916.

278 *Park Region Echo*, Aug 8, 1916.

279 *Willmar Tribune*, Aug 23, 1916.

280 *Willmar Tribune*, Oct 4, 1916.

281 *Willmar Tribune*, Oct 11, 1916.

282 Ibid.

283 Ibid.

284 Robert L. Morlan, *Political Prairie Fire* (St. Paul: Minnesota Historical Society Press, 1985), 22-23.

285 "Nonpartisan League," Minnesota Historical Society: http://www.mnhs.org/library/tips/history_topics/102nonpartisan.html.

286 *Park Region Echo*, Oct 3, 1916.

287 *Park Region Echo*, Dec 19, 1916.

288 *Park Region Echo*, Nov 14, 1916.

289 *Park Region Echo*, Dec 5, 1916.

290 *Park Region Echo*, Dec 26, 1916.

291 *Park Region Echo*, Feb 6, 1917.

292 Ibid.

293 C.J. Buell, *The Minnesota legislature of 1917* (with a charming note in place of date and place of publication: "This Book is not Copyrighted Quote as Much as you Please But Give Credit"), 68-69.

294 "Farmer's League Fought at Capitol," *Park Region Echo*, Mar 27, 1917.

295 *The Labor World* (Duluth, Minnesota), Apr 7, 1917.

296 Buell, *legislature of 1917*, 39-43.

297 Carl H. Chrislock, *Watchdog of Loyalty: The Minnesota Commission of Public Safety During World War I* (St. Paul: Minnesota Historical Society Press, 1991), x.

298 Ibid.

299 *Park Region Echo*, Apr 17, 1917.

300 Ibid.

301 "Free Speech and Free Press Defended," *Park Region Echo*, May 1, 1917.

302 Eva Emerson Wold, "A Short Biography," 20.

303 Ibid., 18.

304 Wold published these notices in successive issues during May and early June 1917.

305 *Park Region Echo*, May 8, 1917.

306 *Park Region Echo*, May 15, 1917.

307 *Park Region Echo*, May 22, 1917.

308 Ibid.

309 Ibid.

310 Papers of Minnesota Commission of Public Safety, Minnesota Historical Society.

311 *Park Region Echo*, Aug 14, 1917.

312 Eva Emerson Wold, "A Short Biography," 18-19.

313 *Park Region Echo*, Aug 28, 1917.

314 *Park Region Echo*, Jul 24, 1917.

315 *Park Region Echo*, Sep 4 and 11, 1917.

316 *Park Region Echo*, Sep 25, 1917.

317 Ibid.

318 Ibid.

319 *Park Region Echo*, Oct 9, 1917.

320 *Park Region Echo*, Jan 1, 1918; *Alexandria Post News*, Jan 3, 1918.

321 *Park Region Echo*, Jan 1, 1918.

[322] *Park Region Echo,* Jan 8, 1918.

[323] Ibid.

[324] Ibid..

[325] *Park Region Echo,* Jan 15 and 26, 1918.

[326] *Park Region Echo,* Jan 22, 1918.

[327] *Park Region Echo,* Feb 5, 1918.

[328] *Park Region Echo,* Mar 12, 1918.

[329] Wold indictment, at Douglas County Historical Society, Book 2, #638.

[330] *Alexandria Post News*, Mar 14,1918.

[331] *Park Region Echo,* Mar 12, 1918.

[332] Eva Emerson Wold, "A Short Biography," 22.

[333] Millard L. Gieske and Steven J. Keillor, *Norwegian Yankee: Knute Nelson and the Failure of American Politics, 1860-1923* (Northfield, MN: Norwegian-American Historical Association, 1995), 312. "Copperheads" was a derisive term for Democrats, harking back to members of the party who had opposed the Civil War.

[334] Carl H. Chrislock, *Progressive Era in Minnesota, 1899-1918* (St. Paul: Minnesota Historical Society Press, 1971), 161-62.

[335] Letter to Knute Nelson from the America First Association, December 28, 1917; Folder "December 28-31, 1917"; Box 144.I.13.4F; Part of the Knute Nelson Papers in the Manuscript Collections of the Minnesota Historical Society Library.

[336] "J. F. McGee Abuses Magnus Johnson," *Park Region Echo*, Oct 15, 1918. Letter to Knute Nelson from the America First Association, December 28, 1917; Folder "December 28-31, 1917"; Box 144.I.13.4F; Part of the Knute Nelson Papers in the Manuscript Collections of the Minnesota Historical Society Library.

[337] "President Frowns Upon McGee's Plan," *Park Region Echo*, Apr 30, 1918.

[338] Carl H. Chrislock, *Ethnicity Challenged: The Upper Midwest Norwegian-American Experience in World War I*, Topical Studies, Vol. 3 (Northfield, MN: Norwegian-American Historical Association, 1981), 91.

[339] *Park Region Echo*, Apr 30, 1918.

[340] "Keynote Speech was Thrilling," *Park Region Echo*, Mar 19, 1918.

[341] Ibid.

[342] "Enemies are Foiled by Nonpartisans," *Park Region Echo*, Mar 12, 1918.

[343] Eva Emerson Wold, "A Short Biography," 24.

[344] *Minneapolis Tribune*, Mar 12, 1918.

[345] Gieske and Keillor, *Norwegian Yankee*, 315.

[346] Ibid.

[347] *Park Region Echo*, Apr 2, 1918.

[348] *Park Region Echo*, May 21, 1918.

[349] Ibid.

[350] *Park Region Echo*, May 14, 1918.

[351] *Park Region Echo,* Jun 11, 1918.

352 *Alexandria Citizen,* Jun 20, 1918.

353 *Park Region Echo,* Jul 4, 1918.

354 *The Warren Sheaf* (Warren, MN), Jul 3, 1918.

355 *Park Region Echo,* Jul 23, 1918.

356 *Park Region Echo,* Sep 3, 1918.

357 *Minneapolis Tribune,* Nov. 16, 1919 (https://www.startribune.com/nov-16-1919-tarred-and-feathered/70155507/). https://slate.com/human-interest/2013/10/photos-german-american-farmer-tarred-and-feathered-in-1918.html. Both of these sites include photos of Meints tarred and feathered.

358 *Park Region Echo,* Sep 3, 1918; list of contributors, Sep 18, 1918.

359 *Park Region Echo,* Sep 11, 1918.

360 Ibid.

361 "Walker gives Kinney pointers," *Park Region Echo,* Oct 16, 1918.

362 "Farmers Unite to Support Lobeck," *Minnesota Leader,* Oct 19, 1918.

363 "Carss and Lobeck Have Progressive Backing," *Minnesota Leader,* Nov 2, 1918.

364 Waldemar Ager, in Lobeck family papers.

365 "Alexandria Celebrates," *Alexandria Citizen,* Nov 14, 1918.

366 "Reorganized W.C.T.U.," *Alexandria Citizen,* Dec 5, 1918.

367 "WCTU notes," *Park Region Echo,* Jan 1, 1919.

368 *Park Region Echo,* Jan 29, 1919.

369 *Park Region Echo,* Mar 25, 1919.

370 *Minneapolis Tribune,* Jul 13, 1919.

371 "An explanation." *Park Region Echo,* Mar 12, 1919.

372 *Park Region Echo,* Jan 22 and Feb 12, 1919.

373 *Park Region Echo,* Feb 26, 1919.

374 *Park Region Echo,* Sep 4, 1919; available at https://www.echopress.com/opinion/columns/1919-chaplin-plays-at-the-howard.

375 "Park Region State Bank," *Park Region Echo,* Jan 14, 1920.

376 *Park Region Echo,* Jul 16, 1919.

377 *Park Region Echo,* Jul 23, 1919.

378 "Leaguers had splendid picnics," *Park Region Echo,* Aug 16, 1919.

379 https://en.wikipedia.org/wiki/History_of_the_American_Legion.

380 "Mob Rule Must Stop," *Park Region Echo,* Nov 5, 1919.

381 *Park Region Echo,* June 12, 1921.

382 *Park Region Echo,* Nov 12, 1919. The Lincoln quotation is from his "Address before the Young Men's Lyceum of Springfield, Illinois," Jan 27, 1838.

383 "Two Thousand at Dedication," *Park Region Echo,* Jun 30, 1920.

384 https://www.census.gov/history/www/programs/geography/urban_and_rural_areas.html.

385 "Park Region State Bank Meeting," *Park Region Echo,* Jan 12, 1921.

386 Court documents.

387 "Lobeck causes Proehl's Arrest," *Park Region Echo*, Jan 18, 1922.

388 *Park Region Echo*, Mar 22, 1922.

389 Court documents Case #5043 Forgery in 1st degree, committed 15 Mar 1920 $400. Case #5007 Forgery in 2nd degree, committed 12 Jan 1921 $500. Case # 5044 Grand Larceny 1st degree, committed 30 Sep 1919 $700. Case # 5045 Forgery in 2nd degree, committed 12 Jan 1921 $800. Case # 5046 Forgery in 2nd degree, committed 5 Jan 1921 $1000. Case #5047 Forgery in 2nd degree, committed 12 Jan 1921 $800. Case #5048 Forgery in 2nd degree, committed 12 Jan 1921 $500. Case #5049 Forgery in 2nd degree, committed 5 Jan 1921 $1000. Case #5054 Grand Larceny 1st degree, committed 5 Oct 1920 $1650.

390 *Park Region Echo*, Mar 22, 1922.

391 *Park Region Echo*, editorial page, Mar 29, 1922.

392 *Park Region Echo*, Apr 5, 1922.

393 *Park Region Echo*, "Special Stockholders Meeting last Monday," Apr 12, 1922.

394 Ibid.

395 "Vale I.M. Kalnes," *Alexandria Citizen*, Apr 27, 1922.

396 Drew M. Ross, "White Supremacy on Parade: The Fight to Stop The Birth of a Nation in the Twin Cities," *Minnesota History*, 68/5 (Spring 2023), 170-180, at 178. Ross provides a detailed and persuasively sourced story of the struggles of the Black communities in Minneapolis and St. Paul (with different dynamics in each) to halt showings of the movie, and of the role of the film in the explosive growth of the Klan in the region.

397 Printed on the masthead of *The Light* [Official Organ, World's Purity Federation and Parents' International League], 150 (Jan-Feb 1923), cover (just above a photo of E.E. Lobeck). https://catalog.hathitrust.org/Record/102628713.

398 *The Light*, 104 (Jul-Aug 1915), 4.

399 https://prezi.com/eehvp32lrtyi/sexual-regulation-and-19th-century-purity-movements/

400 B. S. Steadwell, "Hon. E.E. Lobeck Suddenly Stricken," *The Light*, 150, 5-8.

401 Court document: Minnesota Seventh District Court, Mar 18, 1923.

402 Information about death and funeral of E.E. Lobeck is from the diary of his niece, Ellen Berg. On Dorsett, see Note 123. On Wells, see information at Minnesota Historical Society (https://www.mnhs.org/newspapers/hub/backbone) about the Temperance newsletter, *Backbone* (1897-1906), which became *The Public Weal* (1906-1908): "Its sole editor and general manager was George F. Wells (1853-1934), a Methodist pastor and long-time Temperance advocate. All issues also identify W. G. [Willis Greenleaf] Calderwood (1866-1956), secretary of the State Prohibition Committee and a senatorial candidate in 1916 and 1918, as a contact person."

403 *Østerdalslaget Aarbok*, 1923.

404 *Capital Times*, Madison WI, Mar 26, 1959.

405 https://archiveswest.orbiscascade.org/ark:80444/xv05447.